AF730022

Praise for

INTERNATIONAL FREAK

Part vivid story of the unlikely international making of countercultural London, part bracing account of how freaks and hippies made the modern world we now take for granted, *International Freak* is an entirely compelling account of how a remarkable individual life might make us think again about the recent past.

— Professor Matt Houlbrook, author of *Queer London: Perils and Pleasures in the Sexual Metropolis, 1918-1957*

International Freak explores a neglected side of London, revealing a gritty and often contradictory city that is frequently overlooked or misrepresented in narratives of the Swinging Sixties. This book functions as a guide to an alternative vision of the city, an act of literary recovery that provides an intimate and distinctive portrait of both its subject and a forgotten world that remains significant today.

— Rachel Lichtenstein, author of *On Brick Lane and Rodinsky's Room*

This a painstakingly researched but propulsively readable book that reconstructs the fascinating, often moving life of Robin Farquharson ... It is the biography of a ghost, and to read it is to feel haunted, and at times infuriated, by an uncontrollably talented, finally uncategorisable character.

— Professor Matthew Beaumont, author of *Nightwalking: A Nocturnal History of London*

Even after all this time the 1960s continues to yield up its hidden countercultural histories... Robin Farquharson's mesmerising story has certainly up until now been one of that period's most hidden and unsung and arguably its most crazed. A Zelig-like presence stalks these pages, briefly merging fringe and mainstream before tantalisingly retreating into the margins again. A spellbinding tale.

— Rob Chapman, author of *Psychedelia and Other Colours*

About the Author

M. Syd Rosen lives in London, where he writes about fame, fantasy, and radical politics. Alongside his writing he is the co-founder of Jargon, a non-profit dedicated to diasporic culture. *International Freak* is his first book.

INTERNATIONAL FREAK

Robin Farquharson and the Dream of Psychedelic Revolt

M. Syd Rosen

International Freak by M. Syd Rosen
First published by Strange Attractor Press 2026
ISBN: 9781917674102

A CIP catalogue record for this book is available from the British Library.

Strange Attractor Press
BM SAP, London,
WC1N 3XX, UK
www.strangeattractor.co.uk

Distributed by The MIT Press, Cambridge, Massachusetts.
And London, England.
Printed and bound in the USA by Versa Press.

CONTENTS

Part III

Ruined by the Wrecking Gangs, 1970-1973

All should know the rule by which this game may be won.
— Charles Dodgson, 'A Method of Taking Votes on More Than Two Issues' (1876)

I can dig the skyjacker trip
If you wanna get through, you got to be hip.
— The White Panthers, 'Leila the Hijacker' (1970)

INTRODUCTION
A STITCH IN TIME DISTORTS ETERNITY

As Thursday became Friday, the windows of 21 Platt Street exploded and the road was showered with glass.

Though dramatic, fires weren't particularly unusual in this corner of Somers Town. It was 1973 and the local council were intent on following through on a plan of managed decline. As a result, every second or third house was either squatted or abandoned. Residents constructed improvised electrical systems or made use of old-fashioned gas lamps. Ashtrays were few and far between. Sweet and sticky trails of smoke worked their way through splintered door frames. House fires were a common result, even on a bitterly cold night in late March. Nobody was usually hurt.

On this occasion, though, the sound of exploding windows prompted a handful of concerned locals to step into the late night air. Fire engines roared into view and a tall silhouette emerged inside the burning building. Rather than rushing to safety, the figure calmly moved towards what had recently been the second-floor window and positioned itself against the jagged shards.

The shadow revealed itself to be a middle-aged man with thinning hair and a rough, thick beard. One hand was clenched in a fist above his head, straining at the sleeve of a battered and sooty blazer. His other hand jutted out in front of him, grasping at an imaginary bundle of papers. This dramatic pose was framed by the picture-perfect glow of orange and red flames.

Right on cue, the man cleared his throat. Then, gazing down at his terrified neighbours, he began to deliver some kind of speech, reading from the invisible script he held in front of him. His voice was completely inaudible between the roar of the flames and the cries from the street below. Whatever he was saying, the fire had grown so piercingly bright and so impossibly hot that the crowd were forced to look away.

The emergency services had by now obtained access to the burning building. They were soon seen shovelling the unknown man onto a stretcher and into a waiting ambulance. As the vehicle sped off, a neighbour snapped a picture of the scene.

Two firemen stood on the first floor balcony, feeding a hose into what remained of the building. A third controlled the flow of water from the street. Thanks to their work, the fire was soon over. The crowd dallied for a few minutes longer but without the warmth of the flames it became too cold to stay outside. The drama of the evening was over.

A feverish and short-lived wave of reporting did little to clear up the mystery of the man at the window. As he died of his wounds in a nearby hospital, readers learned that the victim-to-be was a legendary mathematician, an infamous hippie, a pioneering gay rights activist, a fierce opponent of apartheid, a terrorist, a snob, a fantasist, a drug addict, a diplomat, and, nearly everyone agreed, an incurable lunatic. His age ranged from 35 to 50 years old. His first name varied too, fluctuating from Robin to Reginald to Robert. One neighbour reported that his surname was something like Ferguson. No-one was really sure.

It would eventually be established that the man the papers had dubbed the 'dropout doctor' was actually a former academic called Robin Farquharson, aged 42. The victim's distinctive name was shared by a British diplomat, a Jamaican photographer, and a well-known Edwardian actor. The uncertainty didn't end there. Farquharson apparently held one doctorate from Cambridge, another from Oxford, and maybe another one still from a university back in his home country of South Africa. In some photos he looked like a vestige of an upper-class white colonial family, with all the attendant privileges and prejudices. From other angles he seemed more like a pauper, an all-round troubled man and a troubling presence.

In material terms, though, the result of the fire was relatively straightforward. Farquharson's burns were clearly very serious. While he made some initial progress, he would be dead within the week.

Local, national, and international newspapers took notice of Farquharson's death. In the weeks that followed they gamely tried to work out what the heart of Platt Street fire should be: a homophobic killing, a suicide pact gone awry, a horrible accident, an inevitability, a redevelopment opportunity, or an assassination.

In the meantime, clean-up crews moved in and the police took witness statements. Two Irish labourers were eventually sentenced for arson, criminal damage, and manslaughter but not murder. Camden Council, the owners of the burned building, began to demolish what remained of Platt Street. Press coverage gradually tired of depleting returns on what was becoming only a semi-tragic story about a semi-important underground figure. The two books Farquharson had authored—one a short but brilliant mathematical treatise, the other a patchy but beguiling memoir—gradually went out of print. His doctoral thesis, once the talk of academia, sat in Oxford's Bodleian Library untouched. Blackwell's bookshop wrote to a few Cambridge colleges and a handful of the dead man's old squats, hoping to find someone to settle some of his debts. These enquiries came up short. Things grew quiet and stayed that way.

Since that time, Farquharson's life has been almost entirely excised from the over-exposed history of countercultural London. All that remains in circulation are two paragraphs that come

INTERNATIONAL FREAK BEATEN UP & COMMITTED

Mystery fire death of author —young man accused

Author dies after fire

Platt Street case: further remand

Riddle of the dropout doctor

A 50-YEAR-OLD ex-Cambridge fellow has set Scotland Yard a mystery.

For Dr Robert Farquharson dropped out of society—completely.

Some years ago he described his experiences in the twilight world of people living in derelict houses in a book called The Drop Out.

Dr Farquharson who had held a senior research fellowship at Cambridge, was a doctor of philosophy and had held well-paid jobs in both management and as computer consultant.

Derelict

He was badly burned in ...re in a derelict house ... Platt St., Camden ...n, three days ago. ...e died in University ...ege Hospital.

...dropped out so com...ly that detectives can ... no trace of any ...ive who they can ...

SQUATTERS CHARGED WITH KILLING

SUNDAY TIMES, APRIL 6, 1975

‘BRILLIANT DROP-OUT’ DIES OF BURNS

SA eccentric Robin Farquharson trapped in flaming house

SUNDAY TIMES Correspondent

LONDON, Saturday. DR. ROBIN FARQUHARSON, one of South Africa's most brilliant academicians — he held two doctorates of philosophy — died at St. Pancras Hospital in London last Sunday as the result of severe burns.

Dr. Robin Farquharson tells of his life as a tramp

I took LSD, says brilliant S.A. scholar

Writes book on his life in “twilight world”

SUNDAY TIMES CORRESPONDENT

LONDON, Saturday.

LAST year the brilliant South African scholar and don, Dr. Robin Farquharson, opted out of the academic career he had carved and became ...

Ian Aldridge's book jacket for ‘Drop Out’ by Robin Farquharson (Blond 25s October). Last winter Dr Farquharson spended a successful career and ‘dropped out’; his book is impression of contemporary society seen from the bottom up.

EXCLUSIVE STATEMENT TO “CONTACT”

Mandela Calls—“Deliver the Knock-out Punch”

From ROBIN FARQUHARSON

REGINALD ROBIN FARQUHARSON born on the 3rd day OCTOBER, 1930 at PRETORIA.

Farquharson's death drew a line under years of salacious reporting halfway through *Lights Out for the Territory*, Iain Sinclair's 1997 record of 'nine excursions in the secret history of London'. In Sinclair's distinctive psychogeographical manner, the book stitches together a sequence of historical visions prompted by a series of walks and journeys. Wandering around King's Cross with Aidan Andrew Dun, a visionary poet in the Blakean mould, Sinclair comes upon the site of the legendary Charrington Street squat. In a brief aside, Dun recounts his short but formative encounter there with a quasi-mystic named Robin Farquharson, alluding to the suspicious nature of the fire that cost his friend his life. On they walk and on the book goes to other more or less secret histories.

Most other tellings of Farquharson's death, few as there are, take Dun's account as their sole source of information. But Sinclair's 250 words—poetic, well intentioned, and only a fraction of a far larger work—contained enough wrong details for the passage to be downright misleading. At the same time, enough facts were right to make correcting them seem petty. Repackaged, reworked, and bowdlerised as these things often are, Dun's comments have provided future speculators with enough skewed markers so as to make the circumstances of Farquharson's death unknowable.

Suitably enough, my first encounter with Farquharson's story made next to no sense. As if in a reverie, I found myself sitting in a Somers Town haunt named the Cock Tavern when, uninvited, a local character sat down. Putting one drink down for himself and another for me, the man set to recounting a winding chain of anecdotes about his years as a squatter.

While the general outline of the Platt Street fire stood out, the details were hard to fill in. The convivial atmosphere was not conducive to things like names and dates and to this day, I have no idea what this man was called or anything else about him. After a certain number of anecdotes, he simply got up, downed his pint, confiscated the remains of mine, and left the table before I had had the chance to ask him a single question.

It took me some time to link the story I heard that night with the name of Robin Farquharson. Nurtured on time and second- and third-hand tellings, I knew that what had really happened on Platt Street was probably much more prosaic than local lore had it. But try as I might, I couldn't shake the image of the crazed scholar lecturing amidst the flames of his burning squat. The story couldn't be entirely right, but it contained an essential truth—not about Farquharson the man, but about how we remember people like him, as doomed martyrs going out in a blaze of fire. I was drawn to the story and repulsed by it.

I realised that if I wanted to learn how Farquharson had really died, I needed first to understand a little more about how he had really lived. Unfortunately, the main source for this kind of information was no more reliable than the urban legends that circulated about the fatal fire. First published in 1968, Farquharson's *Drop Out!* is a minor non-fiction masterpiece, a brief and mercurial account of life between the fringes of poverty and hip celebrity. It is also perfectly formulated to lead would-be biographers astray.

Ostensibly an account of Farquharson's years in Swinging London, *Drop Out!* suddenly lurches back to the author's childhood and his student days at Oxford. It also jumps forward to the period in which the book itself was being written, operating as a kind of diary of Farquharson's life on the streets. 'Short bursts of manic Morse code' was how the reviewer from the *Spectator* described it. The book keeps on going backwards and forwards and backwards and forwards with little regard for continuity or shifts of speed or style—and then, after 104 pages, the book stops, suddenly and without ceremony.

If there was anything proto-psychogeographical about *Drop Out!*, as Iain Sinclair evidently sensed there was, it was in the book's subtle and contradictory politics of place and power. Farquharson's writing is filled with names, dates, and addresses that refuse any neat map or chronology. Friends and acquaintances come and go. So do a variety of schemes and set-backs. Institutions open their arms. Some then lock him out. Others lock him up. The reader desperately hopes that something greater than the individual parts might come together, if only for a moment. It is not clear whether this clarity ever arrives.

Despite its enormous scope, *Drop Out!* was also filled with holes. It almost entirely ignores Farquharson's career as academic, a period which briefly brought him to the cusp of fame. As I soon found out, though he lacked any formal scientific or mathematical training, the future dropout made a seminal contribution to the theory of elections. By the age of thirty he had secured a network of powerful friends and benefactors across the English-speaking world. Then, for reasons nobody really understood, Farquharson disappeared. As a result, he came to occupy a strange sort of role in the history of mathematics, not really a real scientist and yet considered a kind of unheralded genius by a number of influential figures in the field. It all seemed a world away from the hippies and revolutionaries of Somers Town squats.

At first glance, Farquharson was one of those countercultural shapeshifters who professed to have met everyone and witnessed everything. Here was a man who knew both Rupert Murdoch and Nelson Mandela intimately, a man whose premature death should have landed him in some kind of pantheon. But the Platt Street fire hadn't made Farquharson a legend. It barely even made him a statistic.

Though Farquharson had abandoned mathematics by the time he wrote his unusual memoir, the contradictions of representation and the representation of contradictions had once been his scholarly speciality. As he wrote in *Drop Out!*, 'a stitch in time distorts eternity'—every time you stop to assess your whereabouts, you are in reality dropping a pin and creating counterfactuals. True to form, his book provides a patchy road-map when it comes to hard and fast facts. But for all its flaws, the book captures the broad strokes of Farquharson's life as well as not a small amount of its chaos.

Using the shaky itinerary provided by *Drop Out!*, I tried to go back and construct a detailed timeline of Farquharson's life and scattered publications. Farquharson also produced a small but professionally published body of journalism and poetry. I then broadened my search to news clippings and court records and mentions I could find of him in the glut of pre-existing countercultural chronicles. Concrete information was thin on the ground. After each round of discoveries I went back to *Drop Out!* to see how to join the dots of surname-less friends and address-free crash pads. Slowly a few patterns started to appear, dates began to align, and the first-tellings of later tall tales began to reveal themselves.

In time, my search extended out from London across three continents, twenty archives, and over sixty interviewees, from Nobel Prize winners to notorious squatters, anti-apartheid organisers, radical psychiatrists, politicians, poets, and beyond. Despite these efforts, I was not able to locate a single standalone source who was aware of all of the contours of Farquharson's life, someone through whom I could filter my findings for accuracy. Nobody seemed to have the whole picture. The anti-apartheid campaigner Dennis Brutus, who collaborated intensely with Farquharson in the early 1960s, came to believe that his colleague died in a barn. Friends from London's alternative scenes, meanwhile, had next to no idea about Farquharson's years of anti-apartheid resistance or his short-lived fame as a mathematician.

Part of the problem came in working out where to place Farquharson. He was in many ways a highly privileged man. In other ways he was a victim long before his tragic death, a man trapped between what appeared to the immiscible worlds of the black-and-white Fifties and the technicolour Sixties. I struggled to know what to define Farquharson as and who to measure him against. But again and again in the literature of the day I came across a word for people like him, a word that meant something between fellow traveller, radical, obsessive, and has-been. In the eyes of underground journalists and many commentators since, Farquharson and his kind were freaks.

Calling someone a 'freak' was not intended to be pejorative in Farquharson's world. The word served instead to describe someone who rejected mainstream values or had a particular fixation, like the 'Beatles freak', the 'health freak', and the ever-present 'speed freak'. After some unidentifiable point in history, probably around 1965, these and a wide array of other freaks, freeks, and phreaks stormed into view, from the cartoon adventures of the Fabulous Furry Freak Brothers to the admonition to 'let your freak flag fly'. The libidinous age of the so-called 'freak scene' had arrived.

By the mid-1960s, non-druggy circles were often referred to as being 'straight'—not necessarily heterosexual, but symbolically on the straight and narrow. By contrast, freaks were self-possessed, expressive, and free of normative ambitions. What these varied figures shared could be anything from smoking dope to having long hair or rejecting monogamy. Freakdom was a broad church. The new wave of Christian evangelicals were commonly referred to as 'Jesus freaks', while those undertaking the hippie trail were often armed with just two words to aim for on arrival in Kathmandu: 'Freak Street', the English-language name for a neighbourhood filled with legalised hashish shops.

In 1966, Frank Zappa and the Mothers of Invention named their first album *Freak Out!*, nodding towards another central tenet of freak culture: freaks were freaks less because of any single unifying trait but because of what they did to others. Like McMurphy in Ken Kesey's *One Flew Over the Cuckoo's Nest*, you could recognise a freak because they freaked *non*-freaks out. As freaks themselves saw it, they were negatively defined but positively inclined. Slowly but surely, being visibly and proudly freaky was seen as akin to taking up a political position. Freaks may not have been engaged in planting bombs but they need not have to in order to bring about a change in perception and consciousness. As the students-turned-militants of the Weather Underground stated in their first communiqué, 'Freaks are revolutionaries and revolutionaries are freaks.'

The freak scene presented itself as an amorphous collective that knew no bounds or norms, a familiar space for all those who felt unfamiliar. As the carnival sideshow performers in Tod Browning's cult 1932 film *Freaks* chant to a newcomer, 'gooble, gobble, we accept her, we accept her, one of us.' This phrase became a mantra not just for knowing cinephiles but for fans of the weird and strange, self-professed outsiders seeking a sense of community. Pioneering punk rockers the Ramones later turned 'gooble, gobble' into a signature part of their stage show, leading crowds in a collective chant of 'gabba gabba hey'. One of the band's roadies would then arrive on stage dressed as 'the Pinhead', a look inspired by an actor with microcephaly in Browning's film.

Joey Ramone, the band's frontman, felt a deep kinship with outcasts borne of his own traumatic medical experiences. The Ramones in turn saw the Pinhead act as affectionate, self-deprecating, and provocative. Punk was about exploding history, providing a place for people who felt they had been left out of straight society. But a freak show was a freak show, whether make-believe or not. Encounters with freaks real or imaginary disturb and shock. But they also remind people of what they have in common, of what makes them un-freaky and 'normal'. It can be a fine line between rupturing normative relations and shoring them up.

If the freak scene reached its height in the taboo-busting behaviour of punk, those for whom freakiness was deemed an affliction rather than a choice became an afterthought. For all the talk of revolution in the so-called counterculture and its varied subcultural offspring, the old structures didn't simply die away, nor did old hierarchies and prejudices fade from view. Referring to someone like Farquharson as a 'freak' was a more complicated characterisation than underground commentators typically anticipated. He was seen as a freak from several directions at once: unstable in hard-to-handle ways, prone to godly visions and manic destruction, and also, as his peers would put it, because he was a book freak, a telephone freak, a numbers freak, and, briefly, a rock'n'roll freak as well.

Though hippie scenes attempted to reappropriate the freak label, it took the arrival of gay pride, crip pride, and mad pride in the mid-1970s onwards to bend this process towards more meaningful ends. Freaks existed, suffered, and thrived long before becoming fashionable. As a survivor of psychiatric abuse and an openly gay man in a period where homosexuality was only just being legalised, Farquharson represents an important early bridge between these two worlds of freakiness and proof that they were never mutually exclusive. His experiences in and around the freak scene of the late 1960s illuminate numerous under-explored elements of hippie living, raising uneasy questions of how age, class, race, and sexuality intersected with cultural shifts and utopian rhetoric. That Farquharson also played a central if seldom acknowledged role in the development of the broader disability rights movement only makes him more deserving of our attention, however late in the day.

Farquharson's life also forces us to reckon with how the Sixties' emergent politics of identity interrelated with the collectivity for which the period is often remembered. The man himself was never sure, fantasising about a variety of solutions which moved between liberal, libertarian, communist, communitarian, and anarchistic approaches, from hyper-local ambitions to truly global aspirations. It would be wrong to try to overly justify or retroactively celebrate any one of these attempts or attempt to unify them under one common theory. The misses are part of the hits, the delusions an important part of the visions. Instead, by inserting Farquharson back into the history of the Sixties we can glimpse at the full gamut of the era's freakiness and not just its most performative edges. Only then will we begin to understand what the counterculture truly stood for and whom it truly served and how.

Farquharson's base stretched and flexed all the way to Johannesburg, Oxford, New York, and Glasgow. It was this constant whir of activity that earned him the dubious title of 'international freak' in the underground press. In spite of his regular travels, though, London remained Farquharson's centre.

By the time he arrived in 1965 the capital was on the precipice of a wholesale transformation. Vulnerable from its war years, London was being formed and reformed by mass migration and

MATHS - POLITICS WINS HIM PRIZE

RDM 19/12/61

DR. ROBIN FARQUHARSON (above), research officer in the Marginal Mines Research Unit of the Department of Commerce and Applied Economics at the University of the Witwatersrand, has been awarded the 1961 Monograph Prize in Social Sciences.

the aftereffects of high colonialism. For a few glimmering years one could be on the margins and in the middle at the very same time. The city's residents were comically wealthy and depressingly poor, close to the halls of power and yet party to a thriving alternate structure. A parallel politics of ambition and desperation decided who got to rise and who needed to fall.

It is a London many readers will struggle to superimpose onto the place they know today. But it is a London which rests at the core of the city present and long past, a London in which inequality, justice, humour, and folly are interwoven—a London profoundly tied to its former outposts and yet desperate to reconfigure itself without them. It was this dislocation between past and present which drew Farquharson towards London and which pulled him deep into its core.

Figures like Farquharson drift through formal structures, leaving more traces in the ether than they do on the official record. I went as far as I could, tracking down comrades and collaborators, friends and bitter rivals. Stoned testimonies were prised out of Scottish Deadheads. Skeptical fellow travellers recounted rumours and speculations. These and other voices drift in and out of the text that follows, complementing and contradicting our story.

A stitch in time distorts eternity and despite my efforts it was impossible to unpick all of Farquharson's many loops and double backs. His was a kaleidoscopic string figure of a life. We began by tugging at one end of it. Singed by flames and fantasy, let us now tug at the other.

by Robin Farquharson, Screws of the World Orgy Correspondent

PART I
A DECEPTIVE AIR OF REALITY, 1930-1966

g exhibit, made Interflora, is the dge depicting the cury, in dyed d another is a a luxury liner tions and del-
C.A.B.

that this was the fifth time that the award had been made . . . that he owned the original bronze, sculpted

the pink a on the ta pretty tabl music pla your coffe caviar, savoury ch berry flan del. . . . will not b days and

LEFT PRETORIA: Robin Farquharson, the son of Mr. and Mrs. Reginald Farquharson, who has been on a three-month holiday in Pretoria from Oxford, where he has been studying Modern Greats at Brasenose for the last six years. He was given a grant by the recently established Nuffield College at Oxford to embark on certain research, and was subsequently awarded a fellowship at Queen's College.

He left Pretoria recently by air for Paris, where he will work for six months.

pay

CHAPTER I
MERGING INTO THE LANDSCAPE

Though he grew up a world away from the squats of Somers Town, Farquharson's connection to Britain was highly significant. His ancestors on both sides of the family were part of the famous cohort of 5,000 British colonisers who arrived on the Eastern Cape of South Africa in 1820. This wave of settlers subsequently became a much-mythologised part of South African history, something like the country's equivalent of the Pilgrims who sailed to the New World.

Historically, the British-run Cape Colony had practiced a form of qualified franchise, extending the vote to all men regardless of ethnicity. Though the system of apartheid was yet to exist, discrimination was deeply entrenched in the region's colonial administrations. In turn, the Cape Colony was not subject to the same legal restrictions as the rest of the British Empire when slavery was outlawed in 1833. From that time on, a wave of legislation increasingly disenfranchised non-white voters and enshrined a vast array of racially discriminatory practices.

By the end of the nineteenth century black South Africans were forbidden from buying many types of land, from standing for election, and from practising many skilled trades. To be sure, many white South Africans were uncomfortable with this system. From their point of view, however, the most disturbing racial tension was that which existed between different white ethnicities. In this context, the Farquharsons' British background was more than a point of pride. Though the Farquharsons were white they were not Boers, the Afrikaans-speaking descendants of Protestant Dutch settlers. This was a crucial distinction, and one which would come to shape Farquharson's political trajectory.

By the early years of the twentieth century, the Boers and the British had been fighting over control of the gold-rich Cape Colony for the best part of 300 years. This rivalry had recently come to a violent head in the two Anglo-Boer wars, fuelled by disagreement as to rightful ownership of the Transvaal region. These two conflicts resulted in tens of thousands of combined military casualties. Though the exact numbers cannot be known, tens of thousands more died in British concentration camps.

In 1910, the British finally succeeded in crushing the Orange Free State and the South African Republic, two of the fledgling independent Boer Republics. The result was the founding of the Union of South Africa. This landmark moment transformed the former Cape Colony into a self-governing nation of its own. With this came an increasing degree of sovereignty, even if the new South African state still fell under the jurisdiction of the British Commonwealth. Despite what seemed like a victory for the British, the all-powerful aura of the Empire had taken a serious blow. In turn, an incipient nationalism grew amongst the Afrikaners, the Afrikaans-speaking descendants of Britain's Dutch enemies.

As Farquharson later recalled, his family 'were not exiles from England as it then was, not exiles at any time from the England that was contemporary with them then, but exiles from a far earlier time, a time as deeply sunken and as irretrievable as [the mythical island of] Lyonesse'.

Such was the enduring association with Britain that when Robin was born in 1930, the Farquharson family were still considered British in class, temperament, and ethnicity. As a British-South African family, the Farquharsons were secure at the very top of this power structure and yet vulnerable to a newly-emboldened independence movement.

The world Robin grew up in was largely insulated from these geopolitical issues, at least for the time being. Reginald, his father, was a lawyer-notary and founder of Macintosh, Cross & Farquharson, a prestigious law firm in the country's administrative capital of Pretoria. Reginald was a gifted athlete who made a number of appearances for Transvaal, the region's most successful first-class cricket team. His line of work afforded the Farquharsons a certain prestige in Pretoria commensurate with their racial status.

Reginald, his wife Enid (née Andrews), and their four children—Tony, Heather, Reginald junior (always known as Robin), and Michael—lived at Clan Chattan, a large home in a wealthy part of Pretoria known for its British-originating families. Reginald's job also brought the family into powerful social circles. Deputy prime minister Jan Hofmeyr was a regular guest at Clan Chattan. The family's elevated status was complicated by the fact that Enid was often confined to a local mental hospital.

From this rather proper and inhibited environment, Robin was sent to a series of high-achieving private schools. These started with Waterkloof, an exclusive primary school later attended by Elon Musk. Next he attended Woodridge, another leading prep school, before moving to Michaelhouse, an elite Anglican boarding school in the foothills of the Drakensberg mountains. As recalled by the novelist Wilbur Smith, whose time at Michaelhouse overlapped with Farquharson's, Michaelhouse was marked by an 'obsession with team sports and science subjects' common to many boarding schools. What distinguished it from the rest was the fact that 'the food was awful and the beatings heavier and more frequent'. Adding insult to injury were the arctic temperatures, a result of the school's mountainous location.

Rhodes University, Farquharson's alma mater

Robin would not have to endure many winters at Michaelhouse. At the age of 16 and already with the imposing physique of a man several times his age, Farquharson was ready to finish his schooling and begin an undergraduate degree. Though he went on to a short-lived but influential career as a mathematician, his first degree was in Arts, which he studied at Rhodes University on the Southern Cape of South Africa.

Farquharson majored in English and Latin and took additional classes in Roman Law, French, and German. Alongside this language-heavy curriculum Farquharson took modules in Mathematics and Economic History, though he excelled at neither. He did, however, excel at Esperanto, the so-called 'international language' which had gained a small following amongst linguists, eccentrics, and internationalists in the years immediately following World War I. Appropriately, Farquharson's classes were provided by the British Esperanto Association. He also obtained his pilot's license, itself no small sign of status.

Rhodes was a small but prestigious university named for and endowed by Cecil Rhodes, the British colonialist and founding father of the neighbouring state of Rhodesia. As one historian put it, the university was 'meant to be the engine room of English cultural ascendancy in South Africa'. Nevertheless, despite the atrocities of British rule and the structural racism that undergirded it, the former colonial system was seen to be gradually liberalising. While Rhodes was not legally bound to apply segregation, it came out in odd forms. Students were, for example, more or less banned from attending the university if their backgrounds were 'non-European' (i.e. 'native', 'coloured', or 'Asian', according to contemporary classifications). When admitted, these students were forced to live in separate accommodation. Farquharson joined Rhodes at a time when this kind of uneasy compromise was about to come to a sudden end.

In the middle year of Farquharson's undergraduate degree, prime minister Jan Smuts' ruling United Party were voted out of government. Though Smuts was a white supremacist, he had recently begun to relax segregation, a move that proved unpopular with the white electorate. D. F. Malan's National Party came to power in 1948, in part by pushing back hard against Smuts' proposed reforms. The Nats, as they were known, strongly prioritised Afrikaner interests. The result would be catastrophic.

The new ruling party quickly moved to establish a programme of institutionalised minority rule. This new system came to be known as apartheid, the Afrikaans word for 'aparthood'. Apartheid represented both a wholesale codification of decades of pre-existing customs and a significant advancement of racist policies.

All South Africans were now formally divided into one of four racial categories. Sexual relationships across these categories became a criminal offence. To ensure this racial separateness, millions of non-white South Africans were forcibly evicted from what were now deemed white-only areas. Extreme efforts were also made to ensure that political dissent of any kind became impossible.

As these horrors gradually became enshrined in law, families like the Farquharsons found themselves in an ambiguous position. Many white South Africans of British descent were attracted to calls for unity between themselves and the Afrikaners emboldened by

Malan's victory. At the same time, there was an instinctive hesitancy regarding Afrikaner nationalism, which was heavily associated with South African republicanism, anti-Britishness, and more extreme forms of racial segregation. Reaching the end of his teenage years, and finding himself in an elitist but ostensibly tolerant institution, Farquharson responded by joining the National Union of South African Students (NUSAS).

NUSAS were primarily a liberal, multi-racial, non-violent organisation. Originally intended to deepen connections between English and Afrikaans-speaking students, the group's recent decision to support South Africa's military combat against the Nazis significantly altered the organisation's role. By the time Farquharson joined, NUSAS was explicitly anti-apartheid, standing in opposition to the Christian-Nationalist leanings of the Afrikaanse Nationale Studentebond, a rival Afrikaner student body.

NUSAS's increasingly anti-racist stance attracted an extraordinary array of young supporters, with many of its members going on to form the next generation of South African intelligentsia. For now, though, Farquharson was charged with helping out with the NUSAS newsletter and putting together their annual conference. Despite these mundane tasks Farquharson quickly made a strong impression.

Phillip Tobias

My personal association with him has revealed to me a young man of determination and vigour, possessed of a clear and incisive mind and a sincere and rare spirit.

Ernie Wentzel

He was more than a brilliantly clever man. His was a mind of a genius which one is privileged to know perhaps once in a lifetime. He was a superb conversationalist, a delightful eccentric and a man of deep compassion.

Farquharson only got seriously involved in NUSAS when his time at Rhodes was coming to an end. His burgeoning politicisation drew him to his family's historical homeland, as did the chance to pursue his studies more seriously. True to Rhodes's anglocentric impulses, Farquharson's initial plan was to continue his education at Balliol College, Oxford. An ill-timed bout of tonsillitis prevented him from completing his undergraduate on time. It was likely he'd miss the start of the academic year. Fortunately he had some powerful allies to call on.

Though Farquharson was steadily drifting from the rest of his family, his father was never far from reach. Reginald actively pursued a number of old friends to write Oxford with urgent letters of recommendation for his son. Despite Robin's incipient anti-establishment politics, supportive letters were sent on his behalf to a number of top Oxford colleges by Jan Hofmeyr and Leif Egeland, then High Commissioner of South Africa to the United Kingdom. Though it was too late to join Balliol, Oxford's Brasenose College were persuaded to offer a last minute place to this well-connected student.

In late 1950 Farquharson moved to Oxford to begin his second BA, this time in Politics, Philosophy, and Economics. While he was adored by his friends in NUSAS, Farquharson was not a particularly impressive student. Physically, though, he made a distinct impression. Now entering his twenties, he was tall and broad, his receding hairline further emphasising a large, powerful forehead. He was also faintly handsome, with a strong, slightly cleft chin, floppy hair combed into waves, and a powerful stare framed by an ever-present pair of black oval glasses.

Oxford afforded Farquharson a number of freedoms unknown to him back home. As two contemporary historians have written of this period of gay life, 'power was not just an aphrodisiac, but a shield'. So long as Oxford undergraduates didn't go too far they were relatively untouched by the illegality of homosexual activity. Farquharson began to live as openly gay a life as was possible. But no sooner had he settled in Oxford than he was off again, having been awarded a generous student grant to travel through Germany.

It was an incredibly febrile time to be visiting Berlin, or rather the two Berlins. Across the city were thousands of identikit soldiers

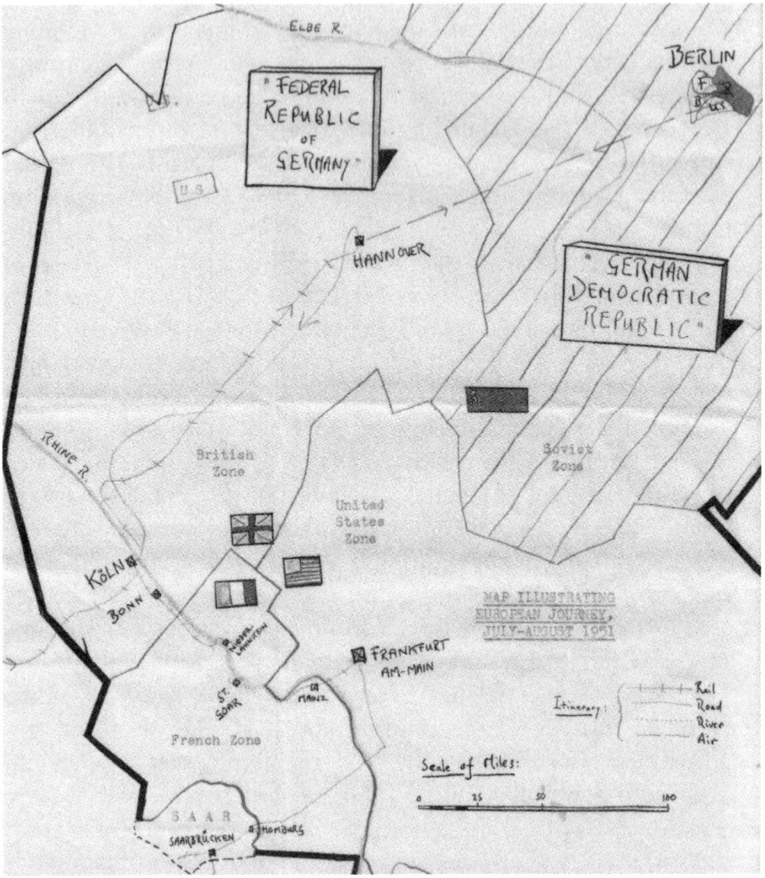

Farquharson's map of his European journey in 1951

distinguishable only by their uniforms. As Farquharson recounted in a report to his college, 'simply observing the look of the two sections of the city' proved to be the most illuminating experience of his trip.

Robin Farquharson

As I explained initially, my principal destinations were, firstly, that strip of the Rhine split by and linking the three Western

> zones of occupation; secondly, the divided city of Berlin; and thirdly, the Saar Territory with its special economic and political status—all with reference to the new internal frontiers which had come into existence within Germany since the war.
>
> One could compare the sharply contrasting effects of economic policy—on the one side, advertisements, hotels & cinemas in abundance, with lavish specialised reconstructions; high prices, no shortages, and considerable unemployment: on the other, nothing on hoardings but political slogans, building largely concentrated on housing & monuments; low food prices but few luxuries, and direction of labour. One could watch the working of an entirely free currency exchange, and link its fluctuations to the varying flows of shoppers. One could stop at two successive station bookstalls, neither carrying a single one of the items displayed by the other. It was a fantastic, and a fascinating, environment.
>
> The Americans seemed curiously reluctant to accept their environment, maintaining an insulated world of shops, restaurants and entertainment, operating on special dollar currency. By comparison, the British had seemed virtually to merge into the landscape.

Farquharson was fascinated by the extreme differences in economy he found—how between West and East Germany the same British money became two distinct currencies, each with not only their own purchasing power but also their own cultural world. He visited the newly-constructed offices of the Social Democratic Party in Cologne. He watched on in horror and amazement as activists readied themselves for yet another election, this time between communists, neo-Nazis, and Christian Democrats. Other organisations were preparing themselves for what they felt was the imminent reunification of Germany. Outfits like the Bund Deutscher Jugend were meanwhile forming paramilitary groups, keen to accelerate the chaos.

Farquharson returned to Britain from his month abroad with a growing sense of his own politics. Everything he had seen on the continent seemed to confirm that political outcomes were

The crest of the Voltaire Society

governed as much by self interest as they were by random acts of chance. Structures formed and reformed and citizens did their best to adapt within them. Moreover, the battle against fascism had revealed democracy itself to be a social construct.

Farquharson felt cynical and absurd and hopeful and hopeless all at once. And so, back in Oxford and still finding his feet, he did what recently radicalised men of his class and inclination had so often done before: he set up a secret society.

The Voltaire Society had all the trappings of a serious and august group. It had elected officers, formal dinners, and boasted of operating both a library and a rather grand sounding 'iconographical collection'. Like everything else about the Society, though, this was a deliberate sham.

> **Ved Mehta**
> The members prided themselves on not following any of the normal procedures of an Oxford society, such as keeping minutes. In fact, many of them were postgraduate foreigners, who were not members of any other Oxford societies, and even most of its English members were aggressively irreverent.

> **John Haldane**
> Its motto was, "If Voltaire did not exist he would have to be invented" and it was generally, if vaguely and superficially, anti-religious. Its main originating purpose seems to have been to boost the credentials of the Society's members by letting them take it in turn to hold the eleven different offices and then list this service on their CVs.

The library consisted of either one or two books, depending on who you asked. The 'iconographical collection', meanwhile, contained a single bust of Voltaire. Farquharson had purchased the sculpture himself from the Louvre gift shop, having cycled all the way to Paris on a dare. Not content with just the one bust, the group's elected iconoclast was charged with stealing those of other societies.

There was final piece missing from the charade. Every Oxford society needed a prominent patron. Like many other tasks, it fell to Farquharson to find one. His number one target was the venerable philosopher and pacifist Bertrand Russell, winner of the 1950 Nobel Prize in Literature. Though Russell was on the cusp of turning eighty and seldom left London, he also had a sense of humour and happily assented to the unlikely honour. The Voltaire Society's inaugural patron duly met with Farquharson and his

Farquharson

Murdoch

Farquharson and 'Red Rupert' during their time on the staff of Cherwell

friends at a Soho bistro. Farquharson lugged the bust of Voltaire along for the ride.

Throughout these formative experiences, Farquharson grew close to a fellow PPE student, a young Marxist from Australia named Rupert Murdoch. The two friends each took up roles at *Cherwell*, the Oxford student newspaper, with Farquharson serving as production manager and layout designer and Murdoch as publicity manager.

Farquharson had been involved in a number of student magazines at Rhodes, but *Cherwell* represented a far bigger challenge. The publication had up to then been an enormously clubby and staid affair, everything that people thought of when they thought of a place like Oxford. Under Farquharson and Murdoch's brief stewardship *Cherwell* reemerged as decidedly more sophisticated, taking its visual cues from the *New Yorker* and featuring a regular supply of short satirical pieces. Murdoch was soon Farquharson's right-hand man in running the Voltaire Society. Despite these adventures, mutual friends were baffled by what the two men saw in each other.

James Mitchell
It's very hard to say what the basis of that friendship was, because they were really very, very different. Robin would talk sixty to

the dozen on any subject and had wild intellectual and political fantasies that he would build up as he was talking. And Rupert never said anything about anything.

Michael Weigall

Both of them were Commonwealth but that's a very minor ground for getting together. Robin had a father who was a bit like Sir Keith Murdoch, reputable Establishment figure in Pretoria. I've seen Robin by the sheer brilliance of his argumentative processes just tying up these chaps in absolute knots and then giggling hysterically like a schoolgirl at how clever he had been. He was the sort of chap who would—unlike so many people at Oxford who would have done it to show off—but he would actually forget to put socks on when he was putting on a tuxedo.

Oxford saw Farquharson blossom into an urbane and somewhat chic mid-century intellectual, with all the attendant eccentricities. Judging by surviving records, he was a magnetic if eccentric presence, entirely aware of and comfortable with his reputation for self-mythologisation. An affectionate profile penned by an unknown *Cherwell* staff writer gives a flavour of both the ironical attitude of the university in the 1950s and Farquharson's mythical status within it.

Cherwell

Radical

Robin Farquharson's aim in life (one suspects) is to become a contradiction in terms. Since childhood he has courted incongruity, and is fondest of extremes when they meet. At B.N.C., he wears corduroys and sandals; in politics, he has moved steadily away from the Labour Party in both directions at once. He has laid out *Oxford Guardian* in the style of 1951, *Clarion* of 1925, *Cherwell* of 1960; he has been heard to support the candidates of Senator Taft and of Aneurin Bevan (for the same reasons). In South Africa, where contrasts are commonplace,

> he finds himself wholeheartedly agreeing with Malan that Government and Opposition policies are indistinguishable. But he will probably be shot if he goes back.
>
> *Rational*
> It is in the Voltaire Society that Robin became definitely established as a figure of his own imagination. First Iconographer, he wrote the original letter to Patron Russell; on the Left Bank, he sought out the life-size bust of the Master, bearing it on his bicycle from Victoria to Brasenose.
>
> His Presidential term was graced by the visit of celebrated anti-clerical Marie Stopes; he devised the clause whereby all officers are appointed by their immediate successors; he introduced the Society to halva, to vodka and to the Index Librorum Prohibitorum. It was with pride that he accepted the dignity of F.V.S.
>
> *Recluse*
> Time was when Farquharson could be encountered any morning, strolling in the Rue Bonaparte or shuffling sectors at the Potsdamerplatz. The Jaffa Road was all one with the Piazza di Spagna, the Palais de Chaillot with the Gallery at Morecambe. But (and how he regrets it!) Political Institutions is not the only paper in the PPE School. Since last October, he has been cutting friends in the street; sleeping alternate nights in mysterious George Street garrets and obscure collegiate crypts. *Cherwell*, Union, Guardian, WUS, NUS, UUIS, & LPG know him no more; but the dogged indomitable soul of him—the fierce, incompatible soul of him—may flame yet forth in glory upon another dawn.

From the distance of seventy-odd years, this all seems rather quaint and otherworldly. When we think of Oxford in the 1960s, we think of things like the Oxford Revue, the radical comedy troupe that would form the basis of Monty Python. For now, though, Terry Jones

Farquharson as featured in the pages of Cherwell

and Michael Palin were just two clever undergraduates. Future international hash smuggler Howard Marks was still weighing up a degree in Physics. Dreams of dope were, for the time being, simply dreams. Though drugs and surreal comedy and revolutionary rhetoric were a part of Oxford life they remained largely under the surface in Farquharson's cohort. For the time being, student journalism and tongue-in-cheek drinking societies were as dissident as things got.

Between the Voltaire Society's antics and the running of *Cherwell*, Farquharson and Murdoch spent a great deal of time together. But the budding partnership was suddenly interrupted when Murdoch's father died. The young journalist returned back to Australia to take over the family's struggling newspaper business, while Farquharson remained in Oxford to finish his degree. Their lives splintered irrevocably. With his closest friend's departure, Farquharson finally began to take the academic side of university seriously. What he discovered would prove revelatory.

CHAPTER 2
A PHONE CALL FROM GOD

Consider rock, paper, scissors or any equivalent version of the classic hand game. Players can use whatever tactics they want in order to win. Some people prefer to select their shape at the last minute; others play whichever shape would beat their previous shape; others try to be as random as possible. Everyone has their own theory as to what works best.

A whole field of study—game theory—seeks to understand decision making through analysing the relationship between tactics and outcomes. But whatever strategy you choose for rock, paper, scissors, the fundamental premise of the game remains the same: no matter which shape you make, you need only be a little bit unlucky for your opponent to win. Even though every shape can defeat another one, there will always be a third shape that is even stronger still. No shape is fundamentally the best, and so even though the game isn't rigged, it also isn't much of a game.

If you understand the problem of deciding which shape to favour in rock, paper, scissors, then you understand the basic problem of running an election. Most accounts locate the origins of modern electoral theory in the work of the Marquis de Condorcet, the eighteenth century French polymath whose eponymous Paradox was a key moment in the birth of game theory. Condorcet's Paradox applies to rock, paper, scissors, but it holds more serious implications when it comes to the management of elections and other group decisions.

For example: sometimes a candidate comes along who would win an election if you placed them in a head-to-head with any other candidate. This kind of candidate is called a 'Condorcet winner'. Compare the candidate with any of their rivals and they'll come out on top. But let's say that there are three candidates, each of whom has their strong points. Candidate A might be highly charismatic. Candidate B is boring but experienced, while candidate C is a complete wildcard. How to identify the most popular candidate now becomes a lot more complicated.

Voters choose whichever candidate they prefer, but democracy comes in many flavours. A group of voters may prefer candidate A over candidate B, and candidate B over candidate C. A head-to-head matchup like the one above makes things seem like a simple yes/no choice, but faced with a choice between candidate A and candidate C, voters might not necessarily prefer candidate A's charisma over candidate C's unknown qualities. Game theorists call these intransitive preferences. The fact that paper can beat rock doesn't mean that it is able to beat scissors.

The solution proposed by Condorcet was an exhaustive process of head-to-head clashes, a complicated and not entirely effective system later dubbed the 'Condorcet method'. Condorcet elections can be costly, cumbersome, and hard to wrap up. Voters might want more representative results in principle but not in practice.

There are also the practicalities of how a regularly shifting multi-party government might actually function and the danger of political instability. Though these questions might seem purely academic, the implications can quickly become very real. Condorcet learned this all too well when the chaos wrought by the French Revolution cost him his life.

In the years that followed, a British mathematician named Charles Babbage began to work on his difference engine, a pioneering template for a mathematical computer that would eventually facilitate calculations and projections on a previously inconceivable scale. While electoral systems were still antiquated and flawed, they could now be studied with increasing precision. But it took until a generation later for the next major advance in electoral theory to arrive. It came about thanks to a Victorian mathematician and Oxford don called Charles Dodgson, better known as Lewis Carroll. Though famous now as the author of *Alice's Adventures in Wonderland*, Dodgson first came to fame as a mathematician, having studied and then taught at Christ Church, Oxford for the best part of thirty years.

Dodgson began to focus his attentions on the problem of elections in the 1870s. The question of suffrage was then becoming of crucial importance in the United Kingdom. Sectarian issues in Scotland and Ireland meant that the distribution of parliamentary seats and the number of electors in each constituency was, to English Conservatives, nothing less than a question of national security. Though we might today associate electoral reform with the aftermath of the transatlantic slave trade and the impact of votes for women, it was neither border control nor egalitarianism which drew Dodgson to study elections. Instead, more parochially, Dodgson's pioneering work grew out of his frustration with how Oxford colleges selected their new fellows.

As one mathematical historian notes, Dodgson 'was devoted to being serious about games and game-like about serious things.' The problem of student selection posed a perfect meeting point between the two approaches. After a short survey, Dodgson quickly saw the inadequacies in the first-past-the-post system used by both Oxford and the British parliament. Under this highly simplistic system, one single winner is selected based on who has the most votes. It makes no difference if other candidates come close to winning or if two opposing voters would rather have come to a compromise on a third candidate: there can only be one winner. First-past-the-post disregards the preferences of all those who don't vote for the ultimate winner, thereby allowing for successful candidates who are disliked by the majority of voters.

After studying first-past-the-post, Dodgson recognised that elections were as much about tactics as they were about desires. As he toiled on his novels and poems, Dodgson also set about trying to devise a system by which the preferences of voters would be precisely represented in the final selection, be it in a parliamentary or a student body. In essence, what Dodgson attempted to do was to create a functional system of proportional representation. He went about this in numerous experimental ways, including allowing candidates the choice of transferring their votes to another candidate as they saw fit. Christ Church eventually made use of one of Dodgson's new systems for admitting members.

Despite this early promise, Dodgson's mathematical work lay unknown outside of this narrow context until the early 1950s. Around this time, a Scottish economist and political scientist named Duncan Black found that Christ Church's archives held a remarkable and largely untapped mass of Dodgson's research, some of which lay unread in a cupboard in the staff common room. Black's diligent research revealed that Dodgson worked on *Through the Looking-Glass* and *The Hunting of the Snark* at the same time as turning his mind to the question of democracy—all without ever referring to Condorcet's work.

Black's rediscovery of Dodgson came at an auspicious time. The early years of the Cold War saw national regimes split into new political blocks. Each had their own increasingly stratified electoral system. Though Black himself was wary of playing up Cold War tensions, accusations of totalitarianism flew across the Iron Curtain. This high-stakes environment led governments the world over to obsess over how best to understand and direct their populations. At the same time, colonised peoples intensified their fight for the right to choose their own leaders and the systems that governed them.

Wartime research into military strategy helped to formalise these questions into the nascent field of game theory. The idea was to study how humans made decisions and how these decisions might be predicted and ultimately influenced. Major progress was made during World War II through the collaboration of Manhattan Project member John von Neumann and his colleague Oskar Morgenstern. An important adjacent field known as social choice theory also sprung up, aiming to understand how these individual preferences might be mapped onto group decisions.

Electioneering was on the cusp of establishing itself as a serious object of study, the indirect result of political instability and government-backed research into strategic decision making. Then, in 1951, the American economist Kenneth Arrow published *Social Choice and Individual Values*. Arrow's principal claim came to be known as his 'impossibility theorem'. This held that there was no way of effectively converting voters' preferences into a fair outcome without ignoring the preferences of some in favour of the preferences of others. The recent ravages of war had revealed the horrifying results of top-down decision making. Now, Arrow had all but confirmed that voting, the purportedly democratic alternative, wasn't fundamentally any fairer.

These were important but distant-seeming developments until Black's rediscovery of Dodgson provided a compelling point of entry for British theorists. By the early 1950s Oxford boasted a particularly strong complement of electoral theorists, otherwise known as psephologists. The field of election studies was now well-enough established to not be intellectually isolated. It was also a new enough discipline for a relative novice to establish a foothold. Farquharson was well-placed to take advantage of this confluence. Silly as it was, the Voltaire Society had given him the chance to play with the pomposity of unearned power and explore the absurdities of privilege. Coupled with his experiences in post-war Berlin and a growing unease towards his family's elevated status, Farquharson's intellectual interests began to pivot away from the humanities and towards the administration of elections. He decided that now was the time to commit himself to a new course of study.

Though Carroll would soon be heralded as a prophet of psychedelia, this was still 1955. While acid was beginning to arrive in the UK, LSD still stood for pounds, shillings, and pence; Alice, Dodgson's best known creation, was still known as a model of Victorian whimsy and not yet the mascot of inner exploration. For now, though, Dodgson's mathematical ideas were revolutionary enough. Farquharson dived headfirst into his new field, reading everything he could lay his hands on. Then, having corresponded with Duncan Black, Farquharson made the brief walk to the library at Christ Church in the hope of studying Dodgson's papers up close.

Farquharson was quickly disappointed: the only known copy of Dodgson's pioneering *A Discussion of the Various Methods of Procedure in Conducting Elections* was located a world away at Princeton in New Jersey. Never one to give up on a lost cause, Farquharson managed to get his hands on a primitive photocopy of Dodgson's text. Ensuring Christ Church took possession of it, Farquharson got to work on some research of his own. He also arranged to meet with Bertrand Russell on a fairly regular basis, hoping to learn what he could from the great man while he was still around. Then disaster struck.

As many Oxbridge students did and still do, Farquharson suffered from a nervous breakdown. In isolation, the episode was a minor enough incident. As a friend wrote to Russell, Farquharson's collapse was the obvious result of 'overwork and anxiety.' In fact, as the friend excitedly told Russell, Farquharson's brief hospitalisation was apparently accompanied by some kind of breakthrough in his work. As to whether the eureka moment had occasioned the collapse or simply coincided with it was unclear.

Farquharson was soon discharged from hospital and returned to Oxford. Undeterred by his bout of ill health, he applied to Nuffield College, Oxford with the hope of beginning a period of graduate research.

Nuffield was one of Oxford's relatively new colleges and lacked the relevant university charter to award degrees under its own name. Despite this, the college held two obvious attractions. It was open only to graduate-level researchers, making it a serious place for serious thinkers. Amongst these researchers was David Butler, the boy wonder of British election research. Being permitted to work alongside Butler would not be easy. The college's standards were high and, judging by the interviewers' remarks, Farquharson divided opinion.

Nuffield interviewer #1
V. able, should get 1st. Lively mind, enormous intellectual curiosity. Full part in coll[ege] life. Midwife to rebirth of *Cherwell*. After travelling on grant submitted excell[ent] acc[ount] of Germany, grasp of political events + prowess of expression unequalled by his contemporaries. Most able undergraduate I have yet come across. Colleagues will like + respect him. No reservations about him. Charming, likeable, good company, outspoken brilliance.

Nuffield interviewer #2
Blue suit. Tall, rather wan, languid look. Glasses. Slight accent. W[ell] inf[ormed]. Intell[igent]. Rather slow spoken. Friendly, businesslike, mature. Balanced view of his own ability but doesn't underestimate either himself or problems. Int[erview] norm[al] with some confidence.

In the end, Farquharson obtained a second-class degree from Oxford, not the first his interviewer had predicted. Doubts and results notwithstanding, Nuffield offered Farquharson the chance to study towards a DPhil, a doctoral research degree. As he began to expand on the series of sketchy papers he had been working on as an undergraduate, it quickly became clear that Nuffield's gamble was going to be repaid handsomely.

Up to now, Farquharson had displayed little aptitude for mathematics, let alone the kind of experimental research currently making bold claims about political systems. But with the support of his supervisor, the economist Norman Leyland, who was soon to found the Oxford Centre for Management Studies, Farquharson began to get to grips with the subject.

Working closely with Dodgson's unpublished materials, Farquharson decided that voters typically had two options. Firstly, they could vote for their preferred candidate with no knowledge of other voters' preferences. Farquharson dubbed this approach 'sincere voting'. He called the other option 'sophisticated voting', because it involved voting against one's short-term preferences with knowledge of other voters' likely actions. Occasionally, the two strategies could overlap, a situation Farquharson referred to as 'straightforward voting'. But inspired by Dodgson, Farquharson discovered that when there were more than two choices at play—like in a hotly-contested election—artificially limiting voters' choices created disagreement at best and the silencing of the majority at worst.

As Farquharson later stated, most theorists were 'concerned with the dropping of the pebble into the urn far more than with the dropper or the reason why it is dropped.' But he and his peers realised that the choice of electoral system bore as much if not more weight than the election itself. As the political scientist William Riker put it, 'most formal analyses of voting now simply assume that voting is a game and voters always vote strategically'. It was Farquharson, however, who saw that voters were more likely to produce a favourable outcome if they voted against what they believed to be their own preferences.

The solution, Farquharson suggested, was that sometimes people are best served not when they vote for their preferred candidate but rather when their vote effectively cancelled out their rival's. Tactical voters were more likely to thrive than those who played by the implicit rules. Elections may be games of chance but that didn't mean that there was no such thing as skill.

Condorcet's contributions to political theory had largely been passed over in favour of the work of Jean-Jacques Rousseau, his revolutionary forebear. But Farquharson's research revealed that the study of tactical voting predated both men by at least 1,700 years. Drawing on a previously neglected letter by the Roman politician Pliny the Younger, Farquharson showed that tactical voting had both a long history and an urgent relevance to contemporary democracy. Suffrage was important—crucial, even—but so long as electoral systems weren't modernised then Western liberal democracy would remain a sham, no matter who got to vote. What passed for democracy was clearly not fit for purpose. What remained to be done was to make it work—or come up with something better.

Speculative theories started to pour out of Farquharson, though he still had very little in the way of formal mathematical training. To solve this, Farquharson paired up with Michael Dummett, soon to become professor of logic at Oxford. In the words of Howard Marks, one of Dummett's later students, Farquharson's new collaborator was 'a chain-smoking, Go-playing, devout Christian'. He was also the world expert on tarot cards, albeit one who believed their roots were in game playing rather than divination.

Dummett and Farquharson made an odd but productive pairing. Dummett knew the maths and the literature inside out, while Farquharson had the feel for ideas. Some time in 1953, Farquharson suggested that they study how the United States Senate voted on the League of Nations Covenant in the wake of World War I.

> **Michael Dummett**
> It struck him that the outcome was a result desired by very few of those taking part in it, and he started devising examples to see how often this happened. All this led him to become interested, indeed obsessively interested, in applying the theory of games to voting procedures, as von Neumann and Morgenstern had not done, and to strategic behaviour by voters, as Black and Arrow had not done. He had little encouragement in this interest from senior members of the University other than Leyland, and there was very little in print to guide him: it was a highly personal interest, which he had developed on his own account.

The head-spinning implications of this work didn't seem to pose a particular problem to Farquharson, at least not at this stage. Friends from Oxford saw him as earnest but not pushy, quiet but not timid.

He was more than capable of holding his own on his preferred subjects and yet also of withdrawing into himself.

> **Anonymous Cambridge referee**
> He is nervous in manner, but at the same time gentle and courteous, and he has a sense of humour of an individual kind. It would be possible to think him something of an oddity, but quite impossible to dislike him.

> **Jonathan Bennett**
> He was light in texture and good fun to be with. Lunching in Nuffield College with Robin and some of his colleagues there, I was struck by how freely they teased and ragged him, all of which he took cheerfully. At one point he said, "I hope your objections to me are personal, not professional."

Only a single generation separated the world of Dodgson and Carroll from the senior academics Farquharson now encountered on a daily basis. Though Farquharson's work was gruelling and challenging, in Dodgson he had found an intellectual role model who celebrated the meeting point of rationality and idiosyncrasy, the melding of linguistic play and mathematical creativity. Despite the changes on the horizon Britain's elite universities were still firmly Victorian, full of Anglican gentleman scholars, dilettantes, and dissolute philosophers. Farquharson was thriving.

The same geopolitical tensions that produced these academic discourses would shortly take an altogether more vibrant form. The imminent rise of the Campaign for Nuclear Disarmament (CND), founded by Bertrand Russell, and the turn from jazz to rock to acid and beyond occasioned what appeared to be a wholesale societal transformation. Dodgson the mathematician would once again be forgotten in favour of Carroll the wordsmith. In the US, two Harvard psychologists named Timothy Leary and Richard Alpert would soon help to develop a very public culture shift. It came in the form of LSD, a hitherto under-examined research chemical first synthesised in the late 1930s. Leary, Alpert, and other public scientists would soon risk their careers to promote LSD as the cure for everything from world hunger to homosexuality. What felt like a new politics was beginning, located as much in the head as anywhere else.

In the UK, students and radicals associated with Oxford and Cambridge would descend on London and be at the forefront of the action, demanding representation that resembled their new world picture. For now, though, this change in consciousness was an intellectual one, proof that the counterculture was only a few steps from conventionality. For the time being, the only route to change was the ballot box.

In April 1955, British voters received an unexpected opportunity to exercise this right: with no advance notice, Winston Churchill announced that he was retiring as prime minister. The sudden departure of this titan of British politics prompted a snap general election in just seven weeks' time. The machinery of electoral politics lurched into gear as the press scrambled for ways to understand the crisis left by Churchill's departure.

As the national broadcaster, the BBC had experimented with televised coverage in the previous two general elections. It was now determined to take this unexpected opportunity to produce its most ambitious programming to date. The result was a mammoth 19 hour-long programme, expertly guided along by the host Richard Dimbleby. With only a few weeks to plan the show, the BBC's landmark election night broadcast eventually made use of some forty studio cameras and numerous local camera teams.

With one in three British homes now in possession of a television, Dimbleby was one of the most recognisable figures in British media. Alongside him, the BBC decided to hire Nuffield College's David Butler as the evening's analytical expert. Butler's job throughout the broadcast was to provide instant statistical information to Dimbleby. These snippets of electoral analysis were provided to Butler by a team of first-class number crunchers led by none other than Robin Farquharson.

It was a testament to how far Farquharson's maths had come that Butler chose him for this high-pressure task. The challenge

Butler (L) introduces Farquharson (in glasses) during the BBC's 1955 election coverage

for Farquharson and his team was to rapidly calculate the shift in votes between the last election and this, a phenomenon Butler had recently named 'swing'. This was then rendered visually on Butler's 'swingometer', a device specially constructed for the 1955 broadcast and which soon became an icon of British election coverage.

Though slow and stilted by contemporary standards, this and other gimmicks made for excellent television. It was a moment of extraordinary visibility for Farquharson, eclipsing by far his brilliant but essentially semi-public appearances on the Oxford academic circuit. At its height, more than one in five people in the United Kingdom tuned in, a total of some 10 million viewers. Farquharson was suddenly a national figure.

By this time nearly all of Farquharson's mathematical work had been written and completed, but his only publication to date was a small text presented by a friend on his behalf to the French Academy of Sciences. The task now was to spread the word. In mid-September, a few months after the election, Farquharson spoke at a conference held at the Royal Institution in London. The other participants represented an extraordinary array of pioneering mathematicians.

Sharing the conference's opening panel with Farquharson was George Spencer Brown, soon to become a hero of the counterculture-cyberculture nexus, and Dennis Gabor, the Hungarian-born inventor of holography. There were also presentations by J. C. R. Licklider, the MIT computer scientist now known as the father of the internet, and Benoît Mandelbrot, the Polish-born polymath famous for developing the theory of fractals. Alongside them was MIT mathematician Oliver Selfridge, who spoke on the subject of pattern recognition. A year later, Selfridge would participate in the so-called Dartmouth workshop, widely considered the founding moment in the field of artificial intelligence.

Data scientists had been proclaiming the coming of the age of computing since the time of Charles Babbage and his difference engine. Now, after many false dawns, this day seemed finally to have arrived, spearheaded by the efforts of a former child prodigy turned MIT professor by the name of Norbert Wiener. For the past decade or so Wiener had been a key figure in the Macy conferences, one of the most influential attempts to date to develop a wholeheartedly interdisciplinary vision of science.

Based in New York, the Macy conferences brought game theorists, data scientists, linguists, evolutionary biologists, and communications theorists together in the hope of sparking new discussions around feedback loops, neural impulses, and information management. Some of those involved in these conversations were even beginning to experiment with the potential of mind-expanding drugs, from the peyote cactus to newer synthetic hallucinogens. These experiences were limited to largely clinical settings, though a small circle of researchers were convinced that these drugs could be a source of great intellectual stimulation. Humphry Osmond, a British psychiatrist with close connections to the Macy group, coined a word to describe the indescribable combination of sensations wrought by these chemicals: 'psychedelic', cod Greek for 'mind manifesting'.

At the Macy conferences the theoretical revelations of Condorcet and Dodgson began to explode into use. From proto-psychedelia to utopian futurism, the common strand linking this motley crew was the new field of cybernetics, the Cold War super-science that sought to master the problem of individual and societal control. Cybernetics held wide-reaching implications for industrial engineering, information sharing, and geopolitical strategy. Though Wiener had by now declared himself a pacifist, some cyberneticists applied their ideas in military contexts, others in computing, others in both. Much lucrative, politically significant, and intellectually compelling work was in the offing.

Electoral theorists and big-money defence contractors were now rubbing shoulders. Pathbreaking discoveries were in the air by the time Farquharson appeared at the Royal Institution conference. The conference was a who's who of the new sciences of decision making. It was therefore only natural that alongside Licklider, Mandelbrot, and the others that Macy conference chair Warren McCulloch would make an appearance. Farquharson held his own amongst this remarkable group of thinkers. He was 24 years old and still lacked any formal training in mathematics.

In spite of his reluctance to publish, Farquharson was primed for a brilliant career in academia, cutting-edge industry, or some yet to be defined media role. Seeking a sturdy institutional base in the weeks after the conference, Farquharson began to seek out academic appointments around Oxford. His first port of call was applying for a job at Queen's College, a process that consisted of a two-part examination he would likely ace. At first glance, the examiners seemed nonplussed. 'I don't think the two answers indicate very much,' Farquharson's assessor noted, 'except that he has some ability.'

Despite the tepid response to his exam, Queen's awarded Farquharson a Laming Travelling Fellowship, a grant intended to fund researchers either planning to teach in a foreign language, conduct business abroad, or otherwise advance the interests of the British Commonwealth. Farquharson snapped up the award, relishing the chance to travel again. The only drawback was that the funding he had been awarded would not be available for a few months. In the meantime, he decided to apply to All Souls, Oxford, a particularly elite college open only to recent Oxford graduates. Successful applicants would be provided with a seven-year salaried position with no teaching obligations, free accommodation, and full access to any programmes of study offered by the university.

A gruelling application procedure determined who would be selected for the college's prestigious fellowship, a process so arcane that it could easily have been taken as an object of study by Farquharson himself.

Michael Dummett

Candidates for All Souls' fellowship examination answer two general papers and two papers on specialist subjects (Farquharson would have chosen politics and economics); they also write an essay on a set topic, not known to them beforehand, and answer a translation paper in Latin, classical Greek, French, German, Italian, Russian and Spanish (of which they do as many as they can). The answer papers are assessed by a team of examiners, but then placed in a room in which any Fellow of the college can read them, which almost all do.

On the day of the election, the Fellows assemble, the examiners' report is read and a discussion ensues, whose upshot is often at variance with the examiners' report. During this discussion only the examination scripts may be referred to. The Fellows then transfer to a different room, in which other relevant information about the candidates may be cited. A vote is taken on which of the candidates should be elected Fellows; these may be none, one, two or occasionally three in number.

The All Souls assessment came just a few weeks after Farquharson's triumph at the Royal Institution conference. Though competition was fierce, the young South African's combination of qualifications, accomplishments, and personal and familial connections meant that he stood as good a chance as anyone of gaining access to this most exclusive of academic environments. It was not to be.

Michael Dummett
On the occasion in question, the Warden of the college received a telephone call on the evening before the election meeting. It started with the words. "Do you have a pen and paper?", and was from Farquharson: he attempted to dictate a lengthy statement in quasi-technical language, expounding a discovery which would have solved many problems in mathematics, mathematical logic, physics, economics and the theory of voting. I know very well what it was like: though I was away for the year in California, Farquharson also telephoned me there in just the same manner. He had had a friend looking after him, to prevent him from doing anything disastrous, but he had contrived to evade this friend to go and make his telephone calls.

Robin Farquharson
The questions had been very fortunate for me; and (as I later learnt) my performance had made me favourite for election to one of the two Fellowships offered. In the week before the election, my mind was a tempest of ideas; I spent forty minutes on the telephone to a colleague in California trying to explain them. On the night before the election, I telephoned the Warden of All Souls, and had him called from his high table to hear that I wanted to give him a message from God. I was not elected.

Michael Dummett
The Warden achieved maximum dramatic effect by scrupulously observing the rules. During the first part of the discussion he made no reference to the telephone call, with the result that,

when Fellows moved to the other room, it was obvious that everybody thought Farquharson far the best of the candidates, and he appeared certain to be elected. The Warden then told them all about the telephone call, from which he inferred that Farquharson had gone mad. The Fellows naturally did not want to offer a Fellowship to someone who was off his head, and so did not elect him. Henceforth every time he had an idea that would lead to some genuinely creative work, it triggered a manic phase; he had a few depressive phases, too, but most were manic.

Robin Farquharson
The next morning my friends took me to the Maudsley Hospital, where I spent a year as a voluntary patient. The Maudsley was hell. I arrived bursting with my divine message and with the discoveries of the last weeks, some of which indeed were genuine and later enabled me to win the Monograph Prize of the American Academy of Arts and Sciences. Expecting the gratitude of humanity, I found myself instead in a wilderness of mirrors staffed by torturers. Appalled, I retreated into a withdrawal close to stupor, from which I was awakened a year later by three sessions of ECT.

Though friends later traced Farquharson's decline to the All Souls debacle, archival records indicate that he had already been admitted to mental hospitals before the fateful phone call to the Warden, not least during the period in which he pursued Russell's mentorship. Farquharson was treated not just for his manic episodes and delusions but also for his homosexuality, something he happened to share with John Sparrow, the Warden of All Souls.

At the time of the phone call from God, mental health provisions in the UK were limited and brutal—ineffective at best, downright dangerous at worst. The hospitals Farquharson experienced were part of the Victorian asylum system: large, purpose-built institutions designed to replace the squalid hospitals of the Regency era. By the mid-1950s the asylums were profoundly incapable of matching the needs of their patients, if ever they could. In 1961, then-minister of health Enoch Powell proposed shuttering the asylums permanently. It would take many years for the NHS to act on this suggestion. For the time being, patients like Farquharson were trapped.

The Queen's College

GILLMAN & SOAME OXFORD

19 57

CHAPTER 3
SYLLABLES OF BRASS

During the period in which Farquharson was hospitalised at the Maudsley, his first major piece of research—'Straightforwardness in Voting Procedures'—was published in *Oxford Economic Papers*, a leading academic journal. On his release, Farquharson then began his fellowship at Queen's.

Despite it all, Oxford was a small town. The grand buildings of Queen's were located in the heart of Oxford. Just down the High Street was Brasenose, site of many of Farquharson's earliest academic triumphs. Walking from Brasenose towards Queen's took him past Oriel College, presided over by its statue of Cecil Rhodes and the colonial order Farquharson had come to loathe. Next he passed the gate of All Souls and the impossible future it represented.

Despite its charged location, Queen's offered Farquharson a chance for respite. Together with a scholarship from the Centre national de la recherche scientifique, the Queen's grant allowed

Farquharson to move to Paris and take in the city of Condorcet and Rousseau. He rented a room just a few metres from the tomb of Napoleon in the affluent 7th arrondissement and tried to rebuild his scholarly identity.

Letters back to senior colleagues at Queen's were filled with positivity and possibility. Reporting a clean bill of health, Farquharson recounted his days working with Condorcet's manuscripts at the Institut de France, his meetings with preeminent scholars, and his pleasure at undertaking a course in French phonetics. He also spent some time at the prestigious École pratique des hautes études, where he presented his research to the important Mathematical Methods in the Social Sciences study group on two occasions, both times in French. Short trips back to England were positive, while return visits to South Africa seemed to show improving relations with his father. Paris was working wonders on Farquharson's wellbeing. The phone call from God began to feel like a long time ago.

Jonathan Bennett

One time when I was lunching with Robin and his mother, and he and I were full of the pleasure of having just completed a difficult bit of work. I said, "This is a lovely lunch; even the water tastes good." Robin's mother rather severely said, "Water is water." Robin said, "You understand that that's the contradictory of 'There is *water* and *water*.'"

Colin Leys

After my wife and I were leaving what was then Southern Rhodesia after I'd done some fieldwork there, we stopped in Pretoria and stayed with him and his father. He was very charming and insisted on presenting me with a copy of a book called *Jock of the Bushveld*—it's a story about a group of trekkers and a dog. It was beautifully illustrated.

At the time of his Paris adventure, Farquharson was at work putting the final touches on his thesis. But this period of productivity was disrupted by the sudden death of his father, prompting an urgent return to South Africa. Nuffield granted Farquharson a three-month extension to finish up his research. But the end result of his repeated absences was that Farquharson had spent the majority of his doctorate away from Norman Chester, the preeminent political economist who was ostensibly his supervisor.

Despite these difficulties, Farquharson eventually managed to submit his thesis. It soon began to circulate around the international game theory community with great interest.

> **David Butler**
> It was the shortest thesis I had ever seen, but four out of the hundred pages were brilliant.

> **Colin Leys**
> My maths was hopeless and my logic was pretty bad too, but I remember his thesis was 27 pages—without a viva.

In truth, Farquharson's thesis was 125 pages, bibliography included, typed and single spaced, plus a 6 page abstract. And though there was no oral examination, as Leys recalled, there was one final hurdle. This consisted of an assessment by R. B. Braithwaite and M. W. Dick, two eminent Oxbridge scholars with deep connections to the Oxbridge of old.

Braithwaite was a prominent philosopher of science at King's College, Cambridge whose career risked being overshadowed not by something he wrote or said but rather something he owned. A decade earlier, the philosopher's college rooms played host to the one and only meeting between Bertrand Russell, Ludwig Wittgenstein, and Karl Popper. These three eminent thinkers had gathered for a meeting of the Cambridge Moral Science Club, where Popper was due to present a paper on the nature of philosophical problems.

Some forty years later Popper published a highly dramatic account of what happened next. Most versions agree that an argument broke out between Popper, who held that philosophical problems were real and demonstrable, and Wittgenstein, who held that philosophical problems were, like everything else, a linguistic phenomenon. As they debated, Wittgenstein held a fireplace poker—either red-hot from the fire or purely ornamental, depending on who was telling the story—with which he was either distractedly toying or jabbing in Popper's direction. Russell served as unwilling middleman until Wittgenstein stormed off, leaving the infamous poker behind. Braithwaite then either hid the item in question or destroyed it, depending on who you ask. Word spread despite Braithwaite's best efforts. Wittgenstein's poker quickly became a mythical object in the symbolic showdown between realism and relativism.

Farquharson's other assessor, M. W. (Marcus William) Dick, was highly influenced by the latter camp. A philosopher and senior tutor at Balliol College, Oxford, Dick was a member of the so-called 'kindergarten' of young scholars associated with J. L. Austin, the pioneering Oxford philosopher of language games. Unlike Braithwaite, whose scholarly publications spanned some sixty years, Dick never published, devoting himself entirely to teaching and mentoring.

Together, Braithwaite and Dick embodied the intellectual might of an entire generation of British philosophy. Farquharson had every reason to feel nervous in their presence, especially given recent events. In the event, Braithwaite and Dick passed the untrained mathematician's thesis with flying colours.

Colin Leys
It was the talk of the town. Marcus Dick said it was the best thesis he had ever read.

R. B. Braithwaite and **M. W. Dick**
Mr. Farquharson's thesis is on a type of subject little studied in British Universities, partly perhaps because in terms of formal disciplines it forms a bridge between two faculties. Mr. Farquharson has applied precise mathematical techniques,

> in particular those of the Theory of Games to problems of voting. We had certain criticisms to make of the detailed presentation which it seemed to us might have been clearer in some places, but we have no doubt that Mr. Farquharson's work, by the originality and excellence of its content, qualifies him for the degree of Doctor of Philosophy. He already holds an acknowledged position as an authority in the literature of the subject.

After the All Souls setback, this degree of praise was highly valuable. If Farquharson lacked the mathematical ability to be considered a true maths prodigy, he was certainly a remarkable ideas man. Though he was increasingly recognised as such, he also began to have episodes like the All Souls attack with increasing regularity.

On one occasion, David Butler was obliged to collect his protégé from Coventry, where Farquharson had called the police in order to proclaim himself the prince of an imaginary African country. In the event, Butler was able to ferry Farquharson home. More often than not, though, the end result was a series of long-distance telephone calls liable to have the young academic indefinitely committed.

> **Frank Cioffi**
> In his manic phase, he would organise all sorts of extraordinarily expensive things like getting the telephone people to install a load of telephones so that he could be in contact with all parts of the world simultaneously.

> **Robin Farquharson**
> I adumbrated vast enterprises, and before one was completely discussed I dropped it to go on to a vaster (clinical term: flight of ideas). I spoke syllables of brass to the walls of an echoing cavern; I was on the throne and in the pulpit and appearing as the Frost Report.

> **Michael Dummett**
> He once succeeded in speaking to [Aristotle] Onassis on the telephone, to tell him to bring whaling to an end. On another occasion he obtained a job as a tour guide, and in the middle of the tour sat down the unfortunate participants to answer an examination on cultural appreciation.

These episodes notwithstanding, Farquharson successfully took up a research fellowship at Nuffield and pursued a further appointment at Merton College, Oxford. The life of an itinerant scholar clearly appealed to him, and as 1956 drew to a close Farquharson began to weigh up the possibility of returning home to South Africa for a short while. Outside the comfort of Clan Chattan, though, things were tense.

In early December, 156 leading anti-apartheid activists were arrested and accused of treason. Amongst their number were numerous leading members of the African National Congress (ANC), South Africa's largest anti-apartheid group. The infamous 'Treason Trial' that followed would drag on for five solid years. Though the defendants were eventually found not guilty, it was clear that the apartheid state would stop at nothing to quash dissident activity.

Until this point, Farquharson had essentially been a political analyst with little stake in what became of his ideas. Oxford's CND branch had recently called on him to analyse the results of some polling they had conducted, but this only hinted at a broad and largely uncontroversial support of pacifism. Farquharson was political but unaligned, but recent developments in South Africa seemed to precipitate a change in his thinking, as hinted at in the introduction to the final version of his thesis.

After explaining the basic thinking behind his ideas, Farquharson's introductory text ended with a quote from Aristotle: 'The goal of political studies is not knowledge,' it stated, 'but action.' In the context of Farquharson's mathematical research, this might seem like a reference to the need for new electoral systems. Given the political context in which he was writing, it's likely that Farquharson was alluding to something considerably more drastic. As his politics hardened, Farquharson returned to his homeland on what seemed like a pro-establishment mission. Within three years he would be on the run, stateless and fearing for his life at the hands of his own government.

CHAPTER 4
BENT BUT NOT BROKEN

Despite the turmoil of the past few years, South Africa continued to present itself to the wider world as a fully-functioning democracy. In April 1958, the country held another general election. The result was another majority for the increasingly brutal Nats regime, which the government held up as proof of the widespread support for apartheid. Given that only white citizens had been allowed to vote, the outcome was unsurprising.

Even as Farquharson began to publicly criticise his homeland, his decision to return to South Africa was part of the country's respectability drive. He had been awarded funding to study the administration of elections in Ghana and South Africa, on which he reported for the *Economist* and South Africa's *Sunday Times*. These soon fed into 'South Africa 1958', a major essay that drew on Farquharson's first-hand experiences of the recent general election and an increasingly journalistic style of writing.

> **Robin Farquharson**
> Elections in South Africa have a deceptive air of reality. Their apparatus of meetings, ballots, and returning officers is so convincing that the psephologist may need a positive act of will to break the spell. It is tempting to suppose that an ordinary election is in progress, under the British electoral system and conducted in a normal Commonwealth fashion. In fact, South African elections operate at two distinct levels of fantasy.

The first and most important level of fantasy, Farquharson explained, was that a vast percentage of South Africans simply couldn't vote. What was known as the 'coloured vote case' had just been resolved, the result of which was that only whites were represented in general elections. This legal hurdle meant that elections now had a veneer of propriety, however unjustly earned.

> **Robin Farquharson**
> For all the shortcomings of its electoral system, for all its racial discrimination and restrictive laws, South Africa in April 1958, was still a country on the hither side of the line between liberty and dictatorship. Many freedoms had dwindled, much injustice prevailed. But it was still possible for opinions to be spoken and printed without prior censorship; those who could vote did not need to fear for the secrecy of their ballots; though laws were unjust, the rule of law at least remained. The Government had bent, but not broken, the democratic conventions within the white community. The Opposition still stood by the compact, and did not dispute the legitimacy of the Government's continuance. Those who did dispute its legitimacy, and appealed to more general principles, enjoyed no significant support from the electorate.

At the same time, popular, non-political resistance to segregation only resulted in further repression, such as when the British teen idol Tommy Steele had recently performed to non-segregated audiences. Farquharson noted that tabloid fears of 'delinquency' gave the authorities the chance to associate rock'n'roll with disorder and disorder with foreignness, which in turn was directed towards South Africa's own 'non-European' citizens. Mass culture was a powerful tool of resistance but apartheid always found a way to justify itself.

The Nats contested the 1958 election under J. G. Strijdom, their new leader. Strijdom died just four months after becoming prime minister and was replaced by Hendrik Verwoerd, an authoritarian Afrikaner nationalist dedicated to vastly extending the scope of apartheid. By the time Verwoerd came to power, Farquharson was back in London and wreaking a fair amount of havoc.

David Butler, the BBC's elections guru, hoped to include 'South Africa 1958' in an upcoming book entitled *Elections Abroad*, which was going to be published by Macmillan. Butler recalled having to spend an entire evening by Farquharson's side to ensure his young colleague would stay still long enough to complete his contribution. Worse scenes were on the horizon.

Colin Leys

My younger brother Roger shared a flat with him and somebody else in London. Roger told me that Robin was a charming but unreliable sort of person to have around. Robin had made a phone call to California which cost something like £180. The bill was on the shared phone in the house and they had to pay it to keep the phone, as he didn't have any money.

Another time Robin got a job as a tour guide. He took a tour party to Norway, and when he was in Oslo, I think it was, he decided to buy them all electric typewriters on the company account.

Robin Farquharson

Returned to the Maudsley via a Norwegian hospital, I found it again intolerable and signed myself out, only to be taken to St. Francis Reception Unit. There I discovered what real brutality could be like when I was dragged into a padded cell by means of a

> twisted sheet around my neck. I soon agreed to return "voluntarily" to the Maudsley.

In November 1958, Farquharson was awarded his DPhil. Though Nuffield first admitted students in 1945, the college couldn't technically award degrees until it was awarded a Royal Charter in 1958. This technicality meant that Farquharson ended up playing a rather historic role as the first ever candidate from the college to be awarded a doctoral degree. In response, Farquharson donated a sheet of writing in the hand of Jean-Jacques Rousseau to the Nuffield College library. It was delivered care of the Voltaire Society, which had by now become a bona fide society. With this gesture, Farquharson's relationship with Oxford was more or less over.

During this time Farquharson once more advised the BBC on statistics, this time for the 1959 general election. The newly-elected parliament welcomed two future forces in British politics: Margaret Thatcher, the former chemist who would eventually lead the Conservative Party, and Jeremy Thorpe, the charismatic child of Tory grandees who oversaw the revitalisation of the Liberal Party. For now, with the Conservatives having won their third successive victory, British politics seemed at a dead end for the left to which Farquharson increasingly belonged. On his release from the Maudsley, he decided that a permanent change of scene would do him good.

Turning his back on a career at Oxford, Farquharson decided to return permanently to South Africa. The pretext was a position in the Department of Commerce and Applied Economics at the University of the Witwatersrand, commonly known as Wits. Farquharson would be heading up the university's new Marginal Mines Research Unit. Gold mines had been South Africa's principal source of colonial wealth and one of the major causes of the Boer Wars. Understanding the factors behind the gradual decline of the mines was a matter of national importance. Whatever the rights and wrongs of apartheid, Farquharson was keen to play his part in stabilising the economy. 1960 also marked the fiftieth anniversary of the Union of South Africa. The South African government were therefore keener than ever to reinforce their ideological and financial independence.

The anniversary of South African independence would not prove to be the defining event of 1960. On March 21st, police opened fire on 7,000 black protesters in the township of Sharpeville. Sixty-nine people were killed and 180 more injured. The Sharpeville massacre, as it came to be known, would soon be seen as the major political moment of the era.

Prime minister Verwoerd's government wasted little time in declaring a state of emergency in response to its own actions. These powers allowed the government to detain without trial some 18,000 people accused of being a threat to national security. ANC leader Nelson Mandela was amongst their number. The ANC itself was banned outright.

White South Africans struggled to look away from these horrifying abuses of power, but Farquharson had reason to keep his head down. For starters, he had an impressive new job. He was also shuttling between Oxford and Johannesburg in order to undergo training on the Ferranti Mercury and the IBM 1620, two early computers with impressive scientific capabilities. As Farquharson readied himself for a career in industry, the leading *Econometrica* journal published an article he had co-authored with Michael Dummett. This publication was a significant accomplishment for a junior scholar such as Farquharson.

> **Michael Dummett**
> Robin Farquharson said we should send it to *Econometrica*, so I sent it to *Econometrica*. That's all. I can't now remember who actually wrote the main body of the text. I mean, we wrote it together, but the machinery, the technical notions and technical vocabulary, that all came from him.

'Stability in Voting', Farquharson and Dummett's joint article, was gradually recognised as a landmark moment in social choice theory. Its principal speculation was that if an election had three possible outcomes, then the only chance it had of not being subject to manipulation was if there was one voter who had undue influence, otherwise known as a dictator. This was well-informed conjecture, for now at least.

A few months after the *Econometrica* article, the American Academy of Arts and Sciences awarded Farquharson's thesis the prestigious Monograph Prize in the social sciences. This award came at the insistence of Harvard games theorist Thomas Schelling, who had been stunned to learn that Farquharson was not part of any kind of research collective or formal intellectual school.

With numerous languages under his belt and a wide-range of contacts which reached into the upper levels of South African and British society, Farquharson seemed well placed to begin a career as a diplomat or colonial administrator. In fact, another Robin Farquharson was then demonstrating exactly where that road might lead. Born in 1925 and a graduate of Cambridge, this other Robin Farquharson had made swift progress up the ladder of the British Foreign Office. Since 1949 he had moved between postings in Moscow, Madrid, and Paris in a career that would culminate in a knighthood. In 1955 he married the daughter of Sir Ivo Mallet, former Consul-General of Tangier and then ambassador to Spain.

Though Robin Farquharson the diplomat was evidently going places, Robin Farquharson the scholarly prodigy was doing pretty well at generating headlines of his own. His electoral theorising was being keenly discussed in South Africa's English-language press, where the activities of the scion of a prominent Pretoria family were considered important news. The job at Wits put him in close contact with government-backed economists and officials. Farquharson's academic outlook looked once again positive with official appointments and research posts in the offing. Instability both personal and political would soon make that road an impossibility.

contact

MANDELA'S STATEMENT TO "CONTACT"

—see page

4 No. 9
5c (6d)
4th MAY 1961
Registered at the G.P.O. as a Newspaper
SOUTH AFRICA'S NON-RACIAL FORTNIGHTLY

South West Africa—

- **Rebellion on Frontier** —page 3
- **New Labour Racket** —page 5

CHAPTER 5
THE PLEASURES OF THE NIGHT ARE GONE

By the start of the 1960s, Farquharson had become a prominent member of South Africa's small but vocal Liberal Party. In spite of their name, the Liberals were further to the left than the Progressive Party, who were themselves considered to be the leftist point of the all-white parliament. Founded in 1953 by the novelist Alan Paton, author of the wildly successful *Cry, the Beloved Country*, the Liberals had become arguably the leading anti-apartheid political party in the wake of the ANC's banning.

Like the incipient field of game theory, anti-apartheid party politics was a new enough world to make rapid inroads. By 1961, Farquharson had been elected to the executive of the party's Transvaal Division, the region which included the nation's administrative capital, Pretoria.

Alan Marcuson

I was, I guess, about 17. I used to go to Liberal Party meetings that were sort of semi-secret and Robin would turn up. At that

> time, he was working for Anglo American and the boss at that time was a fellow called Harry Oppenheimer—very famous, he was the richest man in South Africa. And Robin was doing some sort of study for Harry Oppenheimer to see how they could make these marginal gold mines more profitable. And Robin used to come to meetings, and I remember him coming to one meeting and he sat down right on this guy's very valuable beloved hat and there was a whole commotion.

Farquharson soon came into close contact with a number of key figures working against the state's system of racial hierarchy. Chief amongst them was his old friend Ernest Wentzel. The former NUSAS head had by now become an attorney and had recently been retained by the Bishop of Johannesburg to conduct an independent investigation into the Sharpeville killings.

Through the Liberal Party, Farquharson also befriended Randolph Vigne, who later commented that Farquharson was 'the only Liberal to whom the word "genius" might be attached.' Vigne had reason to feel frustrated with his fellow party members, making this something of a backhanded compliment.

Like many others, Vigne sensed that the repressive post-Sharpeville climate had severely hamstrung the Liberals' ability to organise. By way of response, Vigne founded the National Committee of Liberation (NCL). Though there were mixed-race members of the NCL, the group primarily consisted of disaffected white activists. The NCL sought to help endangered radicals to escape the possibility of torture at the hands of the South African secret police. The NCL also trained its members in sabotage, awaiting the day when such a step would prove necessary

Farquharson now moved between the rarified environment of his day job and semi-clandestine political meetings. Through Vigne he became close with Harold Head, a leading black journalist, and his wife Bessie Head, a prominent Pan-African novelist. Farquharson fundraised for the Heads and attempted to find safe avenues for them to publish their anti-authoritarian work.

Despite his growing radicalisation, Farquharson also maintained his base at Wits. Making use of his status as a respected political analyst, he began to publish critiques of South Africa and its allies.

> **Robin Farquharson**
> The Federation of Rhodesia and Nyasaland is well known as requiring the intending visitor to state the sex of his wife on his Immigration Form. And it outdoes even America's notorious McCarran-Walter Immigration Act by insisting that immigrants should not only never have been members of any Communist organisation, but also should not have been 'supporters' or 'sympathisers' with any. These two characteristics—endearing stupidity and fanatical suspicion—also apply to many white politicians in Rhodesia.

In April 1961, prime minister Verwoerd took another major step towards increasing the passage of apartheid regulations. Following a white-only referendum of the sort to make social choice theorists shudder, Queen Elizabeth II was removed as South Africa's head of state. A new constitution came into force which dissolved the Union of South Africa in order to make the country a standalone republic. Though this marked the final step in ending British colonial rule, many activists looked on in horror as Afrikaner nationalism grew increasingly dominant and isolated.

Farquharson began to freelance more regularly as a journalist. He started to write for *Contact*, a newspaper closely allied with the Liberals, and *Fighting Talk*, another anti-apartheid publication. It was for *Contact*'s May 1961 issue that Farquharson interviewed Nelson Mandela, by now one of the most infamous men in the country.

Mandela had just attended the enormous All-In African Conference, which was held in Pietermaritzburg to mark the first anniversary of the Sharpeville massacre. The conference brought together representatives of 145 different political bodies, representing the largest gathering of African political leaders since the banning of the ANC. The conference's organisers had been harassed and arrested but still put together an extraordinary meeting, the end result of which was a call for a colour-blind national convention. In the event that the government should ignore these demands—which, of course, they would—then the conference suggested a programme of national demonstrations, strikes, and boycotts.

Though these were only printed words, such appeals would not have been taken lightly. South Africa was soon to pass an act allowing for those accused of banned political activities to be jailed for up to 90 days without recourse to a lawyer or a trial. After 90 days, suspects would be freed and, more often than not, immediately re-arrested. Associating with known banned people was therefore a serious risk, not just to one's career but to one's personal safety. The alternative to imprisonment was a visit from the Security Branch (SB), the notorious security police known for their use of torture and extrajudicial killings.

Mandela believed that the time for escalating resistance had come. A month after his call for a strike appeared in *Contact*, the chairman of the ANC's Transvaal branch formed the uMkhonto we Sizwe paramilitary group, known in English as the Spear of the Nation. Violent resistance to apartheid was getting more frequent by the day.

Around this time, Farquharson began to seek to subvert the university system in more active ways. He made a concerted effort to bring known undesirable elements inside the power structure. One of them was Dennis Brutus, a mixed-race poet and vociferous critic of apartheid.

> **Dennis Brutus**
> I worked for him—not always pleasantly, since he was moody, and I was touchy—at Wits as his coffeeboy, for which he paid me erratically, if at all. He was really providing me with a pretext to permit me to study at Wits as a lay student—I was a banned person. When admin learnt they were horrified, and of course I was fired; I was part of the resistance and could have poisoned their coffee.

Dennis Brutus led the campaign to have South Africa banned from competing at international sporting events

Besides helping friends to find employment, Farquharson also used press interest in his work to advance anti-racist views to a more general audience. Writing in the *Rand Daily Mail*, one of the few English-language anti-apartheid newspapers, Farquharson rejected the racial undertones present in suggestions that South Africa was 'full'.

> **Robin Farquharson**
> Finally, and this is perhaps my most important point, people are a good thing. Human beings are not a means to an end, they are ends in themselves. The birth of a child should be the occasion for rejoicing, not for despair.
>
> A standard of living is meaningless unless there are people to enjoy it. As an economist, I think of the blessings of rising population: an expanding market, abundant labour supply, rising land values, all the signs of a boom.
>
> The parents who choose a second child rather than a second car may be making a decision which genuinely gives them greater happiness, and thus validly increases their standard of living.
>
> Rising population should not be regarded as a spectre or a bogey. Rather should we consider it a challenge—an opportunity to develop our resources, and itself a resource: for the one essential to all development and progress is human labour and human talent. Let us be glad that this labour and talent is arising in increasing numbers.
>
> Let us dissuade no one from obeying the precept: "Be fruitful, and multiply, and replenish the earth."

During this time Farquharson also edited the 'Africana' column of the anti-apartheid *New African* magazine, which featured unintentionally amusing extracts from pro-apartheid publications. He also began to publish poetry, some of it featuring the multilingual wordplay that would characterise several of his later manic episodes.

Robin Farquharson
The pleasures of the night are gone:
Jou liggaam was my liefdesbron.
Saad van plesier is wyd gesaai:
The arduous hours went gently by.

Jou speeksel was my blydheidsous:
Completeness flowed from limbs held close.
Each permutation fresh to tell
Die gloei van jou gevlekde vel.

Vreugde sal altyd moet verdwyn:
Lovers must separate again.
Resignedly I contemplate
My tydelike eensaamheid.

This Carroll-inspired poem served another role, alluding publicly for the first time at Farquharson's own homosexuality. The union of English and Afrikaans revealed talk of the 'seeds of pleasure', his lover's 'mottled skin' and the 'sauce of happiness'. Completing a line in English with a rhyme in Afrikaans, or vice-versa, readers required both languages to fully understand the poem's homoerotic and interracial edge. Joining the two rival languages only underlined the irreconcilable nature of white South Africa and the queer undertones of calls for brotherhood and fraternity.

Another poem, published this time in *Fighting Talk*, drew a link between different forms of institutionalisation and oppression and the potential solution offered by radical domesticity.

Robin Farquharson
They said in madhouse:
"Truth is incestuous:
Errors' exogamy
Brings hybrid vigour."
They said in courthouse:

"Keep colour classified:
All shading's subtleties
Blur line to error."
They said in jailhouse:
"We cannot help it;
Separateness serves the
Good of society."
I said in my house:
"Thought is admixture.
Only from opposites
Flows resolution;
Only from difference,
Fertile conception.
Even in madhouse
This is remembered.
Tell it in a man's house
Lest man should perish."

These were the earnest and unstudied words of a man starting to find his creative voice.

An abandoned novel from around the same time hinted at a more suitable outlet for Farquharson's thinking, engaged as it was in an increasingly internationalist outlook. Titled *The Drifters*, the story featured a stark portrayal of the post-war professional class in which Farquharson found himself. He published five briefs excerpts of *The Drifters* in the *New African*, the first of which betrayed Farquharson's keen eye for the arbitrary nature of justice.

Robin Farquharson
Northwards from Johannesburg's Centre there stretch three avenues with the names of three Prime Ministers—Barry Hertzog, Jan Smuts and Louis Botha. Along Jan Smuts and Barry Hertzog avenues are spread the lavish regions of the Northern Suburbs: the large plots, the often-painted houses, from which the Progressive Party, still the party of the upper

> class, draws the bulk of its enlightened but insufficient clientele. But to the east of Louis Botha Avenue, the main road to Pretoria, there cluster the Transitional Suburbs–the homes of newlyweds and pensioners, of those who have just arrived or will soon depart, the dwellings of intermediacy and evanescence. They are not slums, like Doornfontein: many whose incomes are momentarily or even permanently high live there for choice. But they have acquired a special quality, metropolitan and impersonal and hectic. In Hillbrow, in Berea, in Yeoville, in Bellevue, the population drifts. In some blocks of flats hardly a tenant stays a year. A new flat is easy to find: brand new blocks are always full, blocks twelve months old half-empty. Population flows in and out. Purposeless or intensely motivated, inhabitants move across the street or around the corner and back again and on and on. A political organiser is lucky if half the names on the electoral roll are still good. Life surges and life streams.

The drifters Farquharson depicted remain shallow and alienated, hopeful of more meaningful connections across racial divides but incapable of making them a reality. In this regard the subject and the title owe a debt to the concept of the *dérive*, the semi-aimless urban drift made famous by the Situationist International in Paris. This experimental cell of revolutionary Marxists popularised the *dérive* as a temporary solution to metropolitan malaise, allowing individuals to rewire their relationship to the city by chance encounters and acts of imagination.

While their influence grew throughout the 1960s, in material terms the Situationist International consisted of a small but fluctuating membership lorded over by the theorist Guy Debord. Though various international branches were set up, the Situationist International had a small and predominantly white membership and were centred around a handful European capitals. As the group's somewhat ironic name indicated, there was a fine line between utopian ambition and simple pomposity.

Despite Debord's despotic tendencies, the Situationist International harboured a multiplicity of voices on the question of decolonisation, producing a broad range of texts that circulated widely amongst independence movements across Africa. Colonisation, they argued, didn't just impact on life in French-run North Africa, but also the everyday life of the colonisers, with bureaucracy, nationalism, and party political machinations filtering through to the most mundane aspects of daily existence. A later extract of *The Drifters* shows Farquharson's engagement with this other aspect of the Situationists' thinking.

> **Robin Farquharson**
> The drifters waver on many boundaries. The lines between races and sexes and economic classes, sharp as they sometimes are, fade and shift disconcertingly and unpredictably. The strongest advocates of the Immorality Act often find themselves its victims. Nimrod Mkele has drawn attention to the value of white friends to Africans as a status symbol: he has not explored the inverse situation, the significance of social relations with non-whites to whites who wish to make a gesture of nonconformity. Nowhere in the world is it more difficult for a relationship simply to exist between people rather than between members of groups, classified and identified even if they refuse to be stereotyped or segregated. South African society is not a single organism, not a smooth surface: it is a body sliced in segments, a field sewn with trenches and landmines. No wonder the drifters drift.

Passages like these feel sensitive to the complicated interplay of race, culture, and prestige together with an awareness of the author's own fluctuating place within South African society. *The Drifters*, however, was never finished. We can only wonder how these fragments would have slotted together, if at all.

Creative writing remained a sideline for Farquharson. Alongside his scholarly research, his primary occupation came to be the activities of the South African Non-Racial Olympic Committee (SAN-ROC). Founded by Dennis Brutus, Farquharson's

Host refuses police entry to multi-racial party

Farquharson's refusal to follow police orders made the news across South Africa

erstwhile coffeeboy, SAN-ROC was a force to be reckoned with. Knowing white South Africa's obsession for competitive sport, Brutus's singleminded aim was to have the country banned from competing in international competitions so long as its sports teams were not racially integrated. Brutus suffered decades of oppression at the hands of the apartheid state and its allies in what ultimately proved to be a highly disruptive campaign.

Farquharson continued with his research at Wits, participating in prominent policy events and involving himself in Liberal Party meetings. He was also increasingly recognised as an expert on election history. While researching his biography of the statesman Jan Hofmeyr, Liberal Party founder Alan Paton wrote to Farquharson for his advice. Farquharson's father had been one of Hofmeyr's confidants. The prominent intellectual had, in turn, helped young Robin get into Oxford. This was of little important to Paton, who now wrote to Farquharson in order to ensure the accuracy of his analysis of South Africa's fateful 1948 general election.

Coming in the fraught years immediately following Sharpeville, Farquharson's association with Brutus and other black and mixed-race activists was always going to lead to increased scrutiny. When it came, the result would see Farquharson flee his homeland, stripped of his passport.

The first weekend of August 1963, while still employed by Wits, Farquharson was accused of hosting a non-segregated party. Some twenty cops surrounded his house in Johannesburg, making sure to note the license plates of the cars gathered outside. Farquharson then refused the warrantless police the right to search his home. Before the police finally retreated, a journalist named Gordon Winter snapped a picture of Farquharson blocking the doorway with his large frame. Winter's photo appeared in the anti-apartheid *Sunday Express* the following week under the headline 'Host refuses police entry to multi-racial party'. If Farquharson wasn't already on the radar of the South African authorities, this defiant image put him in their crosshairs. His otherwise productive return to South Africa was all but over.

Besides his newly-found revolutionary politics, Farquharson was increasingly open about his homosexuality. Unlike the UK, where homosexual activity was on the cusp of decriminalisation, apartheid South Africa was heading in the opposite direction. In 1966, a raid on a similar but larger party in suburban Johannesburg led to an even stricter codification of the laws banning homosexuality.

Some intimated that the non-segregated parties Farquharson organised were sexual in nature; that if he had played by more of the rules expected of him, exceptions may have been made. In later years Farquharson would concede that he did have a sexual preference for mixed-race men. Though talk of an interracial orgy would surely have gone down badly, the very notion of black and white socialising at the behest of a university lecturer was sufficient cause enough for the party to be broken up. That Winter's picture of Farquharson appeared in the English-language press would hardly have helped calm the authorities, keen as they were to portray racial dissent as an exclusively black problem. The heat was turning up and Farquharson didn't seem to care.

SUPPORT THE WORLD CAMPAIGN FOR THE RELEASE
OF SOUTH AFRICAN POLITICAL PRISONERS
THE ANTI-APARTHEID MOVEMENT
15 ENDSLEIGH ST LONDON WC1 EUS 5786
SAVE
THESE LIVES

CHAPTER 6
THE AFRICAN RESISTANCE MOVEMENT

A few days after word of the party hit the papers, Farquharson published a satirical 'mathematical comment' on the practice of the so-called no trial act. One detention of 90 days equalled 90 days imprisonment. Two detentions of 90 days equalled 180 days imprisonment. Three detentions equalled 270 days imprisonment. And so on and so on until it became obvious that the act in fact allowed for indefinite detention without any recourse to justice.

Farquharson knew of what he spoke, having recently been on the receiving end of a 'quizzing' from the Security Branch. Well aware that he was increasingly unwelcome in Pretoria, and publicly hinting at his likely fate if he remained, Farquharson prepared to leave the country.

Gordon Winter

The next hilarious incident was when Robin took 200 African children on a picnic in the countryside. Spotting two cars trailing the three buses containing the African kids, Robin ordered

> the drivers to leave the main road and drive across fields. The result was something similar to a British comedy film. As the buses drove through bushes and across farmland, the two cars (containing S.B. men, of course) followed doggedly behind, creating a cavalcade of complete craziness. Robin thought it hilarious, but Pretoria did not.

By this stage, Dennis Brutus had amassed a huge and impressive network of public and private allies, meeting with everyone from the Pope to Fidel Castro and Muhammad Ali. SAN-ROC had garnered the support of a huge number of non-white sporting associations, totalling some 45,000 combined members. The campaign to have South Africa banned from international sporting events was reaching its peak and was deemed serious enough to be granted an audience with the International Olympic Committee at an upcoming conference in Baden-Baden.

This was a major opportunity. It was imperative Brutus go and make his case in person, whether or not the South African authorities consented. Farquharson and the teacher John Harris, a close friend and SAN-ROC chairman, had contrived to obtain British papers for Brutus so that the organisation's head could safely travel to the meeting. Farquharson and Harris's efforts were in vain.

Though Brutus managed to leave the country, he was apprehended in Mozambique and forcibly returned to South Africa. Fearing that he would be delivered to secret police in Johannesburg, Brutus attempted to escape. Instead, he was shot and left for dead by ambulance workers for a white-only hospital. Though he somehow managed to survive the ordeal, Brutus would spend the next two years imprisoned on the notorious Robben Island. His friend Nelson Mandela was held in the next cell over.

Brutus's shooting left SAN-ROC in crisis at their moment of greatest need. As Brutus's deputy, John Harris was the natural backup to travel to Baden-Baden. But Harris had also had his passport withdrawn and was soon on the receiving end of a banning order which made political organising nearly impossible. This left

Farquharson next in line to represent SAN-ROC at the make-or-break conference. With little time to prepare for the all-important trip, Farquharson departed almost immediately. He took a circuitous route through Botswana, repeatedly swapping and abandoning cars on his way out of Africa.

In Baden-Baden, the International Olympic Committee heard SAN-ROC's case and ultimately agreed to commit to banning any apartheid state from participating in the Olympics. In due course, South Africa were banned from competing at the 1964 games. It was an extraordinary victory for SAN-ROC's campaign, especially considering what had recently befallen Brutus and his colleagues. One can only imagine what Farquharson's sporting father would have made of his son's participation in such activities.

The IOC's decision was front-page news around the world, as was the role of SAN-ROC, whose leader was now a high-profile political prisoner. But South African newspapers reported on Farquharson's flight from the country with great confusion, suggesting that he had all the requisite documents to come and go as he wished. In reality, his passport had also been confiscated.

After several years of building up a reputation as a Liberal dissident, Farquharson had irrevocably broken with the interests of the South African state. By leaving the country as he did, he risked not only his career but also his status as a South African citizen, which was also duly revoked. It would be six years before he made his next and final visit home.

Around the middle of 1964, Randolph Vigne's National Committee of Liberation took a turn towards guerrilla activity. Having tried and failed to form a working relationship with the banned ANC, Vigne and sixty or so colleagues began to actively step up their campaign of sabotage. Changing their name to the African Resistance Movement (ARM), the group began to plan a new and extreme round of actions. One former South African intelligence operative later alleged that the ARM was on the receiving end of funding from assorted CIA front groups. If true, it was unclear whether the intention was to covertly fund armed resistance to apartheid or to intentionally intensify the situation so as to precipitate a violent crackdown on the anti-apartheid movement. The USA was capable of anything.

Whether or not the ARM were CIA-backed or not, Vigne's group were liquidated as soon as they undertook their first steps towards violent resistance. Under torture, a former NUSAS member provided the names of his ARM comrades to the authorities. Those who couldn't flee quickly enough were rounded up. Several were sentenced to internment on Robben Island.

The authorities began to pick off the rest of this circle. A British-born mathematician friend of Farquharson's named Denis Higgs was kidnapped in Zambia. Five days later, Higgs was found bound and gagged in Johannesburg after a tip-off claiming to come from one of the kidnappers. Anti-apartheid activists believed that Higgs was targeted because the government suspected him of participating in the recent bombing of a white-only railway platform, an attack which killed an old woman and injured two dozen bystanders. Rumours went around that the authorities were unable to prosecute Higgs without formally extraditing him, which would have obligated them to reveal the full extent of their intelligence gathering operations. Higgs managed to flee to London.

Given the context of repression and surveillance, it was highly likely that if Farquharson hadn't fled he too would have been on the receiving end of a banning order or worse. Ernest Wentzel, Farquharson's old NUSAS friend, was arrested in the wake of the fatal bombing. His wife was kidnapped in Swaziland and forcibly returned to South Africa, where she too was placed in detention. SAN-ROC's John Harris, another of Farquharson's close friends, was even less fortunate. Arrested just seven hours after the railway explosion, interrogators immediately set about torturing him.

At first, it seemed that the authorities had made a mistake in targeting Harris. A well-liked teacher with a young family, Harris was an unlikely guerrilla. He was already well known to security services and therefore a tactically unwise choice for any high-risk actions. In the words of his biographer, 'he was probably also the most unpopular white man—among whites—in South Africa' due to his involvement in SAN-ROC. But with his jaw badly broken and his testicles kicked black and blue, Harris confessed to the bombing.

Through the pain, Harris attempted to persuade his torturers that he had never intended to harm anyone. He had in fact dialled in numerous warning calls well in advance of the explosion. The first call was to the police, explaining that it was too late to defuse the bomb and that they should instead focus on evacuating the station. Next, Harris made a call to the *Rand Daily Mail*, making a similar statement, and then, switching to fluent Afrikaans, made another statement to the pro-government *Transvaler*. Both newspapers quickly informed the police of the bomb and the time remaining.

Either through incompetence or complicity, the police did nothing to stop the bomb from going off. Disagreement continues to this day as to whether South African authorities moved the explosive in order to make its impact more devastating, or simply allowed for the bombing to proceed in the hope of justifying an even more vicious clampdown of the anti-apartheid movement.

Whether or not the government bore the ultimate blame, it was clear that Harris had little chance of a reprieve. If nothing else, the bombing was intended to be a final gesture of resistance before the ARM was broken by the authorities. Harris's lawyers attempted the insanity defence, but few were persuaded. 'Moody he may have been,' Harris's biographer noted, but 'mad he wasn't.' Ernest Wentzel believed that this desperate legal tactic may have been inspired by Harris's observations of Farquharson's own erratic behaviour.

The judge was entirely unconvinced. On April 1st the following year, Harris was executed, the first and last white person executed for resistance to apartheid. As the noose was tightened around his neck, Harris sung the words to 'We Shall Overcome'.

Some have speculated that Farquharson was a member of the ARM, but evidence is thin on the ground. Nor was Farquharson believed to have played any role in Harris's bombing. But he was sympathetic to his friend's cause and heartbroken by what had happened. Speaking to the *New African*, Farquharson decried how increasing government repression meant that Harris had been 'denied the chance to continue any form of open activity against racialism.' Farquharson may as well have been describing his own situation.

After SAN-ROC's triumph at Baden-Baden, Farquharson made his way back to London. There he rejoined Bessie and Harold Head and other friends from the *New African*, which now published in exile from the UK. The vocally anti-apartheid magazine's contributors found a strong anti-colonial movement and a ready network of sympathetic activists. Within a few years the ANC would seek to draw on this community, identifying affluent British anti-racists as ideal participants in the construction of a covert international anti-apartheid network. Principally comprised of white students who had left the country in order to study at Oxford as well as young British leftists, these so-called 'London recruits' secretly agitated on behalf of the ANC. It would take several years for the system of recruitment, training, and participation to begin to operate.

For now, London-based South Africans were more or less self-organised. The Berger household in Camden hosted meetings of the South African Freedom Association, the British pressure group that soon renamed itself the Anti-Apartheid Movement. There were also an increasing number of politicians willing to vocally critique apartheid, be it out of personal conviction or a desire to bolster their resistance to the pro-South African Conservative administration.

Farquharson also rekindled his friendship with Gordon Winter, the British-born journalist whose coverage of the interracial party had kickstarted the events that culminated in Farquharson's exile. Winter had returned to his home country and was keen to resume his friendships with the large network of South African radicals now based in London. It is not clear how Winter and Farquharson reconnected, though there is reason to believe the journalist engineered the situation. Winter soon saw that Farquharson's days of advocating for a more sophisticated approach to tactical voting were well and truly over.

Gordon Winter

Soon after his arrival UK-wise, Robin used a substantial inheritance to start recruiting a 'guerrilla army' which he said would cross the borders into SA and secretly set up a revolutionary struggle against apartheid. He found no lack of eager recruits when it became known that he was paying a signing-on reward. Thirty or more men, of all races, enlisted. But he fell victim to a small group of shrewd, hard drinking Irishmen in a Dean Street, Soho pub (The French House) who told him they could, for a price, obtain such 'essential equipment' as machine guns, hand grenades and dynamite.

One month and two thousand quid later, Robin realised his enthusiastic 'army' had only been interested in liberating him from his money. The shock of their treachery and the fact that they had made a fool of him in the eyes of several South African exiles living in London caused Robin to suffer a nervous breakdown.

Randolph Vigne

Robin was a very sick man and could do much less for Bessie [Head] than he would have wished, heavily drugged as he was in the course of the severe mental illness which was to lead to his death only a few years later. Was he a victim of the pressures of the South Africa that had forced out so many of us after our failed challenges to the Afrikaner Nationalist regime?

Winter and Farquharson grew close during this time, though neither man quite knew what to make of the other. As a prominent anti-apartheid journalist, Winter closely documented the London scene, keeping in close contact with all of its movers and shakers. The journalist would later feature prominently in Farquharson's memoir in largely flattering terms. This was in part down to Winter buying Farquharson three pies and a cup of tea during a pronounced streak of poverty. But this fondness went further back. 'I owe Gordon some gratitude', Farquharson recalled, 'because back in '63 in Jo'burg he had played the game over a photo he took of me keeping the fuzz out of a party'. Farquharson acknowledged that Winter had 'a pretty complex reputation', a situation balanced by the fact that Farquharson knew his own reputation wasn't exactly straightforward either. Winter, Farquharson concluded, had a 'heart of gold I *think*'.

Farquharson was right to question his friend's motives. It later emerged that Winter was a convicted criminal whose ties to organised crime and friendliness with anti-apartheid activists had made him a prime candidate for recruitment by the security services. Faced with the threat of deportation from his adopted homeland, Winter decided to spy for Republican Intelligence, South Africa's principal intelligence agency, as well as its successor, the Bureau of State Security (BOSS).

Winter's eventual return to the UK was a direct result of his spying. Shortly before he left South Africa, Winter's gun had been used in the murder of a mob-linked diamond prospector. The security services arranged for the journalist-spy to be very publicly deported to the UK so as not to blow his cover. Safely in the employ of a London-based news bureau, Winter resumed his spying activities, continuing to befriend and betray South African exiles with reckless abandon.

During this period Winter grew close to spy chief Hendrik van den Bergh and John Vorster, the minister of justice and future prime minister. Both were former members of the war-time Ossewabrandwag, the pro-Nazi paramilitary group. Via Winter, South African intelligence were also known to have hired the services of Charles Richardson, the head of London's infamous 'torture gang', who reportedly also took off with Winter's wife.

Winter may also have gotten his hands dirty himself. Winter claimed to have been involved in a convoluted plot to help Nelson Mandela escape prison in order to grant the authorities the chance to shoot him in the back. Though the plot was scrapped, the scheme bore a remarkable similarity to Dennis Brutus's own failed escape attempt. Winter later befriended Brutus's brother, secretly working to

Gordon Winter's reputation as a liberal journalist allowed him to cultivate relationships with many key figures in the anti-apartheid movement

have him detained back in South Africa, and continued to spy on him when he too fled to London. While these relationships began in 1961, they intensified around the time Winter first made Farquharson's acquaintance when covering the interracial party. That Winter happened to be the reporter to hand when Farquharson's party was raided seemed a remarkable coincidence.

Farquharson was now far from South Africa and intent on rebuilding the relationships he had fostered there, Winter included. To what extent Winter spied on Farquharson cannot be known for sure. Winter later claimed that BOSS had commissioned 'an in-depth and concise' volume on the African Resistance Movement as well as 'an astonishing 330-page breakdown of every writer, politician or poet who contributed work to the famous liberal journal the *New African*'. Winter also alleged that BOSS were behind a series of break-ins at the London offices of the Anti-Apartheid Movement and Amnesty International. Farquharson's friend Martin Ennals would found the former and go on to serve as the secretary general for the latter.

Many of these stories were retold by Winter in *Inside BOSS*, his grandiose but plausible tell-all memoir. If *Inside BOSS* was anything to go by then Vigne's suspicions were well founded and Farquharson's breakdowns were indeed related to his political persecution. Later journalists regard Winter's confession as highly untrustworthy, largely because Winter was, at the very least, a convicted criminal turned police informant. Dennis Brutus went so far as to claim that *Inside BOSS* itself was a put-on and that Winter never ceased operating as a high-level spy for South Africa. At the very least, Winter kept close tabs on several figures in Farquharson's circle while back in the UK. He maintained a personal relationship with Farquharson himself and even contributed to a posthumous tribute put together by some of Farquharson's friends.

Winter and his colleagues were therefore in a position to shape how any breakdowns, illnesses, and accidents were reported by the press. For example, on 19 July 1964, Farquharson was apprehended at Didcot railway while on his way to have lunch with a friend in Oxford. The 33-year old academic was spotted waiting for his train when he decided to remove all of his clothes.

Gordon Winter

Robin stood laughing his head off on the crowded concourse as a very flustered ticket clerk ran round his giant frame with a roll of sellotape—sticking pages of the *News of the World* over his bare

> buttocks. "He could not have chosen a more appropriate paper," was Robin's comment.

The police were eventually called after a young child pointed Farquharson out to her mother. As the *Rand Daily Mail* reported, 'Dr. Farquharson said that in South Africa it was the custom in hot weather to take off one's clothes.' A few weeks later Farquharson was again the subject of unwanted press coverage, this time featuring high up in the *Daily Telegraph*'s Monday edition. Farquharson had reportedly been physically removed from the Hilton Hotel in London after refusing to quieten down in the early hours.

Farquharson's background and connections offered him a degree of protection but they also made him more of a target for scrutiny by the security state. Such a climate was enough to put psychological pressure on anyone, let alone someone with a long history of instability. Regardless of his exile, it is highly likely that Farquharson was now under close observation by South Africa's intelligence services. Neither the Hilton nor the Didcot episode resulted in any sort of criminal consequences for Farquharson, making it all the more remarkable that they were subject to news coverage on the other side of the world less than 24 hours later.

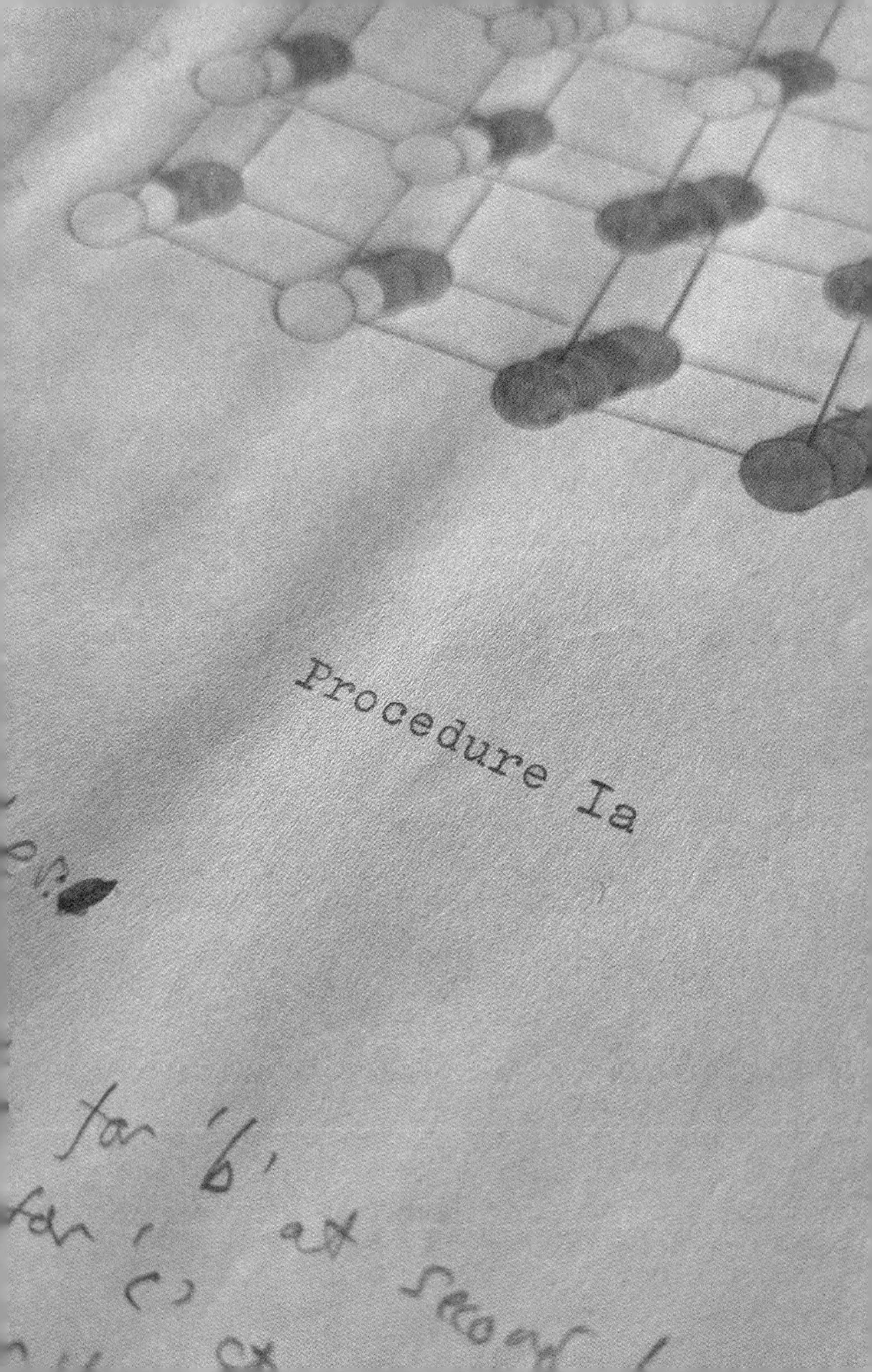
Procedure Ia

CHAPTER 7
THE SUPREME LORD OF CHURCHILL

Despite these incidents, Farquharson continued to seek employment for himself as a mathematician throughout 1964. He also began to take serious steps towards controlling his manic episodes, undergoing two concurrent courses of therapy in London and receiving regular psychiatric care in Cambridge. In September he was well enough to present at an international conference at Gonville and Caius College, Cambridge. The subject was the meeting point between the social sciences and operational research, the most industry-relevant part of Farquharson's work. But as he himself admitted, the research Farquharson presented that day was a decade old already. Though this was an embarrassing thing to admit, his precocious contributions to the field continued to bring Farquharson into close contact with a number of the leading mathematicians of the age.

Friends and advisors included the philosopher of language John Searle, with whom Farquharson shared an apartment, and D. G. Champernowne, the mathematician and close collaborator of the codebreaker Alan Turing. Farquharson also met with future Nobel Prize-winning economist Kenneth Arrow, who took a keen interest in his younger colleague's work. Arrow went as far as to write letters of recommendation for Farquharson who was otherwise a relative stranger. Like many others, Arrow recognised that Farquharson was an unorthodox proposition. At the same time, Farquharson was well positioned to take up a place amongst the interdisciplinary opportunities offered by the new mathematics of game theory and social choice.

Since its establishment in 1960, Churchill College had quickly become a world-leading centre for this kind of experimental work. By the middle of the decade, Churchill attempted to recruit Farquharson as a senior research fellow. The new University of Essex went one step further, offering Farquharson a senior lectureship in Applied Mathematics. Farquharson was also contacted by representatives from Plessey, one of Britain's leading telecommunications companies. Given Plessey's extensive research interests in radio, telephones, and computing, the firm would have held great interest for Farquharson, even if they were also the UK's leading defence contractor.

As word spread of Farquharson's theories and his return to the UK, so too did his connections across the English-speaking world. The pioneering game theorist John von Neumann recommended Farquharson to colleagues at Princeton. Interest also grew in publishing his thesis. The text's rather unwieldy name—'An approach to a pure theory of voting procedure'—did little to put off potential publishers. Farquharson was also very particular about how he wanted his book to look, complaining of how a similar volume contained 'large and horrible diagrams'.

Iain McLean

It was well known at the time that RF's insistence on yellow for a single circle in a single diagram (p. 35) doubled the production cost and may have contributed to the 10-year delay in publication.

Several leading academic presses nevertheless jostled to bring Farquharson's text to market, even if it meant dealing with his strict requirements. At Yale, the leading game theorist Martin Shubik became a strong supporter, volunteering to write a foreword to the published version of Farquharson's research.

In the meantime, Harvard professor Thomas Schelling assigned Farquharson's research papers to his undergraduates. Like Kenneth Arrow, Schelling went on to win the Nobel Prize for Economics. He was a well-connected man; amongst other accomplishments Schelling was responsible for bringing the story behind *Dr. Strangelove* to the attention of Stanley Kubrick. Von Neumann, Shubik, Schelling, and Arrow each moved in particularly powerful circles. Each was at the height of his personal fame and influence when he sought to take Farquharson under his wing. Farquharson seemed destined to make the move over to a major US institution as soon as it was feasible.

Following a successful interview with Frank Hahn, the leading monetary theorist, Farquharson decided to take up the position at Churchill. The Cambridge college offered Farquharson a prestigious three-year fellowship with a healthy salary. Despite their enthusiasm Churchill knew there were a few potential issues.

Behind the scenes, the college had done their research. It revealed that Farquharson had had a few bouts of ill health while at Nuffield, manic episodes in which he rambled and repeatedly made long-distance telephone calls. Farquharson refused his new employer's offer of putting a block on his phone to prevent him from dialling abroad. He did, however agree to see a Cambridge-based psychiatrist, a promise Farquharson did not follow through on.

Instead, Churchill's new hire launched himself back into anti-apartheid activism, taking his lead from SAN-ROC's model of highly-publicised boycotts. Farquharson helped to organise a students and staff boycott of South African goods alongside the Marxist critic Raymond Williams, who was a fellow of Jesus College. Despite the culture of fear and the distance he also tried to keep in touch with friends back in South Africa, including Alan Paton, the founder of the Liberal Party.

> **Robin Farquharson** to **Alan Paton**
> Liberal exiles have a new focus in London at the *New African* office, 12a Goodwin Court, St Martin's Lane, WC2 (TEMple Bar 4283). The slow-grinding mills of Pretoria, after month's deliberation, decided not to renew my passport; so I have applied to the Home Office for a certificate of identity, and hope with it to visit America next month for a mathematical conference. At Churchill I am Senior Research Fellow in management studies, much concerned with decision-making in economics and politics. But I miss you (and 15,999,999 others) pretty badly.

Farquharson made use of these new travel documents in order to take up John von Neumann's attractive suggestion to visit Princeton. Farquharson's plan was to attend a conference on game theory sponsored by the Office of Naval Research, a branch of the US Navy that among other things oversaw research into electronic warfare. Successful inroads here and Farquharson might just land a position at one of the top-level institutions that had been circling him for the past decade.

He landed at the Hilton in New York, and after some inevitable phone-based tomfoolery was obligated to pay for the rest of his transatlantic calls in advance. Though the details are lost to time, the rest of the visit went just as badly. Farquharson wound up in a hospital in Washington and ended up missing the conference entirely.

By the time Farquharson returned to Churchill, it was clear that Oxbridge was not for him. Friends were divided as to the ultimate cause.

> **Peter Johnston**
> At Churchill, he decided that the walk or cycle from digs to college was too much for the undergrads: logically enough he hired a fleet of double deck buses. He didn't tell anyone else. The

idea was that the buses should trundle to and from, 24 hours a day (Robin sometimes went walking in the small hours). Before the day arrived, Robin decided to inaugurate the service with a celebratory outing: a day trip for masters and students to Clacton-on-Sea. Again he neglected to tell anyone else. By the time the irate drivers of the bedecked buses arrived and demanded to know where the bloody passengers were, Robin's logic had incontrovertibly told him that he, Robin, was the supreme Lord of Churchill. From there, it was a very small step in logic to nationalise the buses, to run under Robin's sole direction.

Frank Hahn
I spent one afternoon in his college room trying to quieten him down, but he was very excited about having solved the problem of the 'Farquharson cube' which, I am afraid, I don't know anything about. He did not enlighten me.

Gordon Winter
He also fiddled with a couple of boys while sleeping rough. He admitted he was "born a homosexual" and said he was not at all ashamed of it.

Guy Legge
I think the key to Robin was his homosexuality that resulted in him drinking and then behaving badly. This would result in him being arrested and then attributing things to his "manic depression".

However discreet he may or may not have been about his homosexuality, it was clear that Churchill didn't want Farquharson to come back. The problem was that under their terms of employment, college fellows could only be fired for 'disgraceful conduct or persistent neglect of duty', neither of which would be easy or pleasant to prove.

An extreme breakdown in late 1964 culminated in Farquharson attempting to return to the London Hilton. Friends managed to persuaded him to travel to Cambridge for treatment. A document

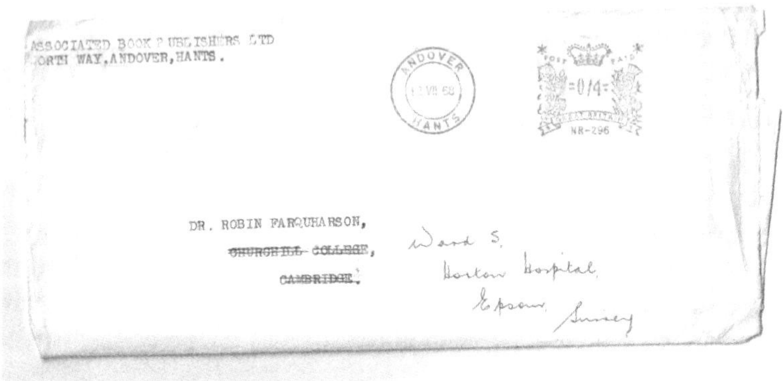

Farquharson's instability resulted in recurrent periods of forced hospitalisation

presented to the college council indicated that a dossier could be put together which might simplify the process of removing Farquharson. Whether this dossier was ever compiled, and quite what it contained, is unknown.

The Cambridge of the early 1960s was ill-equipped to deal with the difficult confluence of problems the South African academic posed. Homosexuality, though inevitably commonplace amongst staff and students, was still a criminal offence. Mental instability was treated with little more lenience.

There were nonetheless some glimmers of a more patient-centric future. The election of a Labour government in October 1964 promised a renewed wave of investment in the NHS, including new hospitals. Though a former sex ed teacher named Mary Whitehouse had recently launched a campaign to 'clean up television'—a euphemism for her desire to crack down on social liberalism, contraception, and gay rights—attitudes towards homosexuality were softening. Though sex continued to be scandalous, the British public were tired by hypocrisy, as shown by the recent Profumo Affair, in which the then-secretary of state for war's involvement with a Soho showgirl precipitated the collapse of the Conservative government. The use of oral contraception was spreading and the sexual revolution was underway, no matter what Mary Whitehouse believed.

After his most recent breakdown, Farquharson spent time at Fulbourn Hospital in Cambridge and at Claybury Hospital in the London suburb of Woodford, two former asylums known for their pioneering therapeutic communities. In a bid to make their care more holistic and responsive, some hospitals were even recruiting cyberneticists of the sort familiar to Farquharson from the conference circuit. But by the end of 1965 a clear pattern had emerged. Each time progress was made in Farquharson's recovery it would be undone by another episode or set back by the traumatic experience of hospitalisation itself.

> **Michael Dummett**
> The most disastrous of his outbreaks was when he rented a suite of offices near Oxford Circus in London on behalf of a spurious company, and engaged the services of a large number of typists, computer operators, etc. How all this was eventually paid for, I do not know; I suppose by the college.

By this time, some of Farquharson's behaviour had begun to be known to the wider world. A scholarly review of a French volume of game theory hinted at an increasing crankiness. He began his analysis in the *South African Journal of Economics* by admitting that he hadn't read the book in question. 'Some carping I shall do,' he continued, complaining that 'the stitching of my copy has already come away.' By the time the book in question was published, Farquharson had left academia for good.

Farquharson stood little chance of riding out his illness from the security of a prestigious fellowship. He was an openly gay and increasingly unstable individual who found himself in repeated trouble with the security services of an ambiguously allied nation. Though he had powerful friends and influential family connections, Farquharson's behaviour was simply too embarrassing for Oxbridge to handle.

While the full circumstances surrounding the end of Farquharson's research career might never be ascertained, it is clear that Churchill successfully persuaded him to resign rather than having to fire him.

In turn, the college arranged for £3,000—something like £50,000 in today's money—to be paid into a trust fund in the care of two of Farquharson's friends, one of whom had co-founded the Voltaire Society. As recounted in *Drop Out!*, Farquharson successfully prevailed on these two men to let him access the money, which he then proceeded to exhaust in a matter of weeks.

A representative from the Ministry of Justice kept a close eye on Farquharson's situation, seeing to it that he received British papers so that he would not inadvertently become stateless. Instead of pursuing a glorious move to the United States, Farquharson decided to settle for good in the UK. More or less burned by his years in Oxford and Cambridge, he tried to set up shop in London, informing the alumni newspaper of his alma mater, Rhodes University, that he was 'to make a full time career of writing.' This was easier said than done.

CHAPTER 8
BASICALLY HOSTILE TO CONVENTION

Once wealthy from the products of Empire, Britain had hit a post-war slump. In the hope of filling large gaps in the labour market, the British government heavily incentivised citizens from its former colonies to immigrate by passing the British Nationality Act 1948. This landmark piece of legislation granted equal citizenship to those born in the British colonies as well as the right to settle in the UK. Over the next 25 years, some 500,000 Caribbeans made the move to the so-called mother country. Together they came to be known as the Windrush generation, named for one of the cruise liners that made the long journey from Jamaica to London.

Ready employment was not the only attraction. As one influential account puts it, rather than moving simply for economic reasons, the Windrush generation surged 'towards the vastness and freedom to self-fashion that England represented.' The call of the mother country was strong, representing the largest wave of arrivals to the UK since the so-called Great Migration of Eastern European Jews at the end of the nineteenth century.

The result was transformative, both in terms of the British labour crisis and the impact it had on the socio-cultural landscape of metropolitan life. Together with the growing popularity of American culture, the arrival of mass migration saw white and black families, artists, designers, hustlers, and organisers of all kinds mingle, feud, and collaborate on a previously unheard-of scale. In the words of Colin MacInnes, one of the most influential white chroniclers of these changes, an 'England, half-English' began to develop.

Though thinkers like MacInnes were often subtle and knowledgeable in the ways in which they discussed race, there remained a strong sense of exoticism in how these newly-arrived migrants were perceived. As the pioneering Trinidad-born filmmaker Horace Ové commented, the Australian-born MacInnes 'was one of the only writers that wanted to write about black people and live among black people, and he got beaten up by black people, slept with them, ate with them, and wrote about them.' At the same time, 'he was pushing too hard,' Ové recalled. 'He was angrier than them.'

The London encountered by the Windrush generation was far from a blank slate. The city was already home to numerous Caribbean communities and had housed many African American and Afro-Caribbean soldiers during the recent war. What was new was the coverage afforded to these communities, much of it in panicked tones. Sporadic racial violence was already a relatively common occurrence. Dyed-in-the-wool racists and professional grifters speculated that a society ruled by drug abuse and loose morals was just around the corner. Many scandalised column inches were spent discussing the perceived relationship between Caribbean pimps and local white women who sold sex. How would the city absorb these new residents—and how would these new residents shape the city?

One ominous answer seemed to come in the form of the Notting Hill riots. In late August 1958, an argument broke out in public between a Swedish woman and her husband, a Jamaican pimp. As a crowd gathered around the bickering couple, Notting Hill exploded into chaos. Roving gangs of anti-immigrant Teddy

Boys began to assail buildings associated with the Caribbean community. Violent self-defence and retaliation followed. Similar conflagrations were sparked in other British cities. It would take over a week for these skirmishes to die down.

Fears grew over what this influx of 'aliens' would mean for the capital's housing market. Bomb damage still ravaged great swathes of the capital, and much of what remained of its housing stock had fallen into disrepair. The problem came into sharp relief in 1966 with the broadcast of the BBC's *Cathy Come Home*, a television play which introduced millions of viewers to the realities of urban homelessness.

The BBC's gritty hit illustrated a number of major challenges faced by the Greater London Council (GLC), a new administrative body tasked with overseeing the city's rejuvenation. Top of the GLC's list of issues was the role played by slumlords. Chief amongst these dubious characters was Peter Rachman. A Polish-born survivor of both the Soviet and German concentration camps, Rachman had transformed himself into a British property baron. His speciality was buying run-down properties in West London and renting them to Caribbean immigrants who otherwise struggled to secure stable housing. Some considered Rachman a kind of noble scoundrel, providing housing to those who were turned away by racist landlords. Most considered him a simple profiteer. Whether the 'Rachmanisation' of the city's housing stock was a symptom or a cause of growing unrest remained up for debate.

As the first signs of social disorder revealed themselves to the black-and-white vision of post-war London, a sudden rush of revolutionary architecture exploded onto the city's imagination. Britain's industrial rise and decline had already fuelled several waves of revolutionary social movements. In the mid-nineteenth century, the members of the Arts and Crafts movement had sought a socialist-utopian alternative to Victorian values, a holistic craft of poetry, architecture, design, and labour in keeping with a modernising world yet with an eye on Britain's romantic past.

Other utopians looked to the East. In the years leading up to World War I, pacifists, labour organisers, and suffragettes worked to bring yoga and vedanta to the city in tension with ascendent humanist values. The so-called settlement movement sought to provide new institutional bases for a global city, as venues like Toynbee Hall, Conway Hall, and Caxton Hall opened their doors to visionaries and rabble rousers. Nazism dawned, leading crypto-fascists and proto-New Agers to retreat to sun cults and countryside idylls. Blackshirts marched through the East End. Upwardly mobile Jews moved up to Finchley and out to Essex.

Small networks of squatters started to spring up in opposition to the Rachmanisation ofWest London, inadvertently facilitated by the degradation of the housing stock he oversaw. The media spotlight shone on Soho and the blend of bohemians, jazz musicians, pedlars, and hustlers who sought sanctuary in the French House and the Colony Room. Shopfronts shifted and shebeens began to spring up.

The utopian urbanists of post-war London responded to these changes in diverse ways. In 1961, architect Cedric Price and experimental dramaturge Joan Littlewood dreamed up what they called the 'Fun Palace', an interdisciplinary 'laboratory of fun' where culture and science could run amok. Inspired by cybernetics, the experimental architectural firm Archigram reimagined the city as a sequence of automated bubbles and pop art fantasies that morphed according to the needs of their users.

New builds were necessarily the only solution: the hulking Centre Point tower on New Oxford Street had been thrown up and essentially forgotten about at enormous cost. Old structures could be reimagined and reinterpreted just fine: playwright Arnold Wesker launched his 'Centre 42' in a disused Victorian engine shed in Camden called the Roundhouse, giving birth to one of London's most important cultural venues.

Nor did new institutions need to have a permanent base. As Cold War defence budgets boomed and universities struggled to balance the books, libertarians and anarchists reconstituted the academy in a series of temporary 'anti-universities'. The most famous of these

A variety of utopian schemes sought to reimagine the London of tomorrow. L to R: Archigram, Centre Point, and the Roundhouse

was the Free University of New York established by the sociologist Allen Krebs and a dissident doctor named Joe Berke. Looking to New York and later Paris for pedagogical inspiration, students and teachers dialogued as peers, or at least tried to.

Scottish writer and revolutionary Alexander Trocchi launched something altogether more extreme. Drawing on the work of his erstwhile friends in the Situationist International, Trocchi's 'project sigma' offered itself as a sort of free-form artist-run revolutionary cell. Sigma's aim was nothing less than a wholesale storming of the hacienda of institutional might via the combined forces of Burroughs, Beckett, junk, and joy. Rather than seeking to overtake, sigma sought to outflank, a procedure Trocchi dubbed 'an invisible insurrection of a million minds'. What sigma really was varied on the day and the gathered adherents, but it seemed to take the form of a post-capitalist consulting agency, a renter's union, an experimental architectural practice, or some variant of all three.

For a while it looked like there was a whole generation of these alternative organisers—those forged in the cradle of bomb culture, as Trocchi's friend Jeff Nuttall had recently put it. In June 1965, they gathered in their thousands at the Royal Albert Hall for an event called the International Poetry Incarnation, which featured readings from the visiting luminaries Allen Ginsberg, Gregory Corso, and Lawrence Ferlinghetti, as well as homegrown talents like Harry Fainlight and Tom McGrath. Conceived by underground instigator Barbara Rubin, arranged by book dealer Barry Miles, and hosted by Trocchi himself, the Incarnation was less a gathering of poets and more a coming out moment for the British underground. Captured for posterity in the cult film *Wholly Communion*, the Albert Hall event saw previously disparate scenes grouped together in one place at one time. Building off the Campaign for Nuclear Disarmament and the pages of *Peace News*, the in-house organ of the pacifist movement, the counterculture began to recognise itself.

Experienced observers were torn between marvelling and mourning the changes London was undergoing. Alongside Colin MacInnes were characters like the journalistic sketch writer

Geoffrey Fletcher, whose books like *The London Nobody Knows* documented these fluctuations. Drug-taking was increasingly normalised, breakdowns were seen as potential breakthroughs, and homosexuality was borderline fashionable if still unlawful. New spaces and new types of spaces sprouted throughout the capital to accommodate and inculcate these attitudes. Chief amongst them was the Indica Gallery, opened that winter by Barry Miles, his wife Sue, and John Dunbar, the artist partner of Marianne Faithfull. But perhaps the most concrete of these London-based experiments in modern living came via a small cohort calling themselves the Philadelphia Association.

Thanks to the efforts of a Cambridge dropout named Phil Cohen, the Philadelphia Association—amongst them the Scottish psychiatrist R. D. Laing and the South African psychiatrist David Cooper—found a site called Kingsley Hall, a derelict building in the east London neighbourhood of Bow. The Hall had been opened in 1928 by Doris and Muriel Lester, two leading pacifists. The Lester sisters commissioned Charles Cowles-Voysey, the son of Arts and Crafts leader C. F. A. Voysey, tasking him with repurposing a disused chapel so that it might serve the local community. In 1931, Gandhi spent three months living at the Hall as part of his campaign to achieve Indian independence, helping to make the British capital a hub of anti-colonial activity in the process.

The Hall had long since fallen into a state of decline by the time the Philadelphia Association took possession of the premises in 1965. Reimagining the space as a centre for communal living, the Philadelphia Association's goal was to run the Hall as a psychiatric community where therapists and patients would live side by side. A similar project had recently been launched at Paddington Day Hospital, which focused on treating former patients of Horton Hospital in Surrey without recourse to drugs or electroconvulsive therapy. Crucially, though, the experiment at Kingsley Hall would run independent of the NHS. It took its leave from earlier experiments at Fulbourn and Claybury but in a more radical direction occasionally referred to as 'anti-psychiatry' by both its supporters and critics.

Rather than trying to avert manic episodes in the typical way, Laing believed in the therapeutic power of madness. This was also not an entirely new idea. The rediscovery of William Blake and other earlier visionary artists had heralded a recent fascination in so-called 'outsider art'. This included a broad range of work produced by untrained amateurs, prisoners, and mental patients whose lack of education or mainstream acceptance seemed to facilitate closer contact with mystical powers of expression.

Allen Ginsberg's 1955 poem 'Howl' had implored a new generation to seek these fraught highs, to turn the tables and 'accuse your doctors of insanity'. By the mid-1960s, government-backed researchers and amateur enthusiasts had spent over a decade speculating that psychedelic drugs—in particular LSD and mescaline—could induce or enhance profound, truthful, or otherworldly experiences. Users could be guided into a state of what Laing called 'super-sanity', a clarity of vision and purpose normally occluded by the shackles of the ego and normative society.

A very public form of psychedelia was blossoming. The discovery of Kingsley Hall seemed an ideal opportunity to put these ideas into action. Laing would, however, have to contend with other interests.

> **R. D. Laing**
> Joe Berke was hanging around trying to set up a free university set-up and trying to use Kingsley Hall for that. He put in his book—or that book with [ex-patient] Mary Barnes—that I was arrogant in stopping him from using Kingsley Hall for a fucking free university. Alex Trocchi came round to Kingsley Hall and pulled out a needle in a public sitting-room and started turning on to heroin—*no*, I said. What we were doing was far more important than you fucking well making a political demonstration about drugs and consciousness. *No way*.

Farquharson had been in and out of mental hospitals during these crucial early years of underground and alternative culture. By 1965 he estimated that he over the past decade he had spent one day out of every five in hospital. Though he missed the International Poetry Incarnation, Farquharson was swept up in its slipstream, corresponding with the poet Harry Fainlight, whose disastrous appearance at the Royal Albert Hall precipitated a decline from which he would never fully recover. Juggling suit-and-tie jobs whenever he could secure them, Farquharson soon entered into a decidedly bohemian-bourgeois milieu.

Around this time, Farquharson became friendly with Anthony Howell, a ballet dancer turned poet and associate of Marianne Faithfull and David Hockney. Howell lived in a greenhouse rented from the head of a mixed-race jazz band across the street from Housmans, the legendary pacifist bookshop and headquarters of *Peace News*. Howell was on the cusp of breaking through as a poet, opening up his unusual living quarters as a refuge for fellow artists. Farquharson was a frequent presence, as likely to stop by to discuss philosophy as to drift in, wolf down some leftovers, have a bath, and head off back into the London night.

Another regular visitor to Howell's greenhouse was a brilliant young poet called Nicholas Lafitte, whose father François had been a prominent figure in the development of the welfare state in the 1940s. Born to an American anarchist and a French suffragette, François was the adopted son of Havelock Ellis, the Victorian sexologist. In a broad career that spanned the promotion of eugenics, the study of homosexuality, and pioneering psychedelic experimentation, Ellis cast a long shadow over the Lafitte family. His adoptive grandson Nicholas was widely travelled, highly intellectual, and profoundly therapised when he met Farquharson in the mid-1960s, probably at Addenbrooke's Hospital in Cambridge.

Anthony Howell

Nick had been two or three years ahead of me at Leighton Park School, a Quaker public school in Reading. Leighton was famous for its pacifism, so Nick and Robin would have naturally graduated to a certain set of agreements about things. They met in some sort of asylum, but I never saw Robin do anything really

> peculiar. Whenever I saw him, he was immensely articulate—I never saw him in any sort of bad spasm of behaviour. What we mainly did is have intense conversations.
>
> There was a very important political implication in Robin's work and so we talked a lot about voting theory. Now, my father was in the Royal Electrical and Mechanical Engineers, a mathematician and a scientist and something of an artist. My great-uncle was Pinchas Rosen, who was the person who brought in proportional representation in Israel. His brother, my grandfather, was Martin Rosenbluth, a tithe collector for the Zionists who picked up money from both Einstein and Freud, though they might not have admitted it. So, though I had been absolutely lousy at mathematics at school, one of the things that Robin bequeathed to me was that that did not necessarily stop you getting a grasp of mathematical concepts.

Lafitte and Howell were less guides to the new London than points of entry. As Farquharson later recalled, 'I considered the flower people and the hippies in a way attractive, people I admired in a way because I had long considered myself basically hostile to convention, though unlike them I had always, or almost always, submitted to it.' Now, with Lafitte and Howell for company, hippie living became a serious possibility.

Turn the right corner and London was a city replete with emigré psychoanalysts, socialist intellectuals, and experimental writers. The environment in which they thrived was underwritten by the benefits system pioneered by Lafitte's father; the dole made it possible to live in the here and now as an artist. Farquharson took notice and began to regularly sign on when he was out of work, which was often.

By the mid-1960s the many factions of bohemian London had fused into a seemingly unified wave of cosmopolitan experimentation, the unwitting progeny of Havelock Ellis and William Blake. These new experimentalists were at home with both the demimonde and high society, as familiar with the salons of Chelsea as the bedsitters of Caledonian Road. Come the middle of 1966 and lacking anywhere

Farquharson's entrée to bohemian London was Anthony Howell (R), pictured here alongside Allen Ginsberg

else to stay, Farquharson took his most decisive step yet into this world and became an early participant in the experiment that was Kingsley Hall.

In many ways the Hall was the ideal home for someone like him. Farquharson was already a disillusioned veteran of both the crumbling asylum system and the more progressive approaches of the NHS. The team behind the Hall were vastly knowledgeable about cases like his, mixing countercultural expertise, radical political thinking, and medical experience. Like Farquharson, David Cooper was an anti-apartheid South African. While the full extent of Cooper's activities prior to leaving South Africa are unknown, Laing suspected that his collaborator had been a Communist Party member. It is possible that Cooper was Farquharson's entrée to the Hall, a connection that likely came via Henry Adler, one of the doctor's patients. Adler was another well-off white South African who had been sent to London to pursue treatment for what his family saw as his mental illness. Instead, he plunged himself into alternative scenes and quickly became an important connector figure as well as a mentor to the young Malcolm McLaren.

Leon Redler, another of the Hall's founders, had also treated George Spencer Brown, the British polymath who had shared a conference panel with Farquharson a few years earlier. Despite these positive signs, it quickly emerged that Farquharson posed a more extreme behavioural problem, not least because he simply refused to stop making international phone calls.

R. D. Laing

Robin Farquharson had a bright idea that what we needed in order to develop Kingsley Hall was to buy about 300 acres of desert somewhere outside of Addis Ababa in Ethiopia. He was a very strange guy, as you can imagine; very intelligent and totally out of his fucking mind. While phoning up places all over the world—in the course of about two or three hours—he rang up two or three hundred pounds' worth of long-distance telephone bills. I said you can't use the phone unless you are going to pay for it, he wasn't about to pay for it. "No, don't worry. The Ethiopian government is going to pay for it." So I tell him he can't use the telephone. So he rips the telephone out; if he can't use the telephone, no one else can. You can see that if someone got in the building who was determined to conduct himself in that sort of way, what could you do?

Everybody had to be able to get enough money to buy food, or scavenge for it. And had to pay for the telephone. He didn't like

> walls, so he went on a rampage, smashing and ripping anything, trying to knock doors and walls down—what are you going to do with someone like that? There was very little of that but when it did happen what were we supposed to do in a context like that?

That Farquharson was asked to leave Kingsley Hall was a testament to the extremity of his behaviour. The nurse and painter Mary Barnes, for example, was not asked to leave, despite having a history of painting on the walls with her own faeces. But Farquharson was a large man who frequently had recourse to violence when manic. Laing and his colleagues were ill-equipped and unwilling to deal with him in that state and knew only too well how harmful further pharmacological interventions would be.

The experiment at Kingsley Hall began to fracture around the time Farquharson left, a victim of competing egos, drugs, and over-ambition. But Farquharson's expulsion nevertheless spoke to the limits of R. D. Laing's work and its ability to propose a genuinely holistic alternative to hospitalisation. If Farquharson was too mad to be helped by the Hall, a space designed for those ill-suited to mental hospitals and wider society alike, then the sorry verdict seemed to be that he was probably too mad to be helped anywhere.

PART II
THE SKYJACKER TRIP, 1967-1970

CHAPTER 9
CONCENTRATING WITH MY EYES CLOSED

Despite his recent ups and downs, Farquharson continued to present himself as an authority on elections, publishing a letter to the editor of the *Spectator* about Duncan Black and electoral paradoxes. He gave his address as 'Nuffield College', an institution he had long since departed. Instead, by the end of the summer, Farquharson was admitted to Claybury Hospital—'hell of hells', as he later described it. Quite what he experienced there is unknown, though friends recall him being subjected to electroconvulsive therapy to little positive effect.

His academic career seemingly over, Farquharson looked once more to reinvent himself.

Peter Johnston

Robin Farquharson answered an ad I'd placed in the *Financial Times*, looking for new customers for my one-man publicity company. The address was a hospital and Robin had signed 'Dr'. Under the impression I was visiting one of the staff, I went to see him, to find that he was a patient in a mental hospital. He was suffering severe withdrawal from a manic [episode] and in a bad way. The idea he had was sound (most of Robin's ideas were sound at the outset) and though it looked highly dubious commercially, I was interested enough to design a letterhead for the projected marketing company—Foremost Electronics. During this exercise I got to know Robin and accepted the fact that the idea was going to fizzle out.

Subsequently I also designed letterheads for: Aardvark Agency (which answered any questions on any subject at any time for 10p a go); Farquharson Associates, S.A., U.S.A. and U.K. (which threatened to be a high-powered computer group in education); Dr R.R. Farquharson, Business Consultant, and Dr Robin Farquharson, Hardware and Software. None of these ever got off the ground continuously for more than 48 hours, though if they fitted in with Robin's manic plans of the moment, they were invoked without hesitation. Requests for any of these became my signal that he was off on a trip again.

Robin Farquharson
World currency stability improves in direct ratio to the number of individual currencies which are accepted throughout the world. There are two—dollars and sterling—(and) if there were 10, there would never be a currency crisis. But the biggest single gain for stability comes in raising world currencies from 2 to 3.

Peter Johnston
As ever, Robin's starting point was true. He telephoned the treasury here and was fobbed off. A supreme (quite frightening to see) effort to retain a grip on his reason (in manic neither his health nor his physical ability was impaired: his judgement and critical faculty hit the moon) and he telephoned the U.S. Treasury. They, suitably impressed by this peremptory professor phoning from the UK not only advised Robin that Henry Fowler (then Secretary of the Treasury) was on holiday, but told him

where. Down with the phone: despite his efforts, his reason slipped a notch and by the time he got Fowler's hotel, he was on the verge of incomprehensibility, but sufficiently impressive to send an aide scuttling to the beach. Fowler came to the phone, realised he was dealing with a crank (which Robin by now was) and told Robin to fuck off.

Robin, almost hysterical, jumps in a taxi, directs the driver to a printers, rushes in there and persuades the driver to print the first batch of the third currency (which Robin had designed in the taxi). It says something for the level of Robin's intellect and introverted humour that he titled his stabilising money 'Far Things'. Somewhere, someone, is storing a suitcase of Robin's with several hundred thousand Far Things in it.

Gordon Winter

I met Robin again in 67 when he had completely tuned his back on society and was living as a tramp, eating out of dustbins, conning commuters for fourpence and sleeping in shop doorways.

Sometimes, he slept in the all night Post Office at Trafalgar Square. One night a constable fuzz tried to move him on but he was no match for Robin, who had taken the precaution of buying an airmail letter. As the cop woke him up, Robin pointed to a ballpoint pen in his right hand—and held up the airmail letter as 'unchallengeable evidence' that he was entitled to sit in the Post Office and write to a friend. When the cop tried to point out that he had been sleeping, Robin answered, "I would like you to prove in court that I was not concentrating with my eyes closed." The cop slunk off, baffled by such logic from a tramp.

Though the Kingsley Hall project was beginning to collapse, other experimental communities were beginning to develop. In 1966, a former Rachman associate named Michael de Freitas helped to source a building on Powis Terrace in Notting Hill for activists to establish something called the London Free School. Though early meetings were held at Housmans bookshop, the London Free

School was rooted around providing a non-hierarchical response to the social problems faced by residents of Notting Hill. Its animating spirit was Rhaune Laslett, a fixture of the local community and one of those involved in organising the first Notting Hill Carnival. Under Laslett's watch, the Free School offered English language classes, legal aid sessions, discussion groups on everything from race relations to housing, art workshops, free nurseries, and more.

A year later, the interdisciplinary Arts Lab was founded on Drury Lane as London's premier independent arts centre and alternative clearinghouse. Visitors to the former warehouse found distinct spaces for theatre, music, and cinema, as well as a gallery and a cafe run by Sue Miles. A short journey east from the Arts Lab, Laing's erstwhile colleague Joe Berke was on the cusp of finally establishing a London anti-university in Shoreditch. Timothy Leary, the disgraced Harvard psychologist, was meanwhile reemerging as an international advocate for LSD, encouraging prospective users to 'Turn on, tune in, drop out'. Acid fuelled fantasies of a collective, international consciousness, a world of disparate freaks joining forces. For a while, it seemed like Trocchi's vision for project sigma was autonomously assembling itself, just like he said it would.

As squatting networks developed and alternative institutions sprung up, so too did a Fourth Estate fit for covering them. Many of the new underground papers had connections both to the world of CND and the new hip scenes that grew out of it. In 1966, an all night rave at the Roundhouse marked the launch of *International Times*, a technicolour continuation of the Free School's newsletter. The paper was founded by John 'Hoppy' Hopkins, a part-time pot dealer, photographer, and London Free School co-founder together with Barry Miles of the Indica Gallery and a host of other new London luminaries including Tom McGrath, the Royal Albert Hall performer and former editor of *Peace News*. Hoppy was soon involved in opening UFO, a psychedelic nightclub whose profits were plowed back into more underground ventures.

In 1967, the psychedelic magazine *OZ* arrived in Britain, having first been launched in Australia. The following year, these new papers were joined by *Time Out*. Together, they charted, critiqued, and constituted the burgeoning scene in equal measure, fuelling the demand for a viable alternative and saturating it with mythic anticipation in the process.

Farquharson had never been prolific with regard to his published work, producing little outside of a few academic articles and an assortment of South African journalism. But he never stopped writing. Friends recall the regular sight of the dissident scholar standing at a window, lecturing a stranger on some obscure topic as his papers fluttered off into the street below. Inspired by the sudden surge in alternative publications, Farquharson now turned his attention to writing something between a memoir and a novel.

As Farquharson later explained, his initial pitch was to write something like *London on Five Dollars a Week*, a relatively hacky guide to cheap living. Such works were quick to churn out and easy to tailor to new countries or themes. In a countercultural vein Farquharson suggested titling his book *How to Live Without Working and Not Get Bust*.

The idea came at the recommendation of a friend named Nigel, to whom the resulting volume was dedicated. There were two main Nigels in Farquharson's life. The first was Nigel Lawson, a former housemate at Oxford and fellow PPE student. Since that time Lawson had begun a career in journalism and subsequently climbed the ranks of the Conservative Party, later to serve as Margaret Thatcher's energy minister and then her Chancellor. Lawson was thanked by Farquharson in the acknowledgments to his article 'Straightforwardness in Voting Procedures' in 1956. Though Farquharson remained in touch with Lawson after their university days, it is hard to imagine the ascendent Tory being too familiar with his old friend's new way of life. The prospect of his being the right Nigel is very low.

The same cannot be said for the second Nigel in Farquharson's life. Nigel Samuel was the heir to an enormous property fortune, an eccentric dilettante whose predilection for funding underground causes brought him into close contact with *International Times* and Michael de Freitas, now also known as Michael X. Samuel's cash was all over alternative London, making him an easy mark for hustlers on the make. Many of them were unaware of Samuel's vulnerable state, at least initially—as Miles recalled, 'you never knew in those days whether someone was tripping out or literally starving to death.' Whether he was coming or going, Samuel's connections and ready handouts meant that he was precisely the sort of person Farquharson would have turned to for advice in finding a publisher, if not a bit of welcome cash.

Samuel's sister was Nicky Waymouth, a socialite who was married to a third Nigel—Nigel Waymouth of Granny Takes a Trip, the legendary King's Road boutique that brought William Morris's aesthetics to the likes of Jimi Hendrix and the Beatles. There were other likely Nigels still: denizens of laundrettes and post offices and bars and squats and collectives, Nigels who no doubt made passing comments to eccentric mathematicians only to see them reemerge as grand Farquharsonian fantasies. Whoever he was, Nigel directed the prospective author to the infamous Doughty Street offices of the publisher Anthony Blond. There he found a place one journalist described as a 'vision of a Pompeian brothel', just the sort of company to take a chance on a man like Farquharson.

The eponymous Blond was a natural risk-taker. Born into a wealthy Jewish family and educated at Eton, Blond did his National Service in the army, where he spent his time enjoying 'the joys of drink, people, parties, fancy waistcoats, foreign travel and falling in love—mostly with young men.' Registering as a conscientious objector, Blond studied at Oxford, where the pattern continued.

After failing at the family business—his father produced the underwear for Marks & Spencer—Blond launched himself as a publisher. In quick order Anthony Blond Limited issued Gore Vidal's scandalous *Myra Breckenridge* as well as the translated works of French novelist Jean Genet, the former petty criminal, unabashed homosexual, and prose stylist par excellence.

Genet's services were secured in an act of iconoclasm typical of Blond: the author's tightrope-walking boyfriend had broken his leg and was short of cash. Blond paid the surgeon's fees in exchange for the English-language rights to Genet's work. Blond was also known

Anthony Blond at a fancy dress party around the time he met Farquharson

to be subsidising the outrageously queer novelist Simon Raven on the condition that the louche belle-lettrist stay out of London. Raven's biographer later described his subject as having a 'robust attitude to Jews'; despite threatening to fall out on several occasions, Raven evidently made an exception for his publisher.

Blond was fond of risk-takers, highly tolerant of homosexuality, wary of injustice, and reckless with money, no doubt abetted by his experience as director of *Private Eye* magazine, one of the most sued publications in Britain. Rightly or wrongly, these instincts combined in late November 1967 when Blond was approached by a gigantic 37-year old ex-Cambridge don with a shrill, upper-class accent and a week's worth of stubble. That this strange man also happened to be gay, mentally unstable, terrible at deadlines, and practically unemployable only made him all the more intriguing a publishing opportunity.

Farquharson may have been a run-of-the-mill character in Anthony Blond's world but this was still something of a sideways move for the would-be don. Though Farquharson had left the world of science behind, the stability that came in the decade following the war had revitalised British industry. The widespread influence of cybernetic ideas had also shown the new science to be inspiring and disturbing in equal measure. Companies like Honeywell and NCR used their expertise in designing thermostats and cash registers respectively to design missile guidance systems and code breaking machines. In the UK a former employee of both companies named Jack Harwell struck out on his own as a computer programmer. British data theorist Stafford Beer would soon meanwhile be hired to restructure the entire economy of socialist Chile along cybernetic lines.

Cybernetics' founding father Norbert Wiener may have become a committed pacifist but the cat was out of the bag. Soon experts in the science of control were testing and refining its theories in every sector of the economy, from forecasting doomsday conclusions to the Cold War to the efficient management of production lines at Ford Motors. President Kennedy had gone so far as to recruit Ford CEO Robert McNamara to be his defence secretary, charging him with applying a data-driven approach to the war in Vietnam.

Though this all felt distant now, Farquharson had until recently been connected to the war machine. As Robin the dropout struggled to work out whether he was coming or going, his namesake at the Foreign Office found himself tasked with normalising British relations with South Africa.

Just in time, having been absent from serious anti-apartheid organising for some years, Farquharson reemerged as a national committee member of the Anti-Apartheid Movement. At the end of May 1967 he attended a formal Anti-Apartheid Movement gathering held at the House of Commons. It was his first involvement in the organisation in some time. Given that the discussion that day included Farquharson's Foreign Office namesake, one wonders if this sudden desire to get involved was not prompted by the other Farquharson's recent promotion.

It was a crucial time in the struggle against apartheid. The ANC's London recruits were then beginning their first actions, exploding bundles of anti-apartheid leaflets over South Africa. But as the militant anti-apartheid organising Farquharson once supported entered its next phase, the movement veteran moved towards more acid-hued undertakings.

Farquharson found himself getting involved in the scene surrounding Charlie Brewster, a pioneering chaos magician better known as Frater Choronzon. Farquharson's friendship with Brewster drew him deeper into the mystic fringes of London life, a scene halfway between performance art and pandaemonium.

Frater Choronzon

One bunch of Brit hippies who were involved in magic on one level or another were the Tribe of the Sacred Mushroom. They affectionately closed down Middle Earth, London's equivalent of Frisco's Avalon Ballroom, with a dramatisation of the Tibetan 'Chod Rite', which was billed as 'The Hundred Drums of Jericho Welcome Icarus', timed to mark the closest approach to Earth of an errant planetoid of that name.

Paul Minns

The Tribe of the Sacred Mushroom held a purported sacrifice of a child. White tunicked with spears, the tribe had set up a dais and we were to provide the music. I think I glimpsed a young girl but before anything could start the doors burst open and in

> swept Covent Garden workers looking for the intended 'victim' to be followed five minutes later by many police. Being pacifists the Tribe offered no resistance thank goodness but the child vanished into thin air in the following hilarious melée.

Brewster took a leading role in the Middle Earth event, specially constructing a new magical device he referred to as the 'Trip Machine'. Farquharson put up the cash for the machine to be made, though accounts of its efficacy varied.

> **John 'Nosher' Neal**
> It was like a coffin. It wasn't a light show, it was just a vibrating box and you just had it in the room with you. It didn't work but he tried to drag it everywhere.

Middle Earth was shut down soon afterwards, reportedly as a direct result of the police raid.

Though Farquharson kept up appearances and sought to fashion himself as a mover and shaker in alternative London, in other circles he still held out hope of being seen as a serious thinker. Only a few weeks before meeting with Anthony Blond, Farquharson took part in an important international conference at the Centre national de la recherche scientifique in Aix-en-Provence. Economist Richard Zeckhauser was there to present his research, one of McNamara's recent hires at the Department of Defense. Other participants included high-level intelligence analysts, several Nobel Prize winners, and Duncan Black, the rediscoverer of Charles Dodgson. When Farquharson took to the podium, attendees were told that the speaker was affiliated with Churchill College, Cambridge, by now a powerhouse in the new sciences of game theory and social choice. Farquharson's Churchill appointment had in truth ended some two years earlier.

His academic career in tatters, Farquharson had recently been fired from a job at a computer programming company and was, for all intents and purposes, homeless. Inspired by the words of Timothy

Leary, he was now also using LSD. Having lost contact with the world of cybernetic proto-psychedelia when he dropped out of the academy, Farquharson was now encountering it again as part of a mass movement.

As he later wrote, 'the LSD insight has enabled me to make sense of what before had seemed simply a purposeless affliction.' Rather than exacerbating his psychosis, he felt that LSD afforded him the 'sights of the same landscape through different windows'. As a result, 'I am also now in a position to accept the fact of the psychosis as something validly and perhaps valuably deflecting my life from its previous direction, and able to apply my energies to finding exactly what that direction should be and following it.'

No matter how insightful Farquharson's LSD experiences may have been, they likely did little to make his behaviour more acceptable to broader society. Arriving at Doughty Street with a sleeping bag slung over his shoulder that had been gifted to him by Anthony Howell, Farquharson managed to overcome the suspicions of the publisher's hostile secretary by brandishing the award won by his thesis. In short order he left Blond's office with £2 in his pocket—more than he'd even asked for—and the promise of £2 more per week so long as he kept on writing.

Robin Farquharson
Robin Farquharson Drop out!
14 003228 2

CHAPTER 10
A DIRTY MIND FOR SUCH A HOLY MAN

The result of Blond's gamble was a curious book written over the course of two hectic months. The author of *Drop Out!* bounced from squats to men's shelters to spare bedrooms to street corners, jotting impressions of his day while leaning against lampposts and postboxes. Miscellaneous friends and rivals made cameo appearances, including Randolph Vigne, Gordon Winter, and London Free School founder Rhaune Laslett and her teenage son, who in Farquharson's view claimed to be psychedelicised but was in fact entirely square.

Ostensibly a chronicle of the author's life as a dropout, the book occasionally flitted back towards Farquharson's original idea, a guide to London-on-the-cheap. It offered a random smattering of advice for procuring budget meals and free public transport, together with reprinting a decidedly non-representative selection of shop signs and wanted ads. These passages were paired with brief sketches recounting Farquharson's first acid trip, a nonplussed account of some opportunistic sex work, a series of brutal episodes of police harassment, and a surprisingly moving sequence that culminated in the author being beaten up by a group of teenage boys.

The combination showcased Farquharson's usual obsessions: the periods of mania and delusion, the quaint otherness of post-war Britain, the thrill of telephonic adventuring, the somewhat embarrassed homosexual fumbling, and the relentless wordplay ('childish of me,' he admitted, 'but then you've read the textbooks'). The result was a unique work which approached some of the paranoia of *Inferno*, August Strindberg's novelisation of his increasingly weird life in fin-de-siècle Paris. While *Drop Out!* matched Strindberg for paranoia, his was a worldview that had been distinctly filtered through the paradoxes of life in the old-and-new London of the Welfare State.

Beyond Strindberg, the obvious comparison was with *The Autobiography of a Super-Tramp*, W. H. Davies' autobiographical portrait of late Victorian vagrancy, and George Orwell's later *Down and Out in Paris and London*. But though Farquharson's book clearly drew on these classic accounts of life on the margins, *Drop Out!* obscured as much as it revealed. It excluded, for instance, any meaningful mention of Farquharson's involvement in anti-apartheid organising, eliding a major part of his recent biography and the motivating factor behind his being in London in the first place.

On the contrary, *Drop Out!* at times seemed at pains to point out that Farquharson's suffering was only temporary—that he was almost undercover as a homeless member of alternative London and could return to his rightful position whenever he wanted. As Farquharson wrote in a rather tacked-on conclusion, 'I am very fortunate in that my personal roller-coaster, though it admittedly carries me rather high at times, never takes me below ground level.'

In some ways, this was true: Farquharson's Oxford doctorate and longstanding social connections were hard to entirely discard.

One encounter with the police ends peacefully because although 'my clothing was a bit bizarre', Farquharson's 'accent was right. They melted.' But in other ways Farquharson's values and instability meant that full acceptance into his social class—indeed, into any social class—lay outside of his grasp. Having been beaten by a group of teenage boys, he explained how homelessness afforded him new insight into the lives of the downtrodden, with a hint of irreverence borrowed from *The Drifters*.

> **Robin Farquharson**
> Born a member of a master race in South Africa, by accent and Oxbridge education a member of the British ruling class, my sympathies for the victims of both systems had been abstract, from the outside. No longer. Now I was a Negro. Now I was a Jew. At last, at last.

Though Farquharson was clearly being somewhat self-deprecating, the kinship he felt with oppressed peoples was typical of his scene. Despite his evident privileges, Farquharson was also oppressed. The Sexual Offences Act 1967 had been passed a few months earlier, decriminalising homosexual acts between men over the age of 21. Gay men were nevertheless still disproportionately policed and bore the mental and physical scars of a deeply homophobic society. Ultra-conservative bigots like Mary Whitehouse still hogged the airwaves and promised to 'clean up' public morals; public allies were few and far between.

True to form, the winter Farquharson wrote *Drop Out!* saw the author subjected to hospitalisation with increasing regularity. Farquharson's favourite hospital came to be Horton in Epsom, which maintained a relationship with the experimental work of Paddington Day Hospital.

> **Daniel Morgan**
> When I arrived I was asked to take a bath and then consigned to a bed in the admissions ward with about fifty other souls. A

> male nurse examined my hands and cleaned and dressed them, which was the first decent treatment they had received. The next day I was interviewed by a staff psychiatrist named Dr Tidmarsh who took my details but appeared to express little interest in my predicament. At one point he was called out of his office and left alone I took a quick look at the notebook he had been writing in as he listened to my woes. The only words on the page were "butter, cheddar cheese, milk, cat food." The guy was writing out his shopping list.

In this stereotypically indifferent environment, consultant psychiatrist Dr Gerald Low-Beer appeared like a ray of light to Farquharson. Though Low-Beer was no anti-psychiatrist, he was an outspoken campaigner for psychiatric reform, publicising the use of psychiatric 'treatment' in the USSR as a punishment for political prisoners. Farquharson and Low-Beer struck an arrangement which allowed the patient to decide for himself when he was well enough to leave.

> **Peter Johnston**
>
> God was speaking to Robin with increasing frequency: for such a holy man, he had a very dirty mind, to judge by some of the commands he issued to Robin. One such was to take off his trousers in the tube, in front of a Mary Whitehouse stand-in.
>
> Robin continued, as was his right, to visit Churchill until he exasperated his few remaining friends beyond reason by encouraging a sing-song and boozing session on the masters lawn, inciting several of the least stable undergrads to cock a snook at the establishment and appearing (minus one trouser leg, minus shoes, very dirty and very high) at high table with his guest—a very hairy young man—whom Robin introduced as his fiancé. Around this time—say '68 or so—I have a vivid memory of C. P. Snow's utter astonishment when confronted by Robin in full flight. Never can so literate a man have been struck so speechless as Lord Charles that day who blessed his own soul in

Gerald Low-Beer during his campaign for the rights of Soviet mental patients

a repetitive monotone while spilling his drink unheeded down his shirt front.

It is difficult to know whether Low-Beer's tolerance of Farquharson was based on progressive medical ideals or the privileges from which Farquharson still benefitted. Either way, Farquharson seemed an unlikely leader in the youth revolution. He was born in 1930, a cultural lifetime before psychedelia, placing him either side of the totemic Alex Trocchi (1925) and Michael X (1933). Youth was fetishised but age was not clearly a hindrance to becoming a hip star.

Farquharson's upper-class mores were not disqualifying either—boarding school kids were everywhere, and not just in Notting Hill's aristocratic circles—nor was his scientific background. The mathematical philosopher Mike Lesser was a regular contributor to *International Times*, a die-hard CND activist, and a committed stoner. The allure of Hoppy's sideline in pot dealing was only enhanced by his previous job working at the British government's atomic energy research laboratory.

Class and status didn't dissolve away despite the new structures, though they interrelated in unexpected ways. Farquharson's name would already have been familiar to Hoppy from the Notting Hill scene, while Tom McGrath, the first editor of *International Times*, would have been abreast of Farquharson in his capacity as editor of *Peace News*. This familiarity might not have been an asset.

Barry Miles

I ran into Robin at the Arts Lab a few times where he was shouting at people trying to eat and sometimes stealing food off their plates. He made Sue's life a misery and that of her staff but she was tolerant to a degree because she recognised that he was deranged. He certainly brought everyone down.

Farquharson's background did little to inculcate him from the consequences of his actions when it came to disrupting avant-garde activity. In quick order he came to be the recipient of numerous bans from the Arts Lab, on one occasion due to what Jim Haynes, the founder, described as Farquharson's 'vibrations'. As Farquharson bitterly recounted in *Drop Out!*, 'I don't see how I can control my "vibrations" until I find out what the hell vibrations are.'

Farquharson was now bouncing between doss-houses, friends' sofas, and church crypts. As recounted in *Drop Out!*, on one of the crypt stays a church warden passed him a few coins. From there the story turned this way and that as Farquharson beat back his authorial fantasies and attempted to tell the reader about 'Shepperton Studios Proper'. He briefly got back on track before deciding to interrupt the main story with an anecdote about *Punch* magazine.

Robin Farquharson

One volume, whose title I don't remember, had an article by A. P. Herbert on 'Wrong Numbers'. His point was that he was so sick of being rung by wrong numbers that he would pretend he was the right number, and play along for laughs. (Say, for example, 'I am putting you through to the Prime Minister now, Sir', and then leave the receiver on the table for an hour.) APH said he realized this wasn't a very nice game but felt he had no alternative. I have found an alternative, however, particularly applicable to crossed lines. I play along for real.

So last Friday when I was making a local call, I suddenly found I was through to Shepperton Studios. So, seizing the opportunity, I asked to make inquiries about studio space, and was put through to Mr Andy Worker. He was most helpful, and said the minimum cost was around £300 per week. He suggested I come down for a chat, on Monday; a chauffeur with a black Humber would be at the station. And that is why I was guarding my pound (the 19s. 3d., the 19s. but thank God never less) for the journey. In fact, the ticket, day return, cost only 10s. 6d., so I had some reserve. The train was, of course, late; but the chauffeur was there, and the Humber up to expectation.

When Farquharson was seen to be in his right mind, he was a former Cambridge don, permitted to cause trouble in keeping with his status; when a homeless man was seen to be in his right mind, he remained a homeless man, vulnerable to all the abuse that came with it.

Despite the chaos surrounding its writing, *Drop Out!* was issued that October with an extraordinary cover by Alan Aldridge, the celebrated 'graphic entertainer' and illustrator. Aldridge's speciality was in taking the playfulness of nineteenth-century graphic design and bending it towards a psychedelic idiom. Obtaining his services was quite a coup on Blond's part. Aldridge had already demonstrated his eye for mass-market imagery in a striking design for the Who's album *A Quick One* and the controversial poster for Andy Warhol and Paul Morrissey's film *Chelsea Girls*. Aldridge's unique style had recently seen him go from shaking up the art direction of Penguin Books to collaborating with Lennon and McCartney in the branding of Apple Records.

The cover of *Drop Out!* was classic Aldridge, linking the Victoriana of Farquharson's Oxford with the lysergised colours of alternative London. The four arms of a dapper man in a pinstripe suit and bowler hat extend out in front of a rainbow. The man—a stand-in for Farquharson himself—prances over melting buildings and bending automobiles, steamers, planes, and sticky foodstuffs. Two of his hands grasp at flowers and hearts; the two others jettison keys and cash, just as Farquharson boasted of doing. A powerful orange sun then pushes its way through purple clouds to illuminate the title and author above.

Blond spared no expense in trying to make the rest of the book a premium offering. The spines were foil stamped and the cover was paired with lavish psychedelic endpapers. But priced at 25 shillings, *Drop Out!* was far too expensive for its 100-odd pages and far too esoteric to be taken seriously. Matters probably weren't helped by the fact that Blond tried to flog the book through *Private Eye*'s mail order catalogue. Two years later Farquharson was still burdened with trying to offload his complimentary author's copies. Instead, the book became a novelty both in London and back in South Africa, where skeptical reviewers read it through a typically shocked lens: as one headline crowed, 'I took LSD, says brilliant S. A. scholar'.

In truth, *Drop Out!* was faintly shocking. It veered from subject to subject and location to location, winding through literary styles with a knowing but unbothered eye on the demands it placed on the reader. Numerous chapters disintegrated down blind alleys. Others, the reader was told, were merely the author's attempt at rewriting earlier, better drafts destroyed after receiving 'instructions' we cannot perceive.

Some of these passages were darkly comic and self-aware. Others were infuriating, and perhaps not deliberately so. The book's best moments came when Farquharson attempted to explain the experience of mania in real time:

> **Robin Farquharson**
> Moving about London under control is just like being the chauffeur of a distinguished but, at first seeming, most capricious passenger, who constantly contradicts himself and reverses his orders to the chauffeur in a way that to the chauffeur can only seem haphazard, confused, and indeed very annoying. 'Turn left, no, I mean right! Take that turning, no, don't! Turn round and go back the way we came! Stop altogether while I look at the map!' It takes the chauffeur a little time to realize that, though the city is new to his passenger and the chauffeur has passed his taxi-driver's knowledge-of-London test, the passenger knows exactly the destination to which they are moving and of which the driver has not, and cannot have, the remotest inkling. (Don't overrate the knowledge-of-London test; I happily remember the day when a taxi-driver asked to borrow my A to Z.) Indeed it only dawns very slowly on the chauffeur that, although he has outraged convention and perhaps the chauffeur by scorning the comfortable and normal back seat and pushing, without even asking, into the front seat beside the driver, his passenger is a most distinguished visitor indeed and from far further than the Magellanic Clouds.

Though few people ended up buying Farquharson's book, Aldridge's dramatic cover sufficiently captured the peaks and troughs of its author's life of poverty and prosperity.

Around this time, the filmmaker Norman Cohen set out to document these twin worlds by turning Geoffrey Fletcher's *The London Nobody Knows* into a documentary. Adapted for the screen by Fletcher himself, the result was an extraordinary record of London on the cusp of something. It flit between vérité footage of street markets to Pythonesque sketches to elegant monologues delivered by the great James Mason—an extraordinary actor with a voice made of silk, but not a natural host. The combination was gently trippy and oddly compelling.

After a whistlestop tour of Kensal Green Cemetery we are transported into a Salvation Army shelter. Mason shares a cup of tea with a few of the residents and balks at the inflated cost of a night's stay. The camera then drifts into a series of gauzy filmed portraits of homeless people, culminating in one of the film's odder set pieces. A group of men and women sit boozing on the steps of the Machzike Hadath, otherwise known as the Spitalfields Great Synagogue on the corner of Brick Lane. Their bottles contain a vivid, purple liquid, the distinctive hue of cheap methylated spirits. Others sip at something more translucent, the denatured alcohol having been watered down into a milky mauve. A middle-aged man with slicked back hair takes a swig from a full bottle, prompting another middle-aged man to swoop in and try to grab it. The other drinkers try in vain to break it up.

One figure in the crowd of inebriated on-lookers looks out of place. He is wearing a beaten-up suit, a red roll-neck jumper, a wool coat, and a pair of heavy glasses. He's clearly a newcomer. Though the man is far younger than the rest of the crowd, he does an equally poor job of separating the brawlers. He throws up his fists and circles the pair of fighters in a fey, inexperienced way, unsure whether to intervene or how. After around 15 seconds the camera moves on, Mason moves on, and this somewhat out of place man is never seen again.

Had he had the chance to speak with Mason, one wonders whether Farquharson could have persuaded the actor that he was being published by Anthony Blond. As for the meths drinkers, they had probably had characters like Farquharson drift through their ranks before. Everybody used to be somebody.

NOTTING HILL
MAP
INSIDE
STOP

CHAPTER 11
BAREFOOT IN CAMDEN UNDERGROUND

Farquharson was homeless and likely sleeping rough in Spitalfields. Just around the corner from the steps of the Great Synagogue was a soup kitchen which operated out of the crypt of Christ Church, the foreboding Hawksmoor church overlooking Spitalfields. The overgrown and flea-infested church gardens were known as Itchy Park and had long been a popular spot for those in need of somewhere to sleep.

By the time *Drop Out!* came out, Farquharson had left the streets of Spitalfields. He was instead living alongside a legendary squatter called Sid Rawle in a former Rachman property at 101 St. Stephen's Gardens, just a few minutes from the site of the London Free School.

Rachman's sideline in brothels and nightclubs had made Notting Hill a source of illicit attraction to artists and wanderers in proto-countercultural London; few were surprised when both Christine Keeler and Mandy Rice-Davies, the two women at the heart of the Profumo Affair, turned out to have been romantically involved with the infamous slumlord.

St. Stephen's Gardens was the heart of Rachman Cool, both its rough edges and romantic middle. A few years earlier, Michael Caine's *Alfie* was shown living at number 29, deigning the eponymous womaniser with sufficient quantities of pseudo-hip. In 1966, All Saints Hall on Powis Gardens hosted some of Pink Floyd's most important early gigs as benefits for the London Free School. Come 1967 and Donald Cammell and Nicolas Roeg were busy shooting Mick Jagger in *Performance* in the same area, repurposing one of Rachman's Powis Square townhouses as the reclusive rock star Turner's hideaway.

It had only been a few years since the summer of 1958, when racially-charged riots broke out fuelled by stories of white sex workers and Afro-Caribbean pimps. The sympathetic white people now navigating the streets of Notting Hill did so with a mixture of naivety, excitement, and confusion. Despite huge internal variances in politics, aesthetics, history, and status, black culture was seen as older and therefore purer and more authentic than others. To embrace this reality was to become, in Norman Mailer's famous and troubling term, a 'white negro'—hip, emancipated, and committed to social experimentation, having 'absorbed the existentialist synapses' of the African-American.

Far from dismissing and indeed brutalising black communities the way normative society was seen to do, bohemians and wannabe anti-racists commonly understood the black experience as the source of what straight white society was lacking: violence, sexuality, and self-expression. This primitivist viewpoint—an update of the long familiar 'noble savage' trope—was wildly influential, and not just amongst white liberals. Michael X's own political awakening was kickstarted by his encounter with Mailer's theory. But as the sociologist Ned Polsky put it in a widely-read rebuke, 'Mailer confuses the life of action with the life of acting out.' Whatever admiration Mailer held for black people, his argument relied on a number of romantic and racist fantasies of its own.

This played out in a variety of ways on the ground in Notting Hill, running a spectrum from simplistic fetishisation to genuine friendship, admiration, and impressive coalition building. All kinds of social and political indicators marked someone out as a potential ally, not least the name by which they referred to the area. To the white bohemians discovering this part of town, it was 'the Gate' of Notting Hill Gate. To the community of Caribbean immigrants, it was 'the Grove' of Ladbroke Grove. Over six short issues the London Free School's newsletter changed its name from *The Gate* to *The Grove*, a move widely seen as attempting to demonstrate the street-smart credentials of a predominantly white editorial team.

The *International Times*, in many ways the successor to the London Free School's newsletter, referred to the area as 'the fertile crescent', repurposing an old archaeological term for the Middle Eastern region deemed to be the cradle of civilisation. The nickname was meant as a compliment, but given the racialised population of Notting Hill the term couldn't help but echo some of the same primitivist tendencies left over from Mailer's thinking.

Whatever the name, the area was also one of the safest parts of London in which to be a gay man. The unique combination of rough-and-ready shopfronts, criminal associations, and proximity to bourgeois Kensington made the area a hub for queer nightlife. The Robin Hood and the Champion, two of London's best known gay bars, were a short walk away from Farquharson's new home. The Blue Moon and El Rio, two of the neighbourhood's most popular hangouts, and ground zero for the sex-and-drugs scandal that became the Profumo Affair, were also both gay friendly—not that 'friendly' was the most obvious word to associate with them, given the violent reputations of their owners.

The transgressive status of these venues in the eyes of white patrons also made them a popular place for white people to encounter potential Afro-Caribbean lovers, whether the target of the attraction was black women, as in the case of Nigel Samuel, or black men, as it was for Farquharson and Colin MacInnes. The writer and cultural critic was now a household name thanks to his bestselling 1959 novel *Absolute Beginners*. MacInnes was known to come from a wealthy background, having been born into a family that included Rudyard Kipling and former Conservative prime minister Stanley Baldwin. Now, with earning power of his own, MacInnes was believed by some to be the money behind the Rio.

Others suspected his friendship with Michael X relied on the latter's ability to provide MacInnes with sexual partners from London's growing black community. MacInnes's preference was for working-class black men to beat him, giving a racialised aspect to the long-standing practice of rough trade. One of Nigel Samuel's intended conquests, meanwhile, eventually stabbed him. As privileged white men knowingly playing with interracial taboos and class dynamics, the possibility of exploitation was never far from view. Neither was violence, be it solicited, retaliatory, or simply opportunistic.

Music, stardom, sexual exploration, and the threat of retaliation and revolution: this alter-vision of West London living exerted a magnetic attraction for men like Farquharson, undergirded by a ready supply of properties and happenings and a broad tolerance for reckless behaviour. Famous faces came and went, some hyper-local, others international. By the time Farquharson moved in, Alex Trocchi had as good a claim as any for being the lord of the area's criminal-dissident culture. The writer and self-declared 'cosmonaut of inner space' had long held court at 6 St. Stephen's Gardens, otherwise known as the international headquarters for what had become the increasingly grand and blurry project sigma.

Trocchi was by now a talismanic figure whose commercial prospects as a writer were so far behind him that his thinking seemed at times to be light-years ahead. He had recently been one of a series of remarkable names drawn to Joe Berke's anti-university, which closed nearly as soon as it had begun. The spectre of heroin hung in the air, as too did accusations of fraud. Names and bodies were churned, melded, and destroyed.

Chemically induced or not, Trocchi was turning his art from the written word to the living word, a master at making scenes and devising plans. He may have 'personified the interface between hustling and the creative arts', as Michael X's biographer later put it, but Trocchi was also increasingly reclusive. Amongst other assorted superpowers and ailments Farquharson came into his own wherever paranoia reigned.

Peter Johnston

Once, I found him barefoot in Camden Underground, hiding from the secret police. Despite joining him in his escape (and thereby gaining first-hand knowledge of how the public at large react) I lost him. He was subsequently done for possession (pot). He said he didn't have it. Probably he didn't. But he had, in the past, tried at least pot, LSD and heroin. I was never 100% sure that he was off it. He was fined, hospitalized (he never paid the fine) and set free.

Woody Haut

Robin was a good friend of my wife Mavis. She used to love telling this story about how a number of very high-powered city businessmen once showed up at her house seemingly unannounced. It turned out that for some obscure reason, Robin had put some kind of announcement or advert in the paper, the result of which was that three or four men arrived expecting someone to prepare them lunch. Robin busied himself talking to these men in a language that nobody really understood but they seemed to take as being part of some sort of serious financial proposition. Then, at the end of the meal, Robin sealed whatever non-existent deal had taken place by handing over a check for £10,000 written on the back of an orange and signed, of course, with a fictitious name. Mavis really appreciated this sort of anarchic side to Robin's personality—the whole thing was like something out of the Marx Brothers.

Anthony Howell

I think the model for him in terms of dress would be William Burroughs. Possibly a bit awry, but formal. It was, "Actually, I'm totally radical but I don't necessarily look it." But there is a difference between intellectual rebellion and something which is, to some extent, unhinged. It's quite interesting, the story of Robin undressing at the station. Now, I did a lot of nude performances, but they were within the context of performance art. The trouble with Robin was that he was often out of context. He didn't frame it right, and that was where it became an episode.

George Firsoff

Robin Farquharson in full cry was able to wreak havoc in a commune of freaks as well as in a straight organisation and when this happened to us and we could not get through to him or calm him down we also ended calling for men in white coats. It must have been a terrible blow for Robin to be rejected by his own tribe and although he did not bear a permanent grudge I understand now he would rather anything than fall into the hands of the men in white coats. I heard he put up a good fight when they cornered him and about ten men were needed to subdue him on this occasion, tho' on the grapevine the story may have growed a bit, I dunno.

By now Trocchi and Berke's sometime friend Laing had fled Kingsley Hall in an acid fugue. The good doctor's published work swiftly moved from clinical papers to memoir to psychedelic dreamscapes increasingly reliant on aphorism and wordplay. But there was also a vagueness and an obliqueness which protected these radical visions from outside infiltration and also made them ripe for parody and misunderstanding. By the summer of 1968 the so-called underground looked to be cresting, a paradoxical position that made it stronger than ever and vulnerable from both inside and out.

FRIENDS

No. 1 DECEMBER 12, 196
UK: 2

CHAPTER 12
THE KING OF ZEMBLA

This visibility created new constituencies, some of which were far more politically turned-on than others. In Notting Hill a creative and colourful underground paper was launched to rival *International Times* and *Time Out* for this readership.

Alan Marcuson

I left South Africa in 1965 when I was 21 and I went up to Leeds University and didn't last long. I'd been in the military and a boarding school and I just didn't want to be at university. I thought I'd love university, but I didn't—I couldn't bear it. And I came down to London and I got involved in a whole underground alternative world. And I ran a London version of *Rolling Stone* magazine for a while and then I started my own magazine called *Friends*. I inherited a bit of money and threw it all into the magazine. And it was an underground magazine for sex, drugs, and rock and roll. Robin lived in some house in Notting Hill and he'd turn up and we couldn't get rid of him

> because he was crazed, absolutely crazed. He was one of these people who was too brilliant for his own good.

As *Friends* slowly became the British alternative scene's radical newspaper of choice, a smaller, Trotskyite-associated paper named *Black Dwarf* carried an exchange between John Lennon and a student radical named John Hoyland. Lennon and his young interlocutor fired accusations back and forth as to correct revolutionary strategy, a discussion which felt increasingly urgent.

That May, Paris exploded into something like a worker-student revolution inspired in part by the teachings of the formerly obscure Situationist International. A text called 'On the Poverty of Student Life' circulated widely, later revealed to be written by the Tunisian Situationist Mustapha Khayati. Inspired by the Situationists, the Sorbonne Occupation Committee went so far as to cable communiqués to the Chinese Communist Party, willing their entry into the constellation of revolutionary parties.

In New York, a group of acid-fuelled anti-war activists took Situationism in a decidedly more psychedelic direction. Led by Abbie Hoffman, Anita Hoffman, Jerry Rubin, Nancy Kurshan, and Paul Krassner the Yippies had recently staged a widely publicised exorcism of the Pentagon, promising to make the Department of Defense levitate, turn orange, and bring about an end to the Vietnam War. Thousands would soon rally around the Yippies' cause, culminating in the Democratic National Convention in Chicago that August, where graphic scenes of police brutality were broadcast the world over.

Things seemed to be speeding up and slowing down. Acid guru Timothy Leary—long since fired by Harvard—was busy getting married, divorced, busted, crowned, and overthrown again and again in some sort of weird self-satirising cycle. In London, drug money poured out of *Friends* as soon as it arrived. Much of it bore the mark of Jim McCann, a reportedly IRA-linked arms smuggler with ties to the gangster Charles Richardson. That an infamous criminal would both freelance for the South African security state and do business

In one of alternative London's weirder publicity stunts, John Lennon and Yoko Ono provided Michael X with some of their hair in exchange for a pair of boxing shorts which reportedly once belonged to Muhammad Ali

with stoned Irish republicans testified to the dizzying, cyclical nature of the alternative scene.

Marcuson would soon spend as much of his time editing *Friends* as trying to get McCann in the same room as John Lennon. Problems and solutions intertwined as hustlers and grifters kept things circulating. Right on cue, Michael X set up a commune of his own called the Black House. A donation of Lennon and Ono's hair kept it in the press long enough to produce reports that the project was to be shuttered amid accusations of torture and extortion. Alternative London was coming of age and splintering all at once, the negative sum of needles, exposure, apocalypticism, and over- and under-theorisation. As put-upon icons struggled to satisfy their own demands, would-be leaders like Farquharson failed to take their place.

By November Farquharson was back in the care of Dr Low-Beer at Horton. One of the reasons was that he had recently been claiming to be the king of Zembla, the fictitious nation at the heart of Vladimir Nabokov's experimental 1962 novel *Pale Fire*. Farquharson was also beginning to spend time with George Hay, a pioneering British science fiction writer. Besides having founded the influential Science Fiction Foundation, Hay was best known for having been an early promoter of Dianetics in Britain. A mixture of hypnosis, psychotherapy, and cybernetic lingo, Dianetics was the brainchild of L. Ron Hubbard, the science fiction writer and founding father of Scientology.

Though Hay would eventually distance himself from Hubbard, he was far from the only futurist seduced by the promises of Dianetics and its process of neo-therapeutic 'auditing'. Hubbard had lived on and off in southern England since the 1950s, where he had accrued many followers in alternative scenes. It was very possible that Farquharson was amongst them, at least for a time.

There is a common trend for conflating mental illness with a specifically scientific kind of genius. Farquharson himself pointed to this tension in a scrap found amongst his papers. 'It's very troublesome being subjected to this kind of mental illness,' he noted, 'but it's written all my books.' Mathematical ability is treated both as something outside of regular human cognition and something buried deep within it, accessed only by those who teeter on the edge of genius and insanity. Sometimes this seems to be true. Duncan Black, who, with Farquharson, rediscovered Charles Dodgson's pioneering work on elections, speculated that Dodgson's mathematical insights were a direct result of his fraught feelings regarding the death of several of the children with whom he was obsessed.

In more recent years, people have pointed at John Nash, the Nobel Prize-winning mathematician whose experiences of schizophrenia were memorably depicted in the multi-Oscar winning biopic *A Beautiful Mind*. Remarkable stories like Nash's help to reinforce the idea of mental illness as commensurate with mathematical insight. To be sure, Farquharson's story does bear some similarities with *A Beautiful Mind*. He drew on Nash's work in his own thesis; the two men had several friends in common and, in many ways, similar mental health crises. Nash, however, recovered in ways Farquharson never sustained, a heroic arc that makes for a more life-affirming theory and a more Oscar-friendly film.

George Spencer Brown, Farquharson's direct contemporary and fellow patient at Kingsley Hall, is another character who has been treated with similar romantic glee by enthusiasts and detractors alike. Spencer Brown's *Laws of Form* was published to a fairly quiet reaction in 1969, the same year that Farquharson's thesis finally came together. Spencer Brown's book gradually gained a foothold in alternative circles, leading the reluctant author out to California for fully fledged guru-fication. When it went badly, Spencer Brown fled back to England, where he grew increasingly eccentric and impossibly obscure. As his following dwindled, those willing to endure him grew only more intense in their faith in the pathbreaking qualities of his mathematical work.

Then there is the case of the geneticist George Price, a one-time member of the Manhattan Project. Price ended up converting to Christianity, engaging in random acts of altruism, and living amongst the homeless population of Euston, not far from where Farquharson would eventually settle. Placing Farquharson in the tradition of Price and other canonical mad geniuses would not prove difficult, particularly given that he completed work on his mathematical opus while confined to a mental hospital. As to whether his mental illness was at the heart of his brilliance or its undoing, caution is needed not to unduly bend his story to fit the clichés.

Altered states can be the root cause of acts of great beauty and innovation, whether induced by emotional turmoil, chemical experimentation, or genetic traits. Instability cost Farquharson a great deal. But it also emboldened him to take severe personal risks in pursuit of collective ends. Manic and deluded behaviour cost Farquharson his chance at a life-changing fellowship at All Souls;

perhaps the same tendencies allowed him to make the breakthroughs that earned him a chance at it in the first place. Like the electoral constituencies Farquharson once studied, personal interest doesn't always neatly align with long-term benefit.

The manic episode that saw Farquharson enter Horton did, at least on this occasion, help him to advance his publishing interests. A flurry of letters resulted in Yale University Press agreeing to publish his thesis in the US. Blackwell's in Oxford handled the British publication, making for a prestigious pair of publishers. The title had been considerably chopped down since the manuscript had been submitted as part of Farquharson's doctorate. It was now known simply as *Theory of Voting*—no 'a', no 'the'. When the book finally went to press its illustrations were reproduced in colour, just as Farquharson had long hoped, albeit at a cost of $1,000, against his royalties.

Reviews were exceptional. According to the Yale political scientist Gerald Kramer, *Theory of Voting* was 'a little gem to read... no serious theoretically-inclined political scientist can afford not to have mastered its contents.' Amartya Sen, future winner of the Nobel Prize in Economics, noted that while the author was 'much more concerned with raising issues than with settling them', the result was ultimately 'both enlightening and delightful.' Harvard political scientist Roberto D'Alimonte came to much to the same conclusion in his Italian-language review, as did the non-specialist reviewer from the *Times Literary Supplement*.

The book obtained a surprising degree of crossover coverage, even accounting for the interest in alternative political solutions then swirling around freaky circles. Farquharson even garnered a mention in *OZ* magazine, with co-editor Jim Anderson praising the 'celebrated London freak' for having produced a book that was 'elegantly printed with lots of totally mystifying black and red diagrams.' Most impressively, *Theory of Voting* was reviewed in *Science*, the journal of the American Association for the Advancement of Science and one of the leading scholarly journals in the world. The review was contributed by Anatol Rapoport, a mathematical psychologist and leading pacifist who had participated in the Aix conference with Farquharson.

> **Anatol Rapoport**
> The great merit of the book is first of all in the rare combination of complete rigor and remarkable clarity, which makes its sophisticated ideas immediately comprehensible to *any* reader motivated to understand them. Secondly, the reader's interest is held at a high pitch by the graceful style and the felicitous examples, some taken from real life, ranging from deliberations in the Roman Senate to the five-year, $18-billion highway program offered by Tennessee's Democratic Senator Albert Gore.

Unfortunately, the extreme delay in publication did little to help with the book's intelligibility, which had already been compressed down into a remarkably small number of pages. The book's mathematical reasoning had always been a little oblique and Farquharson's innovative theories and his intermittent instability had done little to clear things up. A few years later, Richard Niemi, a political scientist, endeavoured to 'collect in one place all of the errors, misleading statements, and assorted problems found in this slender text.' Despite, or perhaps because of Farquharson's brevity, Niemi's results filled nearly seven pages. *Theory of Voting* would prove to be Farquharson's final scholarly contribution.

CHAPTER 13
MOTHER COUNTRY MADMEN

On his return to London from Horton some time in mid-1969, Farquharson was temporarily permitted to return to the Arts Lab. He soon made the acquaintance there of Nicholas Albery, a totemic figure in what was coming to be known as 'alternative London'. Albery came from a privileged arts background, his parents having founded the esteemed Donmar Theatre. Via boarding school, Oxford, and the summer of love in San Francisco, Albery had acquired a robust understanding of institutions and the means to reimagine them. By the time he met Farquharson, Albery had started to cycle through a series of alphabetised pseudonyms in a valiant attempt at shaking off his family ties, leading some friends to refer to him as 'Nicholas A-Z'.

Albery had also just begun to help Hoppy to organise a free information service called BIT, a landmark institution in the development of the British counterculture. Originally spun out from *International Times* and the London Free School, BIT was a volunteer-run office and later commune with a 24-hour hotline, lending library, open kitchen and more, offering tips and tricks to alternative London and beyond.

Richard Neville, the founder of *OZ*, was not impressed, describing BIT as 'little more than a telephone surrounded by stoned optimists, all suffering, as someone once said of an unfortunate actor, from delusions of adequacy.' But to BIT's staff—BIT workers, as they called themselves—the project was something special.

BIT looked back towards romantic notions of communal living and forwards towards the possibilities of a modern, computerised future. Though BIT's name was a clear reference to the initials of *International Times*, it was also a nod to the bit, the smallest unit of information a computer could process. The mind-bending cybernetic ideas that Farquharson had discussed at academic conferences just a few years earlier were now reemerging as trendy markers of countercultural intent.

Free information seemed to be everywhere—whispered in codes, snuck down telephone wires, shared in arcane recipes, and occasionally distributed in cheap mimeographed newsletters. A group calling themselves Zenden—'the degenerate arm of the Zen Bolshevist group'—put out a pamphlet called *Project London Free*, listing 1001 tricks and scams people could pull to get the city to march to their own beat, gratis. 'Information is free,' the pamphlet's editors declared, 'but it's feedback that keeps us together.' Technical terms like 'feedback'—the circular relationship between input and output—had now become buzzwords. So too had 'signal' (the intended content of a message) and 'noise' (the extraneous matter it picks up on the way).

Information centres were spreading across the UK, publicising one another and morphing to local needs and desires in the process. These sometimes bore a resemblance to BIT, like the suitably named Feedback in Bristol. Others took their inspiration from the Old Left, like Birmingham's Peace Centre. There were impromptu community spaces, like Better Books on London's Charing Cross Road, run by Tony Godwin, who had headhunted Alan Aldridge to work at Penguin. There were also experimental new environments,

The headquarters of BIT on the corner of Westbourne Park Road

like the legendary Unicorn Bookshop in Brighton, Glasgow Advisory People (GAP), and other assorted 'growth centres'. Supplementing it all was a growing network of independent arts labs modelled on and reacting to the first centre on Drury Lane.

Having made Farquharson's acquaintance at the original Arts Lab, Albery decided to take him straight to the offices of BIT. 'As we walked and talked,' Albery recalled, 'Robin got higher and higher, and began to see stars in the pavement, and had to take a pill to stay down.' Unperturbed, Albery arranged for Farquharson to man BIT's late-night hotlines.

Nicholas Albery
Robin Farquharson was a BIT night shift worker & general disruptive influence, who used to work here back in 1970, in the bad old pre-collective days. Robin was ideally suited for working at BIT in that he was a complete communications-freak—with never a penny to his name, he used to think nothing of, say, phoning up the White House for a half-hour discussion on the Irish problem; he used to charter airplanes at the drop of a hat (he once ordered two Concordes and two Boeing 747s for the Electric Cinema Club's new charter flight company); he bought a factory by cheque for the manufacturing of radio-telephones out of cocoa tins and bits of string, etc. etc.

Stephen Lee
BIT was set up very, very specifically by Hoppy to help people who were really confused in life and had maybe been kicked out of their homes or whatever. But the irony is that the people who actually ended up working at BIT, apart from Nick Albery, were probably the people who actually needed the most help.

In many ways, Farquharson joining BIT was a masterstroke. In recent months he had been telling anyone that would listen that all he really wanted was to open something he referred to as 'the

University of the Air'—a riff on Harold Wilson's description of the Open University—and now here he was at the heart of an exciting alternative networking project with a state-of-the-art (if messy) telephone system. The same obsession with strategy and problem solving that made Farquharson liable to fixate also made him an ideal BIT worker. The whole thing sounded like project sigma with wires.

Farquharson had, it seemed, finally met both his people and an institution designed for someone with his unique experience and obsessions. But after just a short time at BIT, Farquharson was forced to jump ship. His brother had been killed in a road accident in South Africa and Farquharson was forced to return home for the funeral. Short of cash, he told friends around the office that his airfare had been covered by his old comrade Rupert Murdoch.

It came as a shock to be back in Pretoria for the first time since he had fled the country. Reeling from the sudden change in surroundings and no doubt suffering from the trauma of his brother's sudden death, Farquharson repeatedly attempted to mail drafts of his latest manuscript back to England. He was arrested and taken to hospital.

While hospitalised, Farquharson learned from an imported issue of *International Times* that a new group was forming back in London called People for a New Psychiatry (PNP). Though details were thin on the ground, the name was intriguing to this jaded veteran of Kingsley Hall. Farquharson decided to get in touch with its organiser in anticipation of a hasty return to the UK.

Michael Barnett

Robin had written to me soon after the start of PNP from a mental hospital in Pretoria, South Africa. Typically he had a copy of *IT* to hand there less than two weeks after it reached the London streets. He drew such happenings to him. Power surrounded him. Once it had been academic, this power. I

> sensed his dilemma was that he failed to see how he could realize his own full being in this world. Everything was against him, including himself. His power could find insufficient purchase in society to satisfy itself. Therefore he was forced to abandon most of it, leading to a stormy centre which took him from time to time into mental hospital. You might say he was invulnerable to social conditioning.

Once he had been freed from confinement, Farquharson moved around South Africa, attempting to fuse his telephone mania with his anti-racist politics.

> **Nicholas Albery**
> Perhaps his most inspired venture was the time he launched a multi-racial BIT in Johannesburg: for one month he got round the Apartheid laws by arguing that he couldn't be expected to tell if a person telephoning in was black or white; when they finally arrested him, he managed to persuade them to fly him back to Britain to see his psychiatrist.

As Farquharson's state changed and he mistook noise for signal, the organisations around him shifted. Telephones, headphones, tape decks, and bits of broken or defunct computer equipment began to show up around the place, ready for fixing or repurposing in light shows and meditation environments. More often than not, these machines for exploring consciousness and community were themselves by-products of bloated defence budgets, pointing towards an uneasy connection between resistance and domination.

Alongside a growing air of militancy and communitarianism came a parallel sense of increased individualism. Drug use produced temporary communities and led seekers both outward and inward. Increasing numbers of families and communes began to retreat from the city and attempt to set up their own independent societies.

In the midst of this period of reconstitution the UK began to catch up with the hype-making capacities of the American alternative scene. A music festival organised 40 miles south of the town of Woodstock showed the power of combining rock'n'roll and good publicity. Though the Woodstock Music and Art Fair was itself something of a washout—traffic was so bad that 10% of ticket holders never even made it into the festival site, while Pete Townshend memorably bonked a stage-invading Abbie Hoffman on the head with his guitar—the festival's companion LP quickly became a bestselling record. The ensuing concert film grossed $50 million, confirming Woodstock as the byword for an entire era of socio-cultural production.

The most famous of the early British festivals was organised in 1968 on the Isle of Wight by three inexperienced brothers named Ray, Ron, and Bill Foulk. These events understandably struggled to compete with the scale of American festivals. But word spread fast, and by the 1969 edition the organisers of the Isle of Wight Festival had managed to book Bob Dylan for his first live performance since his infamous motorbike accident. Dylan's participation—and his decision not to join the revellers at Woodstock—led to huge press attention and enormous crowds. Within a year of its founding, the Foulks' festival had become a runaway hit and a fixture of the British summer.

Dylan's high-profile reemergence at the Isle of Wight put the UK firmly on the international countercultural map. *International Times* also began to live up to its name, operating more like a worldwide psychedelic gossip column than a traditional newspaper. Readers and contributors spanned the known world and beyond and money began pouring in and out of alternative London. From inauspicious beginnings, BIT spawned the Community Levy for Alternative Projects, otherwise known as CLAP, a backronym intended to allow proponents to state that 'BIT gives you the CLAP'. Despite the puerile name, the CLAP was a serious undertaking, providing a sort of investment network for matching alternative businesses with potential funders.

Despite their differences in scale and ambition, both the Isle of Wight Festival and the CLAP spoke to the potential of a small but determined group of enthusiasts. The alternative society saw the music festival as a model of change built for a mass audience, more often than not based around the idea of the affinity group. Radical, non-hierarchical cells united by a shared cause, affinity groups sprung up all over the place. As was often the case, the most famous example came from the United States in the form of the Black Panther Party for Self-Defense. Originating in Oakland, California, the Panthers' call to arms, ethnic pride, and striking look inspired radicals the world over, often in conflicted ways.

Various other groups explicitly riffed on the Panther model and not always in support of the Panthers' original goals: there were the Brown Berets (militant Chicanos from Los Angeles), the White Tigers (New York cops united in their hatred of the Panthers), and even a group of nonconforming Christian retirees from Philadelphia who called themselves the Gray Panthers.

But some of the Black Panther Party's most devoted followers outside Oakland's African-American community were a group of white radicals with whom Farquharson soon became obsessed. They dubbed themselves the White Panthers. Their leader was a Detroit-based poet named John Sinclair, who also served as the manager of the innovative noise rockers the MC5. Sinclair's goal was to unite the MC5's powerful sound with explicitly political lyrics, communal living, and, if it came to it, revolutionary violence.

Detroit was one of the most populous cities in the United States, home to America's automobile industry and a thriving music industry best known for Motown Records. The city also had a long history of racial tension, most recently given form in the 12th Street Riot of 1967, which resulted in 44 deaths and more than 7,000 arrests. This was the context in which the MC5 were born, with blues music the soundtrack to armed resistance. Originally called 'Motor City Five', the band abbreviated their name so that it 'sounded like a serial number… stamped out of the auto factories', as guitarist Wayne Kramer put it. This down-and-dirty style was reflected in their music, a combination of garage rock and heavy psychedelic jams that would presage the arrival of hard rock and punk.

Though Sinclair had a relatively comfortable childhood, the group's founding members each came from white working-class families. They saw in the power of blues and rock'n'roll a common language able to transcend racial categories and to form unions across class lines. The band themselves testified to this possibility: Rob Tyner, the band's frontman, had Native American heritage, while Pun Plamondon, a leading White Panther, would later discover that he did too. Some historians have pointed to the band's active engagement with black musicians and deep commitment to the cause: if rock united them, maybe it could unite an entire generation to change its destructive ways.

The MC5's look was distinctive and theatrical, captured in dramatic detail by the photographer Leni Sinclair, the White Panthers' 'minister of education' and wife of John Sinclair. For all their performative rage, the White Panthers were also highly committed, not just to rock but to revolution. 'We are not playing', Sinclair insisted in 1969. 'The only thing we play is music.' But at its core this meant assimilating black identity—a very primitivist and macho vision of black identity—into an idealised model of radical resistance, as made clear by the final words of the White Panthers' founding manifesto.

John Sinclair

The actions of the Black Panthers in America have inspired us and given us strength, as has the music of black America, and we are moving to reflect that strength in our daily activity just as our music contains and extends the power and feeling of the black magic music that originally informed our bodies and told us that we could be free.

I might mention Brother James Brown in this connection, as well as John Coltrane and Archie Shepp. Sun-Ra. LeRoi Jones. Malcolm X. Huey P. Newton, Bobby Seale, Eldridge Cleaver, these are magic names to us. These are men in America. And we're as crazy as they are, and as pure. We're bad.

The White Panthers were Norman Mailer's fantasy put into conflicted action, 'mother country madmen in charge of our own lives', as Sinclair put it.

This was, of course, a very different understanding of the 'mother country' to that of British South African families like the Farquharsons or the Windrush generation. These were white radicals who felt adrift in their own society, who felt a closer kinship—whether real or imagined—to African-American culture, and therefore to questions of African-American identity. They were 'madmen' because of the risks they took, because of their marginalisation, because of their separateness from normative society. Whether this all derived from earnest affectation, racist projection, or both depended on your point of view.

Sinclair's thinking was that if white working-class people couldn't participate in the actions of the Black Panthers, the very least they could do was back them up with the propaganda of the deed. As in Ned Polsky's earlier critique of Norman Mailer, this sometimes meant confusing the life of action with the life of acting out. In a striking parallel to South Africa's doomed African Resistance Movement, Sinclair and his White Panthers often seemed in more of a rush to extreme action than the oppressed peoples to whom they professed allegiance.

Whatever the complicated racial politics at play and the allure of costumes, rhetoric, and raucous music, the US authorities took Sinclair and his peers as a serious threat. Numerous White Panther spinoff groups emerged across the US, leading the organisation to be put under close observation by the FBI. Plamondon, the White Panthers' 'minister of defense', decided to flee the country after being accused of bombing a CIA office in Ann Arbor. Sinclair meanwhile was sentenced to ten years imprisonment after offering two joints to an undercover cop. No sooner had the White Panthers made their name than two of the group's leading figures were out of action.

In the UK—a deeply racist country, albeit one with an altogether different history of racial conflict—white organisers were also grappling with the urgent need to form alliances across ethnic lines. British troops had been deployed to Northern Ireland in the summer of 1969 to suppress sectarian uprisings. London had its own long history of interracial organising, not least in the scene around the recent London Free School in Notting Hill.

Michael X grew close with Alex Trocchi and came to be associated with a non-partisan, hip vision of anti-racist organising, though he maintained some links with older struggles. Michael even published some of his poetry in the *New African*, likely making the connection to this decidedly un-trendy publication through Farquharson, Trocchi's onetime neighbour on St. Stephen's Gardens. Michael had even once mailed his poetic well-wishes to Mao. Despite this ostensibly internationalist outlook, even Michael still looked to the US as the cutting edge of racial pride, closely studying Malcolm X and Muhammad Ali and assiduously courting their attention on visits to the UK.

Given the publicity Sinclair had garnered and the Panther knock-offs that already existed, it was perhaps just a matter of time before someone took the White Panther idea and ran with it. In the UK, a former UFO doorman and sometime *International Times* journalist named Mick Farren heeded the call. A grammar school student turned art school kid, Farren had worked his way up the slippery slope of countercultural fame, enduring a period of homelessness in the same Spitalfields churchyard Farquharson once called home.

Farren now sought to import the White Panthers' hodgepodge philosophy and apply it wholesale on the other side of the Atlantic. Alongside the chutzpah Farren had serious underground bona fides. The Deviants, his new band, were being bankrolled by Nigel Samuel, even though members deemed the benefactor to be 'off his trolley.' Farren was also currently sleeping with Germaine Greer, then best known as a writer for *OZ* magazine.

Farren idolised Alex Trocchi and Michael X and yearned to join them at London's internationalist high table. Part of the goal of the British White Panthers seemed to be to turn Farren into a rock'n'roll superstar, or at very least the British Abbie Hoffman. Beyond this, it was never entirely clear to what extent Farren's White Panther Party were real. 'The British White Panther Party was a very secret society', he later observed, 'the primary secret being that it didn't exist at all.' It was, Farren said, 'the organisational equivalent of Zorro', a means of subversion that insulated *International Times* and other sympathetic publications from the consequences of his actions. 'Within weeks' of announcing the British White Panther Party, he claimed, 'over a thousand freaks had written in with enquiries and ideas.' In truth, the British White Panthers were whatever gaggle of Farren's pals happened to coalesce at a given moment.

Farren's fake-it-til-you-make-it approach was not uncommon. It was fun to pretend to be a big-shot, and if enough people took you seriously, you'd end up becoming the real deal without a lot of the legwork. From his prison cell Sinclair supported the development of the various White Panther outfits, his own group having themselves been some kind of spinoff organisation. To Farren's credit, he did grow close with the MC5, corresponding for many years with their guitarist Wayne Kramer, through whom he came to know Sinclair as well.

Farren's White Panthers were far from the only experiment in radical politics that existed more in name than in practice; project sigma still offered supporters little more than a semi-regular newsletter. But Farren was no sooner a recognisable underground provocateur as he was booted out of his own band. In a one-two punch, Farren was sacked from the Deviants and then made the subject of a scathing *OZ* editorial by none other than Germaine Greer. As Greer wrote about the man who was until recently her lover, 'Mick ended up hating nearly all his audiences. He meant to yell at their parents, but he ended up yelling at them.' Farren seethed but set himself the task of finding a new way to intervene in radical proceedings.

1970
UFO+TV
PRESENT
FUTURE
PAST
INDIVIDUAL
REDSTONE/
INJECTION
SHIP
VANGAURD/
INSERTION
SHIP
This could be the beginning of something else
is it?
COMMUNICATIONS NETWORK
Bachdenkel
14,15 FEB at 7pm MEMBERS 7'6
LOVE+
PEACE
make peace make love make television. we're limiting the number of people in the studio area to 100 at any time. a continuous situation. it starts at 2pm on Saturday and Sunday and we'll start charging about 7pm. Goldsmiths College TV unit, Bachdenkel making videotape, life support functions, a party, a pad, loving people. Made possible by John Yoko Ringo George Sony Ampex

CHAPTER 14
A COMPUTER PROGRAMMED TO PUBLIC

By 1970, the Philadelphia Association's lease of Kingsley Hall had expired and the building was shuttered for good. An increasing number of other communes were popping up to fill the gap in stable housing for victims of psychiatric abuse. Looking to France and the long shadow cast by the Situationist International, Farquharson moved to set up something like this himself. The problem was, as ever, one of space.

Squatting seemed like one potential solution. That summer a group called the London Street Commune had set up shop for ten days at a premium location on Hyde Park Corner, taking over a squatted mansion at 144 Piccadilly. This was surely on Farquharson's radar: apart from being front-page news, two of the squat's leaders were his old housemate Sid Rawle and Phil Cohen, the dropout who had been integral to the founding of Kingsley Hall.

Though Farquharson had missed out on the chaos of the London Street Commune, the stunt did succeed in capturing the attention of the GLC. Then under Conservative rule, the GLC had a difficult balancing act on its hands. If they weren't careful, other, better-organised groups would spring up in the wake of 144 Piccadilly and turn squatting into a mass movement. At the same time, the authorities were tasked with rejuvenating London's housing stock while slashing their operating budget. Allowing would-be squatters the short-term use of abandoned property might pave the way for redevelopment at little cost to local councils.

The GLC's engagement with community housing schemes was therefore not born simply out of altruism. Horace Cutler, then chairman of the GLC's housing committee, has since been called the 'prophet' of British privatisation. In response to London's ongoing housing crisis, he made the sort of calculated decision that would one day make him the head of the GLC. Under Cutler's guidance, the GLC began to promise that they would cut the red tape required for community groups to take possession of abandoned or condemned properties—so long as tenants adhered to a strict set of requirements. Hoping to bend the system's reformist impulses to his own ends, Farquharson promptly announced the launch of what he called the Situationists Housing Association.

> **Robin Farquharson**
> Horace Cutler suggested that if we formed a housing association we might then receive some houses. For a long time nothing happened. The Situationists paid its £37 to register as an industrial and provident society and evolved a committee which can hardly be described as drop-out.

Farquharson was right: the committee of the Situationists Housing Association succeeded in roping in both Leon Redler from Kingsley Hall and Amnesty International secretary general Martin Ennals, whom Farquharson knew from the Anti-Apartheid Movement. Despite these prominent names, Farquharson's scheme sounded fantastical and confused, not least because its name kept on jumping between 'Situationist' and 'Situationists' and from 'Associated' to 'Association'. But records showed that the group really was registered

144 Piccadilly was briefly known as 'Hippiedilly' during the London Street Commune's occupation

as an industrial and provident society. Cutler likewise kept up his end of the deal: within its first year of operation Farquharson's group secured the short-term use of at least four houses, some from the GLC, one of which was turned over for use as a growth centre called Kaleidoscope.

A journalist from the *Guardian* named Raymond Gardner took note and arranged to interview Farquharson at his Notting Hill squat. Gardner described his subject's voice as 'cooly cultured, the phrasing slow and deliberate… it belongs better to the upright world of an Oxbridge debating chamber than a grubby, damp, basement room in Westbourne Park Road.' A recent photo showed a different man to the one featured on the BBC's election coverage some fifteen

Farquharson and his 'friend' pictured in the Guardian *in February 1970*

years earlier. Thin tufts of hair shot up from the very top of Farquharson's head, his faintly curly locks having long since disappeared. The glasses were gone too. In their place was a face now defined by a bushy black beard. Farquharson was shown roaring with laughter, though Gardner observed he seldom made anything like a straightforward joke.

Photographed alongside Farquharson was an unnamed male 'friend'. The former don now spoke openly about both his queerness and his drug experimentation. As Farquharson put it, when drugs and homosexuality collided, they permitted access 'into the secret garden—or perhaps the perfumed garden would be a better term.'

What the *Guardian*'s interviewer heard of Farquharson's underground world impressed him, even if it left him a little confused. Farquharson was giving form to the themes that had dominated his mind since his undergraduate days, shifting from the Dodgson of mathematical paradoxes to the Carroll of rabbit holes. He was now all talk, hinting at the allure of insider knowledge and the hidden codes with which power operates. The whiff of dissidence and dissonance was alluring.

As Gardner noted, though, 'Robin's feet are still planted, however loosely, on the topsoil of conventional society.' He still had his remarkable CV, his academic publishing credentials, and, whatever else happened, his refined voice. Quite how Farquharson would square tensions was not immediately obvious, but in the long, sympathetic interview that followed—which admittedly misspelled Farquharson's surname—the semi-famous dropout was given plenty of space to lay out his plans to thrive both within and without the system.

In the early months of 1970 Farquharson also began to meet up with some of his long-distance correspondents in the hope of forming another experimental grouping.

> **Michael Barnett**
> He stood out, dressed in a dark suit, a tie and a white shirt, from the casually draped people around him. He stood out because of his size too: he was a large man; tall, broad, with a magnificent head. His eyes and face are usually afire, yet that night they were not; they were soft and tranquil, almost demure. He must have been in a strange part of his being, or in disguise.

Barnett's People for a New Psychiatry had by now renamed themselves People, Not Psychiatry as part of a more proactive, separatist stance. With this new approach came the need for space. Through Farquharson and the Situationists Housing Association's dealings with London Free School founder Rhaune Laslett, PNP found themselves a house at 18 Russell Gardens Mews, near Holland Park. In quick order Farquharson formed part of the small group of PNP members that came to make up the new commune's first tenants.

Michael Barnett

From the moment they moved in the world shuddered. Robin, I heard, was going berserk. Nothing could stop him from celebrating *continuously.* Like a lion let loose he went wild. At once the balcony outside his window collapsed as he lodged his iron bedstead on it to make more space in his room for a party he was throwing for twenty or thirty people he had picked up here and there—in parks, in tube trains, on the streets. The house was full of strange people night and day.

Jenny James

His energy was frighteningly high. My strongest memory is of going downstairs at midnight to see what the racket was and finding him dancing naked and maniacally in the very small kitchen which had huge picture windows open to the public, the light on and some of his young sexual partners in the kitchen too, plus loud music blaring. That really wasn't what the house was set up for and I had to keep some kind of control on our reputation else we'd be evicted.

Michael Barnett

Robin never slept, or hardly ever, and the stompings and bangings and bellowings went on through the nights. Music incessantly. His way of appeasing Jenny was to bring her tea in bed at three in the morning then another cup at four and perhaps a third at five. At six the partial peace would be shattered by Robin's booming bass voice in the bath.

I saw Robin only once during that first two weeks of the house's existence, and that was at the Inn on the Park, at a large party launching Quaesitor, the growth centre, at which many members of the Esalen Institute were present. Robin burst in dressed in his BIT vest and jeans, his feet bare over the lush carpets, and proceeded to invite about fifty people to the latest party to celebrate the opening of the first PNP house. His hair was tousled, his eyes afire, his energy bursting his boundaries. He began dancing, talking, declaiming, drinking, all at once. Then he vanished into the night.

A vote was taken among the PNP housemates. The result was unanimous. Farquharson would be asked to leave the house when he returned from wherever he was. Such decisive action proved unnecessary.

> **Michael Barnett**
> Robin had (at last) been picked up by the police and was back in mental hospital in Surrey. It appeared that he had been whirling around the streets in the early hours like a stoned dervish, had punched a policeman who had tried to interrupt his dance, and that was that. Back at the PNP house his things were moved into a corner and, by unanimous agreement amongst the tenants, his room let to someone else.

Around this time, Farquharson began to develop a party trick. He would wait until there was a large gathering—a Saturday night at the artist John Latham's house, as often seemed to be the case—and suddenly declaim that he could predict the name of the song playing on the radio before it was turned on. A crowd of hipper than hip disbelievers would stare and mock, the radio would be turned on, probably to Radio Caroline, and sure enough, the correct song would be playing.

Spectators were left divided over whether this was a parlour trick gleaned from old Oxford or the sign of a serious occult tendency. Farquharson for his part insisted it was simply an act of magic, 'a gift queers often have' which LSD 'had beefed up to quadruple strength.' A few variations on the theme followed.

> **Frater Choronzon**
> One evening he turned up at the Westbourne Park Road flat which I shared with some friends, carrying a large portable radio receiver under his arm. The door was opened and he seemed agitated. "You don't trust me", he said, the speech tumbling out in a flurry, "you all think I'm a spy. Well, I'll prove to you that I'm not!" With that he assumed entry. Seated on the floor in the front room he started singing a song loudly; with imperfect

pitch, but recognisable. All the while he was fiddling with the tuner dial on the portable radio, but with the set switched off. We couldn't figure out what he was up to, but suddenly he turned the radio on loud and the song he was singing came forth over the airwaves, exactly synchronised with his voice. He roared with laughter as we scratched our heads, not completely taking in what we were witnessing. He switched the radio off and lapsed into a learned sounding commentary on a topic of current news interest, all the while twiddling the tuner dial. After a further ten or fifteen seconds he switched the radio on and the commentary programme he had located continued what he was saying.

Next Robin started speaking in German. He tuned the radio again, switched it on and out flowed the Deutsch, absolutely contiguous with what he was saying. "I told you I would prove that I wasn't a spy." We thought it was a conjuring trick, some stunt with a tape recorder. But no, he really did appear to have some bizarre ability to pick up radio waves in his head.

In later years, having got to know him better, we occasionally discussed this offbeat talent. He explained that it only occurred infrequently at a particular stage in the progression of his manic state, and it seemed that the drugs administered interfered with it. I asked if he had ever done any scientific analysis of the process involved, and he said that he generally kept the ability to himself, because he appreciated the sort of pressures and experimentation he might be subjected to if he admitted it or demonstrated it to the wrong company.

Richard Lancaster

In 1970 Robin was living in a basement commune in Westbourne Park Road. I visited him and found six other people there, Robin announced he could get some liquid acid if everyone put some money in—he collected £5. Came back with a jar of orange juice that he said contained the orange juice acid. I and one or two others in a fairly reserved mood; four others amused by it all, humouring Robin and I thought egging him on; Robin clearly in a manic state and laying fairly heavy/speedy vibes on everyone. I became very anxious about tripping in these circumstances. But after 1 ½ hours no-one had come on; Robin then announced the failure of an experiment to induce tripping in a group of people by suggestion alone, with a placebo—there was no acid in the orange juice.

Michael Barnett

He rang me up one night at about 4 a.m. to tell me he had just bought Centre Point, that uninhabited architectural ghost of Tottenham Court Road, for many million pounds. Also he had been granted limitless power, and was prepared to fulfil for me three wishes. Tiredly I gave him three—end poverty, sweep the roads clear of cars, and turn back that year to the beginning. He rang back in an hour to say one of my wishes was proving hard to implement. Would I wait or would I prefer to substitute another? I answered him in a dream. Soon he rang again and wanted to discuss some detail, poverty in Haiti or something. I told him to fuck off and let me sleep, whereupon he exploded at my lack of faith.

Richard Lancaster

By now Robin was getting quite freaky; he got into a rap about how money could be produced by people with overdrafts writing cheques for one another—that money was purely a matter of writing and telephoning—and one only had to do this to be financially able to do anything.

The four freaks who were making fun of him arranged to go with him to Centre Point the next day in a taxi to take up tenancy and he was then due to fly from the roof in a chartered helicopter to visit his bank manager in Cambridge. Robin split to go to the Arts Lab. I was watching a TV programme on Alternative Society organisations later that evening, when Robin suddenly came up to the camera looking quite freaky, pulled out a fiver, announced that no one needed cash ("we need housing and food, not money"), and tried

> to rip the note to pieces. It wouldn't rip properly, so he borrowed a match and set light to it… It was the £5 we had given him earlier.

Quite how Farquharson expected his various money tricks to pan out is unclear. As Richard Lancaster put it, 'he made money seem like electricity that only had to be connected up'. The authorities would probably take a different view, classing Farquharson's habit of paying off one phony cheque with another as a common kind of fraud known as 'kiting'. In this case, however, it wasn't the dodgy cheques that got Farquharson into trouble. The day after his escapades on the BBC, Farquharson returned to Centre Point and set to arguing with the security staff. An ambulance was called and he was once again carted off to Horton.

This was just another minor setback in a period of intense activity. In early 1970, Nicholas Albery was visited at BIT's offices in Notting Hill by a researcher named Andrew Rigby, who was preparing a PhD on communal living. Albery advised Rigby to swing by the Westbourne Park Road commune to interview Farquharson.

> **Andrew Rigby**
> Nicholas was a very organised person and I recall how patient he must have been if he had folk like Farquharson coming round to the office everyday. I did wonder whether Nicholas arranged the encounter just to get Robin off his back. When Robin offered to sell me a copy of his book I protested that I had no money to pay him. He replied that this was no problem, I was just to write a version of the wording on a piece of paper (pay Robin Farquharson the sum of £x etc.) and this would be sufficient for him to obtain the money. I don't recall any mention of such a payment in subsequent bank statements – so I guess I got it as a gift.

Whatever the reasoning, Rigby met with Farquharson and conducted a slightly terse interview. Though Farquharson's replies were blunt, traces of his old obsessions shone through.

Andrew Rigby
How do you see Communes having an influence on social change?

Robin Farquharson
Well, communes are microcosms of the form of government of the future, and the Federation of Communes is the archetypal future state.

Andrew Rigby
Do you feel that it would ever be possible for someone to fully understand you?

Robin Farquharson
Yes, I'm a computer, programmed to public.

Andrew Rigby
Generally speaking, how would you describe yourself politically?

Robin Farquharson
Revolutionary anarchist, with a preference for non-violent methods.

Andrew Rigby
What does the term mean to you?

Robin Farquharson
Someone who wants to replace the present system by a new system in which coercion will not be relevant.

Andrew Rigby
Do you feel that turning to drugs holds any revolutionary potential?

Robin Farquharson
That's right. If you want to make converts, give them some acid first.

Andrew Rigby
In seeking to bring about social change, what kind of strategy do you hold out most hope for?

Robin Farquharson
Well, the basic theoretical problem is to devise a proper large scale decision-making procedure which does not have the disadvantage of the voting system.

Andrew Rigby
What are the disadvantages of voting?

Robin Farquharson
Well, first of all it leads to a gross over-simplification of the nation's will. Secondly, it means that most alternatives cannot be discussed. Thirdly, it leads to the party system. I'd like a system in which there was much more frequent consultation and a much richer range of alternatives available, in which the decision was taken directly by the electorate and not indirectly through the parliamentary system.

Andrew Rigby
Do you have any coherent vision about what your ideal society might look like?

Robin Farquharson
Yes, central communication facility, telephones; it's rather like a society in which the only government is BIT.

Andrew Rigby
What do you think is the greatest advantage and the greatest personal disadvantage of membership of a community?

Robin Farquharson
The major appeal is simply the emotional and physical presence

> of other people. There are many other advantages, such as catering in common—gives you cheaper and better food, people to talk to, people to sleep with, a constant flow of people. The major disadvantage is no privacy, and my papers get fucked up. I would like to move to a commune where I had a room of my own.

A few weeks after Rigby's interview, Farquharson's increasingly visible status as an elder statesman earned him an invitation to participate in a new creative venture. Mixed-media theatre had been making waves in the United States for the past few years, utilising newly-available portable video cameras to mix and remix live footage in immersive environments. These experimental techniques were now being championed in the UK by Hoppy, the founder of BIT. Hoppy saw multi-channel camerawork as more than a new art form: it was a way of unleashing the untapped cybernetic possibilities of human communication.

Hoppy announced himself as a pioneer of these techniques at an event he co-organised at the New Arts Lab in mid-February 1970 called 'UFO+TV'. As reported in *International Times*, TVX, Hoppy's new video collective, invited Farquharson to participate, making merry with live video equipment alongside *OZ*'s Richard Neville and a soundtrack from Birmingham psych-rockers Bachdenkel. Funding for the event came from the Beatles, while corporate support for the project came from Nigel Samuel and Michael X's management company.

BIT opened all kinds of doors for Farquharson. But the organisation constantly lurched between countercultural fame and precarity, a combination that proved to be its undoing. Amidst the excitement and chaos, Farquharson's tenure was never likely to be longterm.

> **Nicholas Albery**
> Unfortunately, like some of the rest of us in those days, he had difficulty getting through to our 'directors' and after one particularly exhilarating nightshift he struck one of the

> directors with a telephone in a symbolic attempt to establish closer communication—however, she was not amused, and eight policemen came into the BIT office & carted him off to mental hospital.

Farquharson's name was now in circulation in London's artistic scenes, no matter his bans from the old Arts Lab and his dramatic departure from BIT.

Shortly after the UFO+TV event, the *Arts Labs Newsletter* planned to publish a 'confrontation' between Farquharson and John Hoyland, the student radical last seen feuding with John Lennon in the pages of *Black Dwarf*. It was not to be. Having headed to the airport in order to fly to Chicago, for reasons unknown, Farquharson missed his flight. He jumped into a taxi only for the driver to kick up a fuss once he spotted that Farquharson was shoeless.

Alan Marcuson

I was no longer working in the underground press because by this time, I'd become a carpet and textile collector and dealer. I was leaving to go to San Francisco and I was at the check-in desk of British Airways and to my absolute horror, Robin turned up in his pyjamas with a mini-cab driver chasing him who wanted the money. He'd obviously blagged the guy that he would get him paid. I paid the mini-cab driver for him and he was demanding my help. I wanted absolutely nothing to do with him. He was clearly off his rocker and I wanted to just get away from him. He recognised me and people said, "Do you know this man?" and I said, "Yes, only slightly..."

It got really out of hand and you know, he was a big bloke. All of a sudden there were several airport security people around him. They were rather afraid of approaching him because he was so mad and he looked dangerous and was demanding a first class trip to New York because he wanted to go and speak at the United Nations or some crazy idea like that. Police eventually came and they started tackling him and I just went through

> into departure. I didn't want to hang around at all and so I left. That's the last time I saw him.

It reportedly took ten policemen to subdue Farquharson. Then, according to the *Arts Labs Newsletter*, 'because the police had nothing to charge him with, they beat him up and had him committed to Horton Mental Hospital.'

CHAPTER 15
THE MINISTER OF PROPAGANDA

After years of busts and raids, the British underground press was heading towards a reckoning. May 1970 saw the release of *OZ* magazine's 'schoolkids issue', a special one-off publication assembled with the support of a handful of precocious teenagers. The resultant issue featured an erotic cartoon by R. Crumb doctored to include the all-too-innocent face of Rupert Bear, the children's comic book character. Farquharson was familiar with the culprit behind Rupert's pornification: sixteen-year old Vivian Berger, whose mother Grace had been the host of the Anti-Apartheid Movement's earliest meetings in London. Berger's provocation worked only too well: the enormous court case that followed felt to many like the counterculture itself was on trial.

Though Farquharson's time at BIT had come to a premature end, he remained on good terms with Nicholas Albery. BIT now had its own newsletter: *Bitman*, 'the degenerate offspring of BIT'. Albery duly asked Farquharson to contribute to the new publication's very first issue. A detailed article soon followed, inevitably delivered to *Bitman*'s volunteer editors from the other end of a telephone. Farquharson's subject was hype, a commodity which was in no short supply.

The relentless and brutal treatment of *OZ* garnered huge sympathy from free speech activists and concerned public figures. The obscenity trial had been catnip for traditional newspapers whose journalists delighted in exposing the underground press as corrupt at best, fraudulent at worst. At the same time, the commercial realities of running a print outfit were hard to avoid, however outspoken the politics contained within. *OZ*, *International Times*, and most other major underground papers tended to survive not as a result of selling papers but rather from regular injections of cash from celebrity benefactors, occasional drug deals, and the reliable placement of advertisements from commercial record labels. In turn these companies relied on young, well-connected staffers—known colloquially as 'company freaks'—who would turn executives on to exciting bands who were potentially worth signing.

The notion of there being an underground independent of the mainstream seemed a thing of the past, if ever it had truly existed. Countercultural fame was now a mainstream event. An anthropology student, Carlos Castañeda, had recently rocketed to stardom with a series of books purporting to share the wisdom of a shaman named Don Juan. Rock'n'rollers broke bread with gurus and analysed cloud formations. Trends were hard to untangle and longevity was hard to predict. Suddenly any passing busker was a superstar just waiting to be discovered. Moondog, 'the Viking of Sixth Avenue', was hailed as a compositional genius of the first order. Others, like Hollywood's Larry 'Wild Man' Fischer, promoted by Frank Zappa, were held up more for mockery than praise.

In the midst of this attention came a rush of guides to hip culture, some of which were hipper than others. The most infamous of these was Jenny Fabian and Johnny Byrne's *Groupie*, a lightly fictionalised account of a sexually voracious teenage girl's experiences in Swinging London. *Groupie* was a curiosity, at once a remarkable on-the-ground account of an important scene and a lurid dramatisation of sex, drugs, and rock'n'roll. Farquharson didn't feature directly, though the Tribe of the Sacred Mushroom did, at least under a pseudonym: 'a community of bearded freaks' known as 'the Oaxaquahatl Peyote People' whose poor Trip Machine gets smashed up during a police raid.

As the author of a recent countercultural memoir himself, Farquharson decided to contribute to *Bitman* a review of three other recent books that claimed alternative living as their own: anti-university founder Joe Berke's *Counter Culture*, *Play Power* by *OZ* editor Richard Neville, and American academic Theodore Roszak's *Making of a Counter Culture*.

Robin Farquharson

April has been the month of the head book boom. As well as the above-mentioned we must welcome the Paladin paperbacks of Jeff Nuttall's *Bomb Culture* and Timothy Leary's *The Politics of Ecstasy*.

First point: Joe Berke's book is a beautiful thing and the only one of the three to have incorporated visual techniques in the design of the book. If it had only had colour, it would have been a mind-blower indeed. £4/10/- is just sick and especially since it's printed on bog-paper. However Joe tells me that he has worked a deal whereby it will be out in paperback form in six months or so at 13/- or less and that's cool. Club together communally and buy it then, it's crucial.

Play Power has no illustrations except Martin Sharp on the dustcover and some Gameheadopoly sketches supplied in a pocket at the back. This is a beautiful book but unlike Joe's it is addressed to the straights and not to us. It will entertain you much more than inform you. But if you have a papa or a mama who won't know where you're at and who wants to know where you're at, this is the book to recommend.

Both Joe and Richard reprint most of that standard Zenden work, *Project London Free*. Regrettably, both delete any of the most interesting and valuable sections, especially those relating to telephones and automatic ticket machines. I am sorry that

> such revolutionaries or their publishers should be so chicken. Maybe they heard the rumour that someone was fined £25 for passing a copy of the original first edition.
>
> The Roszak book is called 'quite sympathetic' by the *Guardian*. Only a straight could think that. Theodore Roszak is an academic who knows a lot about the underground and doesn't like it. His book is worth having from the library if you are exceptionally interested in the U.S. scene and if you can stomach his dense lecture-room style. Though he has read *IT* religiously, he doesn't say anything of much note about the English scene. Not a book to worry about much.
>
> I haven't read them yet, but I understand that the American editions of *Woodstock Nation* by Abbie Hoffman and *Do It!* by J. Rubin are available at Compendium Bookshop, 240 Camden High Street. This might be a place to go if you want more of the real Lebanese.

Having been through the Anthony Blond production mill, Farquharson had an eye for freak scene cash-ins and an easy and thorough grasp of the rip-offs and sell-outs then occurring. He evidently had a level of knowledge about the international countercultural scene and a personal familiarity with many of its major players. When the baffled *Sunday Times* prepared a report on the unexpected popularity of Rupert Bear in hip scenes, they turned to 'Dr Robin Farquharson, one of its gurus' for an explanation. 'A cartoon like Peanuts shows society as it is, riddled and racked with guilt,' Farquharson answered. 'In contrast Rupert is about a dreamworld in which everyone is innocent. Rupert's world is the Underground goal.'

Though Farquharson's *Bitman* review and his appearance as the *Sunday Times*' expert-in-residence were clearly intended to frame him as a wise old head of alternative London, the truth was altogether sadder. May that year saw the suicide of his friend Nicholas Lafitte, the poet who had once opened the doors of bohemia to him. That summer Farquharson was himself confined to

Horton, sliding deeper into the slipstream of the underground just as other acquaintances cooked up their grandest schemes to date.

Mick Farren and his friends had just staged the one-off Phun City, an infamously debauched free festival held in a field in Sussex. The live sounds came via the MC5, the Pretty Things, and a host of other prominent acts, each of whom agreed to perform for free—each, that is, except for the hard rock band Free, who demanded a fee and were promptly shown the door. Balancing out Phun City's spirit of charity and cooperation was the presence of the Hells Angels, brought in to provide security for the weekend. William Burroughs, Alex Trocchi, and J. G. Ballard knocked about and took in the full spectrum of a decidedly weird scene. Acid and speed flowed. Questions were formulated but few were answered.

Farren was far from the only well-connected figure who realised that music festivals could be a source of great power. The summer of 1970 saw the third incarnation of the Isle of Wight festival, the sheer scale of which promised to top all the preceding years. Fiery Creations, the Foulk brothers' promotions company, had put nearly £500,000 into that year's event, a serious but worthwhile investment if the projected profits proved to be accurate. The scene was set for an enormous spectacle featuring Jimi Hendrix, the Who, and nearly every other major rock and psychedelic act going (including the appropriately remunerated Free).

With expectations suitably raised, a huge percentage of the alternative crowd decided to make their way to the Isle of Wight, journalist-participants included.

Mick Farren

We could plainly see that Fiery Creations were protecting their box-office with every security device short of a minefield, and appeared to be deploying the ambience of the East German frontier. Double walls of scaffolding and corrugated iron, with what looked uncomfortably like a freeform zone between them, were patrolled by security men in shabby, badge less, ill-fitting coppers' uniforms, accompanied by equally ill-trained and tense-looking Alsatian dogs.

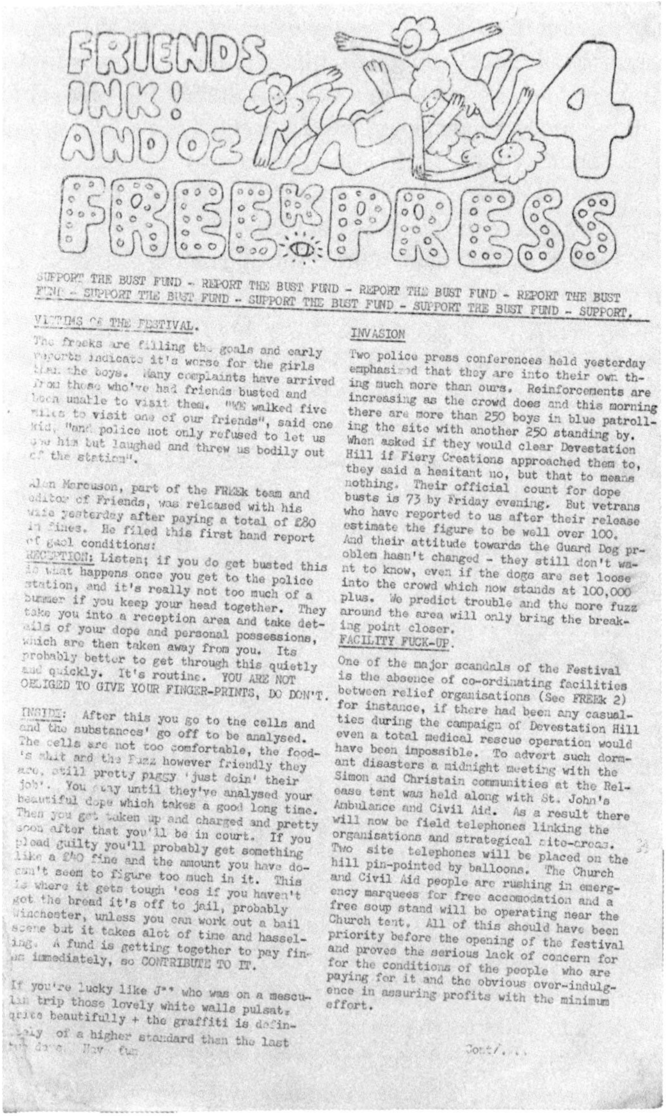

SUPPORT THE BUST FUND - REPORT THE BUST FUND - REPORT THE BUST FUND - REPORT THE BUST FUND - SUPPORT THE BUST FUND - SUPPORT THE BUST FUND - SUPPORT THE BUST FUND - SUPPORT.

VICTIMS OF THE FESTIVAL.

The freeks are filling the goals and early reports indicate it's worse for the girls than the boys. Many complaints have arrived from those who've had friends busted and been unable to visit them. "WE walked five miles to visit one of our friends", said one kid, "and police not only refused to let us give him but laughed and threw us bodily out of the station".

Alan Marcuson, part of the FREEk team and editor of Friends, was released with his wife yesterday after paying a total of £80 in fines. He filed this first hand report of gaol conditions:

RECEPTION: Listen; if you do get busted this is what happens once you get to the police station, and it's really not too much of a bummer if you keep your head together. They take you into a reception area and take details of your dope and personal possessions, which are then taken away from you. Its probably better to get through this quietly and quickly. It's routine. YOU ARE NOT OBLIGED TO GIVE YOUR FINGER-PRINTS, DO DON'T.

INSIDE: After this you go to the cells and and the substances' go off to be analysed. The cells are not too comfortable, the food's shit and the Fuzz however friendly they are, still pretty piggy 'just doin' their job'. You stay until they've analysed your beautiful dope which takes a good long time. Then you get taken up and charged and pretty soon after that you'll be in court. If you plead guilty you'll probably get something like a £40 fine and the amount you have doesn't seem to figure too much in it. This is where it gets tough 'cos if you haven't got the bread it's off to jail, probably Winchester, unless you can work out a bail scene but it takes alot of time and hasseling. A fund is getting together to pay fines immediately, so CONTRIBUTE TO IT.

If you're lucky like J** who was on a mesculin trip those lovely white walls pulsate quite beautifully + the graffiti is definitely of a higher standard than the last [illegible]. Hav fun

INVASION

Two police press conferences held yesterday emphasised that they are into their own thing much more than ours. Reinforcements are increasing as the crowd does and this morning there are more than 250 boys in blue patrolling the site with another 250 standing by. When asked if they would clear Devestation Hill if Fiery Creations approached them to, they said a hesitant no, but that to means nothing. Their official count for dope busts is 73 by Friday evening. But vetrans who have reported to us after their release estimate the figure to be well over 100. And their attitude towards the Guard Dog problem hasn't changed - they still don't want to know, even if the dogs are set loose into the crowd which now stands at 100,000 plus. We predict trouble and the more fuzz around the area will only bring the breaking point closer.

FACILITY FUCK-UP.

One of the major scandals of the Festival is the absence of co-ordinating facilities between relief organisations (See FREEk 2) for instance, if there had been any casualties during the campaign of Devestation Hill even a total medical rescue operation would have been impossible. To advert such dormant disasters a midnight meeting with the Simon and Christain communities at the Release tent was held along with St. John's Ambulance and Civil Aid. As a result there will now be field telephones linking the organisations and strategical site-areas. Two site telephones will be placed on the hill pin-pointed by balloons. The Church and Civil Aid people are rushing in emergency marquees for free accomodation and a free soup stand will be operating near the Church tent. All of this should have been priority before the opening of the festival and proves the serious lack of concern for for the conditions of the people who are paying for it and the obvious over-indulgence in assuring profits with the minimum effort.

Cont/...

New issues of Freek Press *quickly circulated information around the festival site*

Like most of his peers, Farquharson made his way to the festival site, which was being held at a farm by a chalky hillside on the western side of the Isle. Alongside him were 600,000 other attendees, many of whom arrived ill-prepared and lacking tickets. Farren's White Panthers had not-so-quietly spread the word about a large and rather intriguing nearby hill. Known either as 'Devastation Hill' or 'Desolation Row', the hill overlooked the festival site and provided an excellent and free view of the stage. Most of these ticketless attendees made their way to the hillside and did what they could to set up shop.

Matthew Hilton
I spent the summer of 1970 as a newsreel maker at Butlin's Holiday Camp, Minehead. I skipped off to the Isle of Wight, and of course immediately when my back was turned, a stills photographer took my job. But I went with my girlfriend to the Isle of Wight and we constructed a plastic tent. We got there in the middle of the night, King Crimson was playing, and we put the tent up, and of course, I had forgot to put in any respiration holes, so we were basically sleeping in a plastic bag.

London's alternative papers had also gathered their things and descended on the Isle of Wight to take in the music, witness history, and report on it from portable printing presses. Alongside representatives from *OZ* and *Friends*, Farren helped to churn out a special news sheet during the festival called *Freek Press*. From the relative safety of an accredited press tent these broadsides attacked festival conditions in near real-time and shared gossip from across the campsite.

Farren seemed to come and go, helping to write what he later claimed were deliberately pompous articles for *Freek Press* and then darting off to play with his new band in an unlicensed inflatable tent. The festival's organisers were naturally keen to downplay his importance.

> **Ray Foulk**
> While Farren and his associates caused us, the organisers, considerable difficulty, their impact on the experience of the hundreds of thousands attending was negligible. Rather than the event being violent, riotous and worse, the festival was a wonderful peaceful occasion and their resultant impact has been woefully exaggerated.

Not everyone shared the Foulks' view. Despite the star-studded line-up and breathless publicity, neither the organisers nor the local community were well-equipped to deal with what was about to follow. The amplifiers couldn't keep up with the crowds and the winds, and that was only when the speaker system worked at all. When it didn't, the PA system produced eerie effects, like when Jimi Hendrix's amps picked up radio transmissions between security staff and ended up broadcasting them across the entire Isle.

In his account of the festival, penned for publication in the next issue of *International Times*, Farren pointed to the hypocrisy of 'a society where a man can be paid £500 a minute for playing a guitar, yet protests that people need to be fed are shouted down.' Farren was alluding to the festival's numerous and widely discussed stage infractions. Some of these had been tolerated: early on a crowd member was voluntarily handed the mic, using his platform to describe the festival as a 'psychedelic concentration camp'. Later a man known as Yogi Joe stormed the stage in the middle of Joni Mitchell's performance, hoping to speak about the condition of the ticketless festival goers camped on the hillside. Once the man had been carted away, an evidently shocked Mitchell responded by chastising the crowd for behaving like 'tourists' and then proceeded to play one of the greatest sets of her career.

All the while the controversial ring of galvanised iron fences was being attacked from inside and outside the festival grounds. At various stages, White Panthers helped to rip sections of the fencing

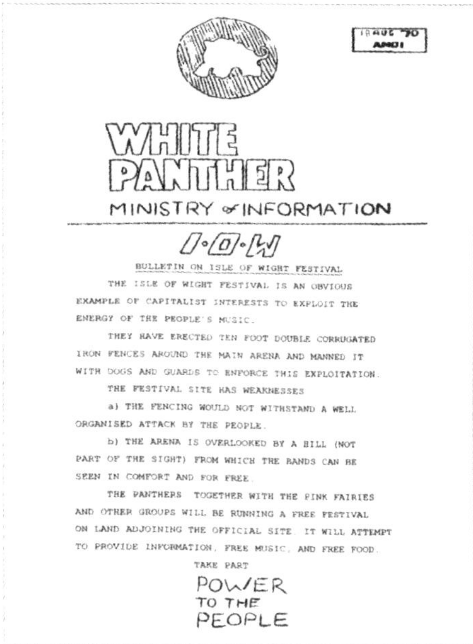

WHITE PANTHER
MINISTRY of INFORMATION

I·O·W

BULLETIN ON ISLE OF WIGHT FESTIVAL

THE ISLE OF WIGHT FESTIVAL IS AN OBVIOUS EXAMPLE OF CAPITALIST INTERESTS TO EXPLOIT THE ENERGY OF THE PEOPLE'S MUSIC.

THEY HAVE ERECTED TEN FOOT DOUBLE CORRUGATED IRON FENCES AROUND THE MAIN ARENA AND MANNED IT WITH DOGS AND GUARDS TO ENFORCE THIS EXPLOITATION.

THE FESTIVAL SITE HAS WEAKNESSES

a) THE FENCING WOULD NOT WITHSTAND A WELL ORGANISED ATTACK BY THE PEOPLE.

b) THE ARENA IS OVERLOOKED BY A HILL (NOT PART OF THE SIGHT) FROM WHICH THE BANDS CAN BE SEEN IN COMFORT AND FOR FREE.

THE PANTHERS TOGETHER WITH THE PINK FAIRIES AND OTHER GROUPS WILL BE RUNNING A FREE FESTIVAL ON LAND ADJOINING THE OFFICIAL SITE. IT WILL ATTEMPT TO PROVIDE INFORMATION, FREE MUSIC, AND FREE FOOD.

TAKE PART

POWER TO THE PEOPLE

Mick Farren and the White Panthers did their best to disrupt the Isle of Wight festival

down alongside knife-wielding French anarchists and Hells Angels. Ray Foulk tried to keep things ticking over, shovelling bundles of loose cash in the direction of nervous performers. May '68 leader Daniel Cohn-Bendit skulked around and LSD gadfly Michael Hollingshead plotted further mischief with Farren. Then, as the fences went flying, Farquharson turned up in a state of some distress at the offices of the local council.

Freshwater Parish Council administrator, internal memo

1. Gentleman, in state of apparent agitation, black eye, bruised swollen knuckles, knocked on door.
2. He said, "I'm Doctor Robin Farquharson. May I use your phone to contact my family. I'll reverse the charges."

3. Permission was granted, as I supposed, erroneously, that there had been an accident.
4. He phoned a Fleet Street number which proved to be the *Sun*.
5. He asked them to give a message to "his mate", 'Deyv Shaap'. He repeated the message in rhyme, "in code," he said. The *Sun* would not accept it without investigation, so he rang off.
6. He then rang another number and revealed that he was a White Panther and that the Panthers and Hells Angels had pulled down the fence etc. The last lines of the coded message were, "See you in Wight, Saturday night, mission accomplished."
7. When challenged about the cost of the calls he offered to write on a piece of paper that he owed us five shillings, or he would give us a ballpoint pen. He departed, leaving an empty boot box, and declaring "Peace and love."
8. I phoned the police, but nothing transpired.

Rupert Murdoch had recently bought the *Sun*, leading some witnesses to believe that 'Deyv Shaap' must have been Farquharson's pseudonym for the Australian mogul. Equally mysterious was how Farquharson had obtained his injuries. According to an account in *Friends*, Farquharson had claimed to be the White Panther's 'minister of propaganda'. He was then 'chased by dogs on Thursday night and taken away by police when he assaulted a guard. He was back at the festival on Monday morning, clean shaven and giving away free food.'

Another witness held that Farquharson was on his way to distribute *Freek Press* when 'he himself freaked out and scared bystanders. He was quickly ejected from the site and just as quickly returned on the hood of a taxi shouting, "Right on, right on." He was beaten and taken to St John's [ambulance] by security men. He was removed in a Land Rover as no one got an ambulance. Many of the St John's team have not dealt with drug cases before.'

A subsequent broadside indicated that Farquharson had in fact been engaged in challenging three Hells Angels to a fist fight before fleeing the scene of the crime. 'The Angels responded with remarkable composure,' the anonymous observer noted. 'At this stage, no one knows Robin's whereabouts.'

PART III
RUINED BY THE WRECKING GANGS, 1970-1973

VEATHER :
Rain later.
ighting-up time :
.5 p.m.
Details—Back Page.

Evening Standard

45,472 London: Monday September 7 1970 7R 6d.

CLOS PRIC

SKYJACKER LEILA: DO WE LET HER GO?

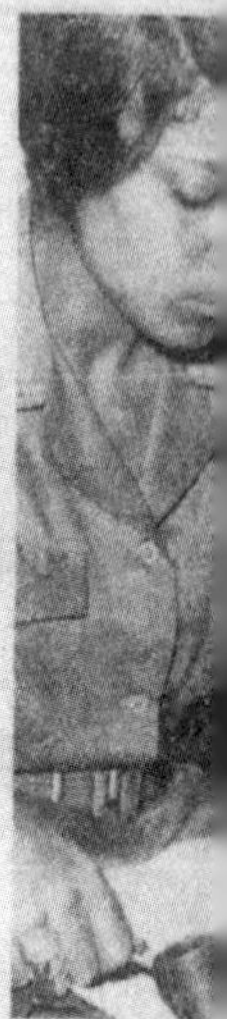

LEILA KHALED, Heathrow yesterd New York bound E landed following attempt in which shot dead. The Po for the Liberation gave Britain 72 release h

Standard Reporter

RGENT talks ere called in hitehall today to ecide what should done with hijack irl Leila Khaled.

The 24-year-old Pales- ian has been moved ider heavy guard to Eal- police headquarters fter yesterday's abortive d to hijack an Israeli rliner.

Arab guerrillas today manded the release of the enade-carrying brunette, hose companion was killed fore the jet made an ergency landing at athrow.

Responsible

The Popular Front for the eration of Palestine warned British Government that it uld be held responsible for harm to Miss Khaled.

This touched off fears that tish airliners could face a ack threat if Britain did not the young guerrilla—who hijacked a TWA jet to mascus in August last year.

s Cabinet Ministers and itehall officials tackled the mma all day. **SWITZER-ND** caved in to the rrilla's demands.

The Swiss decided to release ee imprisoned Arab com- ndos as part of an exchange l for 300 passengers and of Swissair and TWA iners hijacked to Jordan erday.

volved in today's London s were Mr. Reginald Maud- Home Secretary, Mr. hael Noble, President of the rd of Trade responsible for l aviation, and the Foreign ce.

Surrender

enior Whitehall officials who e in the talks met later this rnoon to complete their rt and were later reporting ct to Mr. Heath.

The Swiss Government's sur- der to the guerrilla demand increases the dilemma in ning Street. If the threat to safety of the remaining host- is to be taken seriously, e may be pressure from r Governments whose citi- are involved, for the British ernment to release Miss led.

Strong pressure

COVERED with a raincoat, Leila Khaled, 24, seized at Heathrow after yesterday's hijack of an El Al Boeing, is led from West Drayton police station today.

the heat of a hijack attempt, might do them more harm than good in world public opinion in which there still exists some sympathy for their aims.

Miss Khaled is also in the centre of a tug-of-war between Britain and Israel who wants

jacking began is not yet clearly established and neither is Bri- tain's jurisdiction over the event.

The Israeli Government has not formally asked for the extradition of Miss Khaled. It is understood that the Israeli

Hostages in 'We'll blow you up' peril

Standard Foreign News Desk

ARAB GUERRILLAS today warned that the two hijacked airliners held in Jordan will be blown up if Britain does not release within 72 hours the girl commando seized at Heathrow yesterday after an unsuccessful attempt to hijack a third airliner, an Israeli Boeing 707.

There were conflicting reports about the fate of the 300 passengers involved.

'Women, children free'

In Amman the Popular Front for the Liberation of Palestine announced that women and children passen- gers on the two airliners—a Swissair DC-8 and a Trans- World Airlines Boeing 707—would be released later today.

A Front spokesman said that all Israeli, American, British and West German male passengers would be held until a four-point ulti- matum had been met.

In another development, the Front in Beirut said the commandos proposed to hold American passengers in exchange for Sirhan Sirhan, the Jordanian-born convicted assassin of Senator Robert Kennedy serving a life sent- ence in the U.S.

Earlier a Front spokesman said the hijacked airliners would be blown up with the passengers on board and that boxes of ex- plosives had been put inside the aircraft.

But a report received in Beirut by TWA said the passengers had been taken to Amman and were believed to be resting in a hotel.

The Front warned the British Government that it would be held responsible for any harm to the girl held at Heathrow, Leila Khaled—a warning that sparked off fears that British airliners could face a hijack threat.

Guerrill destroy Jumbo

NEWS ON CA PAGE THE

If a gun is held a a pilot's

BACK PA

Amman by guerr

BACK PA

TV and radio - Royal Trainer, p Crossword, strips

Entertainment

CHAPTER 16
LEILA THE HIJACKER

The three brothers behind the Isle of Wight festival lost £50,000 and never staged an event again. The promoters' loss was the underground's gain. The Isle of Wight proved a formative moment for the British alternative scene of the 1970s, providing its founding legend and predicting its ultimate fault lines. Some derided the festival as the clearest example yet of filthy lucre taking over the alternative society. Others hailed the fall of the fences as the first public iteration of people power. It was the cathartic end of the sixties, the troubling start to the seventies, and maybe even the arrival of revolutionary violence on the all-too-tepid shores of Britain.

What became known as Third Worldism offered a thread between what was occurring in parts of North and Central Africa, Vietnam, Korea, China, and, many hoped, in the United States and United Kingdom. Already widely influential, the Black Panther Party aimed to cement these connections. In the summer of 1969, the Panthers' minister of information Eldridge Cleaver fled the US via Cuba. Cleaver settled in Algiers, where the Panthers were granted an embassy of their own by the newly-independent Algerian government. The Black Panthers' embassy hosted radicals and runaways, including, for a time, the White Panthers' Pun Plamondon, who was now on the FBI's ten most wanted list.

Though a real alliance between European radicals and post-colonial revolutionaries seemed some way off, violent revolt was spreading throughout the West. The Situationist Mustapha Khayati left Paris and involved himself in the activities of the Popular Front for the Liberation of Palestine. In the USA, the Weather Underground emerged from the embers of the USA's largest student activist group and transformed into a radical bombing cell, hoping to precipitate societal collapse from within the belly of the imperial beast. In Germany, the Red Army Faction—better known as the Baader-Meinhof Group—began a similar campaign.

The 1970 Isle of Wight festival seemed to demonstrate how British radicals could form part of these revolutionary struggles. In the weeks immediately after the festival, Londoners were afforded an even closer look at what radical violence might entail. A Situationist-inspired group in Britain calling themselves the Angry Brigade began a bombing campaign, targeting banks, embassies, and Conservative politicians and emphasising their connection to armed struggles the world over. Michael X would meanwhile return to his native Trinidad, where he hoped to entice Alex Trocchi with the idea of bringing sigma to life. Third Worldism was becoming the radical scene's organisational logic, even if there were wild divergences of analysis and approach.

London-based underground newspapers began to see themselves as part of a global resistance network. International revolutionaries were linked in editorials, think pieces, collages, and advertisements, whether they wanted to be or not. Then, at the start of September, the British press reported with a mixture of fear and excitement how members of the Popular Front for the Liberation of Palestine had begun to hijack a series of aeroplanes. The first two groups of hijackers successfully redirected planes from Frankfurt and Zürich to land in Jordan, hoping to force the release of Palestinian prisoners in the process. Another group of four would-be hijackers were split up by passport control in Amsterdam. Two of them managed to board another plane, successfully hijack it, and land in Cairo.

The other two hijackers succeeded in boarding the original flight. They proceeded to attempt to hijack the plane as intended, but it went wrong. One of the hijackers was shot in mid-air, and instead of following instructions to proceed to the Middle East, the pilot landed the plane at Heathrow Airport. The surviving hijacker, Leila Khaled, was duly arrested by British authorities and carted off to Ealing Prison.

Khaled had already been involved in a hijacking in 1969, redirecting a Tel Aviv-bound airliner to Damascus. After making her way to Lebanon, the photojournalist Eddie Adams captured an extraordinary photo of Khaled which cemented her international fame. In Adams' portrait, the Palestinian revolutionary was clad in army fatigues and clutching at an AK-47. With high cheekbones and a *keffiyeh* swept across her glossy black hair, Khaled seemed to embody an idealised vision of Palestinian independence. As if to emphasise the union of femininity and revolutionary commitment, the third finger of Khaled's right hand sported a homemade ring constructed out of a used bullet and the pin of a hand grenade.

Adams' portrait turned Khaled into the closest thing to a revolutionary pin-up since Che Guevara. But between the first and second hijackings Khaled had undergone extensive plastic surgery, hoping to shed her earlier image and go under the radar. In turn, white Western radicals found themselves torn between sympathy, skepticism, and intense feelings of association with Khaled. The hijacker appeared to pair revolutionary praxis with unabashed femininity in provocative, compelling ways. Quite how her actions could meaningfully inform Western revolutionary activity was far from clear.

The Weather Underground embodied this conflicted stance most of all. The group viewed sexual experimentation as just as important a part of the revolution as overthrowing capitalism. The Weather Underground's female members were highly outspoken and mediatised. But robbing banks and running up debts could only carry their campaign so far, and so the group were occasionally forced into putting their increasing criminal expertise up for tender. In 1970 a crime syndicate formed with the purpose of cornering the market for high-grade LSD paid the Weather Underground $25,000 to break Timothy Leary out of prison. Leary was smuggled out of the US and deposited in Algeria under the care of Panther leader Eldridge Cleaver.

Underground papers around the world tracked Leary's every movement as best they could, feeding on rumours, deliberate misdirection, and occasional communiqués. Suddenly the hitherto relatively tranquil Leary issued a statement, possibly crafted by his liberators, which endorsed the Weather Underground's strategy of violent upheaval. Republished in *International Times*, Leary's message ended with a call intended to ring out around the world: 'Right on Leila Khaled!'

By now a further hijacking had taken place in the hope of pressuring the British authorities to free Khaled. Newspapers across London showed two policemen manhandling Khaled, an overcoat thrown over her head to keep her face from the press. The hijacker was transported to Ealing Police Station while Britain decided what to do with her. Reports circulated that the authorities had tried to placate Khaled with a selection of glossy women's magazines for reading material, an offer she rejected. It was at this stage that Farquharson decided to intervene.

According to his friend Peter Johnston, Farquharson tried to deliver Khaled a meal of brown rice and a handful of alternative newspapers. Another account stated that he tried to bring oranges, apricots, and porridge with fried apples.

Whatever the contents of the meal, the authorities weren't interested in granting Farquharson an audience. Phase one of the plan to free Khaled in mind if not body had been frustrated. Speaking to the Associated Press after being turned away—and giving his age as 29, rather than 39—Farquharson explained that "we all think what Leila did was very heroic. She took her life into her hands for the sake of the cause." Not content with one thwarted publicity stunt, Farquharson moved on to phase two: agitprop. He decided that what Khaled needed was an attention-grabbing campaign of the sort his Situationist associates were always managing to put together.

It was an unexpected move from a man whose recent mathematical treatise had two days earlier been favourably reviewed in the *Times Literary Supplement*. But Farquharson knew that there was no such thing as a finishing school for revolutionaries. Che had been a medic before the revolution called. Ho Chi Minh had once been a lowly kitchen porter. If Timothy Leary could move from professor to acid evangelist to PLO supporter, then so could Robin Farquharson.

Farquharson had recently moved into a building on Newport Street, a small backstreet just off Lambeth Walk which ran parallel to the railway arches of Waterloo Station. From these inauspicious headquarters, he decided to gather alternative London's finest and stage a pop culture intervention. Farquharson had spent fifteen years trying to make it as an academic, three years toiling as a data consultant, and two miserable years attempting to become a professional writer. Now he moved through the trajectory of burned out rock star at double quick speed.

There would be sound and light and chaos and joy. Press attention and political reverberations would recall the way British rock'n'rollers struck fear into the hearts of the South African authorities, only now it would be magnified beyond anything Tommy Steele ever did, anything Mick Farren ever did—anything anyone ever did, because pulling the strings above it all would be the singular figure of Dr Robin Farquharson, bona fide mother country madman, possessor of two undergraduate degrees, one masters, one DPhil, and the coveted title of the British underground's leading impresario. But first, he needed help.

Matthew Hilton

After the Isle of Wight, I went back to London and stayed at my mother's house in Woolwich. I went to the Arts Lab and put a notice up on their board which said: 'I have a 16mm camera,

> does anybody want to make a film?' A few days later my mother told me someone had rung for me and gave me a number. It was Robin. He asked me to come over to Lambeth and talk about making a film.

Lambeth's proximity to the Houses of Parliament and the area's relative deprivation had long made it a focus for do-gooders and philanthropists. Back in the 1850s, when the zone around Waterloo Station was widely considered a slum, Henry Beaufoy, the wealthy MP for Hackney, decided that poor children needed access to free education. He selected an unpaved stretch of land called Newport Street for his new institution. Known as the Lambeth Ragged School, Beaufoy's building cut an imposing figure on the edge of an otherwise desolate area.

The Ragged School became redundant as free education became more common in the early years of the twentieth century. In 1903, the site was sold to the local railway and much of the once-grand building was demolished. By the time Farquharson arrived, the Ragged School was falling into disrepair and mainly served as somewhere for the London Fire Brigade to repair their engines. Though Lambeth Walk was immortalised in a popular show tune of the same name, the street's famous market was slowly dying out. Newport Street had meanwhile become more of an alleyway than a street, home to a stretch of one- and two-storey industrial units and garages. One of them was Mara's Scene Painting Shop, a carpentry workshop with the capacity to build a theatrical set in-house. The rest of Newport Street was fairly quiet, boasting enough abandoned buildings for Farquharson to simply walk into one and take occupancy.

In the end, he chose a small building next door to the former Ragged School. 23 Newport Street fit the bill perfectly, 'a tiny little Dickensian place' as Matthew Hilton recalled. Though the ceilings were low and the building was cold, the space gave Farquharson a suitable base for enacting his Situationist-style fantasy-prank. All it took was a shift in mindset for an abandoned building like this to become a global hub of political action.

Farquharson around the time he made his film about Leila Khaled

Matthew Hilton

Robin was in a manic phase and my main impression was the bustle and absurdity of six bright red telephones being installed upstairs and downstairs in this miniature headquarters: his intention was to telephone to world leaders. He was trying, in a sense, to be a supercharged version of who he just kind of missed being.

Robin was a tall stringy fellow with a shock of black hair springing from the back of his jerky swivelling head. He spoke in rapid bursts and there was much grinding of his jaws. Spittle was evident at the edges of his mouth. He was commanding and authoritative, he struck me with his fist when I got a trivial

> mathematics sum wrong. I do not remember that he had a sense of humour.

At one stage Gordon Winter swung by, and, camera in hand, snapped Farquharson in situ. In a way, Winter was the right man to document this new adventure. His candid shot of Farquharson blocking the entrance to the South African police had kickstarted the events that led the academic down the path of political radicalism. Though he still sported a raggedy suit, Farquharson looked otherwise transformed. In his hand he clasped a copy of *Soledad Brother*, a book of prison letters by George Jackson, a recently martyred Black Panther. Farquharson brandished the book like a passport to a new realm.

But this was no time for posturing. Farquharson explained the urgency of his project to Hilton the cameraman and told him that their film was to be called *Leila the Hijacker*. Farquharson also explained that he had no experience making films, let alone commissioning them, so it was left to Hilton to cobble something together. An outline given to the distributors at the London Film-Makers' Co-Operative gave a sense of what the two men cooked up, the numerous typos speaking to the haste with which it was put together.

> **Matthew Hilton**
> everytime you start to make a film as much happens off the cameras as on. action accretes geometrically. you cut the curve somehow so evry film is a formula film. the formula for this one was: leila khaled's skyjack times robin farquahrsons mind plus my camera. commissioned as a promo for a demo this short is a by-product of the high of a manic depressive, the plot is this: an arab girl meets a jewish boy, they are happy for a while but then they quarrel and fight. africa reconciles them with a gift of fruit and they make love.

Though Hilton struggled manfully to put Farquharson's vision into words, his producer—his director?—had in fact made one film before. While in South Africa, Farquharson directed a short film entitled *The Frog Slave*. While the film itself is long since lost, the British Film Institute retains a brief synopsis which describes it as 'an allegory: a magician transforms a frog into a servant; the servant revolts and is transformed back into a frog.' Though it would appear to be some kind of comment on the futility of opposing apartheid, the ambiguity of the allegory makes the film's political implications unclear.

Farquharson's next cinematic effort would be rather more on the nose.

> **Matthew Hilton**
> He turned his attention to the film. He was wearing a mid-thigh length purple tie-dyed dress and would play Leila (aka Palestine). My friend Robert, lent a little hat, was to play Israel, and one of the GPO telephone engineers, a black guy, was to play Africa. We shuffled off down to Lower Marsh and then there was a lot of running about and shouting directed spittily by Robin, with me covering the action as best I could.
>
> There was this kind of knockabout Keystone Cops-type scenario, though nobody wrote anything. Robin just said things like, "Okay, I'm going to chase you down there." The film ends with Israel pinning Palestine to the ground and making thrusting buttocks movements. It was really like Richard Lester meets Jean Genet, without the pace or depth.

The finished film came in at 150 seconds and was probably only ever screened a few times at most. It would appear that the London Film-Makers' Co-Operative never got around to distributing it. This was unsurprising: the true purpose of *Leila the Hijacker*, if not its original purpose, was to function as the music video for a rabble-rousing anthem written specially for the occasion.

CHAPTER 17
HIGH ON DYNAMITE

Farquharson somehow decided that the song's lyrics should be provided by Adam Kisch, one of Matthew Hilton's childhood friends. True to Farquharson's unique organisational abilities, neither of these collaborators was aware of the other's involvement, despite their longterm connection.

> **Adam Kisch**
> I had books of poetry but I had never been a musician, but I thought, "Well, I could do that," so I wrote a bunch of lines. They're a bit wishy-washy because a Marxist-Leninist I'm not. I'm not unequivocally a revolutionary nor am I a pacifist. A revolutionary wouldn't make a statement like that: they'd be absolutely certain of their purpose, as she was and as Robin was.

The backing band were put together by Kisch's friend Nick South, who also took on bass duties. Despite only being in his late teens, South was something of a music industry veteran, particularly when compared with Farquharson and Kisch. The previous year, South played bass for Alexis Korner for the influential bluesman's set at the Rolling Stones' tribute concert to Brian Jones in Hyde Park. Korner's group served as a clearinghouse for young British rockers, amongst them members of the Stones, Led Zeppelin, and Cream; the teenage South was one of his latest discoveries.

For now, South's task was to provide Farquharson with a pair of original compositions, one for each side of a 45-rpm record. South assembled a small group of up-and-coming London musicians for the session: Keith Trowsdale on lead guitar and vocals, Mickey Finn Waller on rhythm guitar, and Roy O'Temro on drums. As the musicians began to come up with a tune, Farquharson and Kisch saw to the logistics.

Adam Kisch
He rents Pye Studios in Marble Arch on a cheque—that was how easy it was in those days—and he demanded a song. So we were on Oxford Street and he was drinking a bottle of milk and he sort of put it to the left of him like there was a shelf there and just let it go. I'm surrounded by stoners and general lunatics, but this guy's out to lunch. It's really obvious.

Farquharson managed to arrange a three-hour session, leaving enough time for only a quick rehearsal before laying down the songs for real. His unlikely group quickly got to work. Kisch's lyrics, delivered by Trowsdale in an affected American accent, gently mocked the premise of a rock'n'roll revolutionary to a melody that could easily have been concocted by Free.

'Leila the Hijacker'
Leila the hijacker, what you done wrong,
To make action be your only goal?
I can dig the skyjacker trip

If you wanna get through, you got to be hip.
Standing on the edge of a stormy sea
Wondering how the future will turn out to be.

Well my brother, she done got it on
You're sweatin' findin' out that it ain't gone wrong.
A woman's still waitin' in a lonesome jail
If she ain't out soon then I guess you've failed.

(Repeat first verse)

You got your rights and I got mine
Who's gonna say where we draw the line?
The whole world watched while you got it on
But you still don't know it ain't gone wrong.

(Repeat first verse)

Well, maybe I'm wrong,
This a story, here in my song,
I'm getting high on dynamite
Well, maybe it's wrong, or maybe it's right.

(Repeat first verse)

Though the musicianship on show was perfectly able, the song clearly hadn't been rehearsed very much and got a little sloppy towards the end of the first and final take. The track would work well for the film Farquharson and Hilton were making but there remained the question of the other side of the record.

If the A-side was a pretty professional rock offering, albeit one with semi-ironic lyrics, the B-side offered the chance to do something decidedly weirder.

Adam Kisch

He's got these three sessions musicians in there who are just playing some kind of riff, like they automatically know how. And Robin steps up to the microphone. I mean it actually sounds very painful, now that I listen to it, but it was inspired at the time.

'Let Us Return (Free Palestine)'

If you had a country and they took it away, what would you say?
Let us return!
If you were in exile and couldn't go home, what'd you do?
Hijack and burn! Let us return!
We come from a country called Palestine, the land and the people are mighty fine.
Let us return!
We was born in the land but we can't go there, human declaration says, "That's not fair!"
Let us return! Free Palestine! Honey and wine! Let us return!

It says in the United Nations Universal Declaration of Human Rights
"Everyone has the right to a nationality. Everyone has the right to leave any country including his own and to return to his country."
We want to return to our country. Let us return!
Spirits of the brave who have died for knowledge, truth, and freedom,
Spirits of plague and pestilence, knowing the bitter price to be free,
Make me strong and brave, make me too the bruised and ripe and ready fruit.
Let us return! Let us return! Let us return! Let us return!

Farquharson's more-English-than-English upper class South African accent made the track sound decidedly rougher than the A-side's pseudo-American thing. The lyrics were earnest, pedantic, and aggressive in equal measure, some of them screeched so forcibly as to be unintelligible.

The track's unique vocalisations and rough-and-ready instrumentation made 'Let Us Return' a real musical one-off. Farquharson managed to both spit out and roll the first letter of 'rights' in 'human rights', sounding like a boarding school Johnny Rotten, albeit seven years ahead of the Sex Pistols' formation. It was also a complete anomaly as far as Farquharson was concerned, the one and only musical effort from a man otherwise dedicated to poetry and literature. More surprisingly for someone who struggled to keep his ideas to himself, the track also represented the only known recording of Farquharson's voice.

As the new group's frontman-manager, Farquharson was keen to find out whether his band of hired hands had stumbled upon a winning formula. He decided that he had the perfect name for his group: the White Panthers. Mick Farren would not be best pleased.

Neither John nor Leni Sinclair had any idea what Farquharson was up to or even who he was, though by this stage there were White Panther factions all over Britain. Precisely how many, and how large they ever were, it was impossible to ascertain. Farren wasn't entirely against this development, regarding the Abbey Wood faction as 'very serious cats.' But Farquharson was a threat, a disruptor of an unwelcome kind. His choice of band name was either a firm nod to Farren's semi-serious revolutionary group or a wholesale appropriation of their brand, one Farren had admittedly borrowed from someone else in the first place.

Where Farren adopted a permanently tongue-in-cheek approach and Sinclair insisted that his Panthers weren't playing around, Farquharson was someone who boasted a secret power: as he wrote in *Drop Out!*, he liked nothing more than to play along for real. What Farren had not accounted for was Farquharson's commitment to a joke. Considering his allies in the African Resistance Movement back home, Farquharson was also a more obvious contender than Farren for leading a guerrilla army of white sympathisers, for better and for worse.

Despite the rather flippant attitude with which Farren had settled on the White Panther moniker, the radical was worried about what having a record like this would do to the credibility of his guerrilla franchise. He may also have taken a dislike to Farquharson due to his association with Sid Rawle, whose London Street Commune had staged a raid on the *International Times* offices and pissed Farren off in the process. Whatever the cause, Farren did everything he could to make it clear that Farquharson's single was very much an unofficial offering, no matter what name it came out under.

> ***International Times***
> Robin Farquharson—Britain's answer to Wild Man Fischer—is currently embracing the White Panther cause; to the merriment & frequent embarrassment of most of the British party. He's just produced a single—'Leila the Hijacker'/'Let Us Return'—by a group predictably called the White Panthers on the Panther label. The single sounds equally good (or bad, depending on your point of view) at either 33 or 45 rpm. Yet another technological breakthrough for the British recording industry!

In early November, Farren took his campaign to even greater heights. Together with Richard Neville, a gaggle of visiting Yippies, and a handful of friends from TVX, Farren disrupted the broadcast of the popular *Frost Programme*. Farren and his group squirted water pistols, smoked joints, and shouted down the evergreen David Frost, the show's bewildered host. Others brandished bells and whistles and handheld cameras and promised to make a broadcast of their own. Frost and his team struggled to regain control, a situation not helped by the first ever live broadcast of a certain four-letter word. Swearing had arrived on British television.

The *Daily Mirror* dubbed Farren's invasion the 'the Frost freakout', repeating the participants' scandalous claim that Frost had secretly encouraged them to disrupt the broadcast. National prude-in-chief Mary Whitehouse bemoaned the fact that 'American revolutionaries have declared that TV is their platform.' Farren and his friends couldn't have put it any better. Given the circumstances, he needn't have worried about Farquharson stealing his thunder.

Robin Elliott

I was very young—about 13 or 14 years old—and was hanging along with Nick. As I recall we went to a kind of office. I think Nick was there to speak to him about the session. There were stacks of printed matter and Farquharson was in charge and feverishly directing people. He was very excited and busy, sweaty and red in the face with this high, excited voice. My overall impression of the man was one of a kind of brilliant, intelligent guy who was on the verge of a mental breakdown. Someone who was pushing a proverbial boulder up a mountain, a guy with a thousand thoughts and things to do and barely managing to keep up.

I remember really liking the track they made, with Nick hammering out a great, strong rhythm section with Roy. I also remember being very much for the release of Leila and pro the Palestinian cause, so maybe that's where my respect for Farquharson came from and maybe why I was so shocked when he hit me. He suddenly turned to me and told me to pass him something which I sort of did, not really understanding what he was on about. Anyway, whatever I did, I got it wrong and he immediately shouted at me and slapped me in the face—a good, hard slap. I remember standing frozen in shock as he continued. I was still living with my mum at the time and she had a relationship with a musician called Davey Graham who was schizophrenic so I immediately recognised the situation Farquharson was in and made sure I didn't react or push him further.

Matthew Hilton

Robin wanted this to be a pop single with all the razzmatazz of a single on *Top of the Pops*, so he ordered me to go out to Dagenham where the record was being pressed to collect the nine hundred and ninety nine copies. He explained that it was necessary to press that many in order to be accepted into the top ten rankings. I remember coming back on the tube with this heavy load, thinking perhaps for the first time, "What have I got myself into?"

In order to marry the record and the film I needed money to complete the editing. I think this was the reason for my visit to Horton. Robin was sitting with two other patients, drugged calm. One of the other patients was non-stop talking. I came away empty handed.

Khaled had by this stage been freed by the British authorities, who were desperate to avoid inflaming an international incident. Press attention promptly switched to Canada, where the Front de libération had bombed and kidnapped their way to making the Quebec independence movement front page news.

Jonathan Bennett

At the height of the Front de libération crisis in Quebec, I was settled in Canada and Robin phoned me from a hospital bed in London. I remember thinking how lovely it was to hear his voice, but it turned out that he was calling to beg me to pass on to prime minister Trudeau his 'analysis' of the crisis. He was enormously upset at having an understanding of the situation but having no way to get it to the relevant authorities, this phone call being his last chance.

The analysis began, "First, they are not after money." This was so trivial that I was sure he was unhinged. The connection became bad, Robin complained about it, and a man's voice from somewhere along the line said, "That's what you get if you try from a hospital bed to reach a phone 6,000 miles away through three exchanges." Robin picked up that he wasn't going to be allowed to continue and said, "Well, I did my best." He was crying.

ANTIUNIVERSITY OF LONDON

CATALOG

October-December 1971

01 LOGIC
02 POETRY
03 COMMUNICATION & ANTI-SOCIALWORK
04 ALTERNATIVE LAW
05 THE I CHING

REGISTRATION MEETING:

2 pm Saturday October 2

43 King Street WC2

(Old Middle Earth)

Outlines of all courses

Will be given

Membership of the Antiuniversit
is free. Apply to the Secretar
Robin Farquharson, 17a Rendle S
W10 5RL,) 01-969 8137.

An optional donation of £1 give
you credit at our bookshop to
that amount.

01 LOGIC (Hugh Dickins)
An introduction to mathematical logic & set theory - paradoxes? non-standard analysis (lateral reasoning?) intuitionism.
Monday evenings? More often?
Who are you?

02 POETRY (Keith Armstrong)
Poetry as his master's voice.
Smile & your world is our universe.
Poetry is mistaught in schools & universities. Poets use & have used all forms of media communication. Poetry is all/all is poetry. The course will use written, lavatory-wall, concrete, kinetic, sound, participation, street, guerilla & found poetry. Everybody's a poet/ nobody's a poet. Students are asked to bring some of their own work with them.

03 COMMUNICATION & ANTI-SOCIALWORK (Jane Gemini) Communication between individals, verbal, non-verbal & psychic. How words can be a handicap to communication: bodily tension, repressions & movements as unconscious communication. Wilhelm Reich character armour. Parapsychology; the effect of LSD & meditation; creative listening. The gamesmanship of a professional social worker. Jung's theory of psychological time eras.

0@ 04 ALTERNATIVE LAW
(Tom Fawthrop)

}

05 THE I CHING
(Robin Farquharson)

}

If you don't see a course
that you like, ask us &
maybe we can lay something
on for you.

We are dolphins;
We swim in the human sea.
We do not breathe its water;
We breathe air.

\- R.F.

Venues & times of all courses
to be arranged.

CHAPTER 18
HEADMASTER ROBIN

Jeremy Thorpe had been an outspoken opponent of apartheid ever since his election in the early 1950s. Though Britain's Liberal Party was larger and older than its South African namesake, they had struggled for leadership for the best part of a century. In 1967, Thorpe became party leader and revitalised the Liberals' electoral fortunes, further amplifying the reach of his anti-apartheid rhetoric. If Thorpe could mastermind the Liberals' return to power—and many thought he could—then it was highly possible that Britain would become more hardline towards South Africa's racist regime.

But Thorpe had a secret. In the early 1960s, he had conducted an affair with a former male model named Norman Scott who now appeared to be blackmailing him. Desperate to go public with the story, in the summer of 1971 Scott arranged to meet with none other than journalist-spy Gordon Winter. Given Winter's ties to the South African security state, he took the opportunity to meet with Thorpe's former lover very seriously. Two investigative journalists who wrote a book on the Thorpe affair believed that Winter went as far as to sleep with Scott himself in the hope of securing his collaboration.

It soon emerged that in addition to his hidden homosexual life, Thorpe had been involved in a complicated and fairly clumsy attempt to have Scott murdered. Though Thorpe was eventually acquitted, the resulting murder trial destroyed his political ambitions. The eventual revelation of Winter's involvement led Thorpe to believe that BOSS was involved in a plot to destroy him.

Despite the legalisation of homosexuality, the shocking revelations of the Thorpe affair revealed the extent to which homophobia still fuelled British society. Whatever progress was made can be attributed at least in part to the steadfast campaigning of the Gay Liberation Front (GLF). Formed in 1969, the GLF saw themselves as part of a lineage of independence movements just as vital as any armed political conflict. The group's name was itself an explicit allusion to the anti-colonial battles fought by the Vietnamese National Liberation Front and the Algerian National Liberation Front. Though initially formed in New York City as a response to the police riot at the Stonewall Inn, the GLF soon had branches all over the UK. The group were well-represented in London, conducting important early meetings at All Saints Hall on Powis Gardens and beginning to stage annual marches in 1970.

Due to the longstanding treatment of homosexuality as a medical disorder the British factions of the GLF were closely linked with anti-psychiatric organising. But the London group was never monolithic and was instead divided into local and ideological groupings. Soon enough there were two rival factions: an older, non-hippie, and perhaps more bourgeois wing and an altogether younger, more psychedelic, and uninhibited wing.

In many ways this split was predictable, though attitudes towards homosexuality in explicitly countercultural scenes remained divided. Quite where those who had historically been deemed 'freaks' fit in with hip society was not always clear. It had, after all, only been a few years since Timothy Leary had insisted that acid could cure users of same-sex desire. At the same time, the pink pound had become

A Very SPECIAL Freak

This is a very special Freak. It is the edited result of a series of taped interviews with a young man who works in a London travel office.

Surprisingly as it may seem, I am not completely opposed to the capers of today's young. I'm 26 years old in December and that means I collect on an insurance policy which my father took out for me when I was five. With the £1,000 I intend making some sort of business investment. Perhaps I'll buy some growth stock or put some money into a small business. You can't do much with a £1,000 as you know, so [illegible]

the principle on which our civilisation is founded.

What would happen to my life if I suddenly decided to stop work. First of all my wife would almost certainly leave me. She wouldn't have any time for a man who wasn't prepared to pull his weight. (And I wouldn't blame her!) Secondly, my family would ostracise me, and I can hardly think of anything more devastating than losing the respect of my close relatives by becoming a sponger. [illegible]

[illegible] try to live in peace particularly with the neighbours. To this end, we try never to mix with them; I always think it's best to keep out the hair of your neighbours otherwise you're just asking for trouble. So we keep our own counsel and don't bother anybody around us. What more can you ask a man to do? I'm loving. I'm giving peace a chance!

A VERY ABBREVIATED DIRECTORY OF INTERNATIONAL FREAKS – not all of them beautiful.

USA: Tuli Kupferberg, Emmett Grogan, Frank Zappa, Abbie Hoffman, Paul Krassner, John Wilcock, Valerie Solanas, Louis Abolafia, The Living Theatre, Little Richard, Ken Kesey, Reverend Jefferson Fuck Poland, Jerry Rubin, Playmate of the Month.

EUROPE: Simon Vinkenoog, Robert Jasper Grootveld, Jean-Jacques Lebel, Danny Cohn-Bendit, Fritz Teufel.

AUSTRALIA: Mad Mel, Bea Miles, Rosaleen Norton, Richard O'Sullivan, Francis James, Barry Humphries, Zara Holt.

UK: Michael Chapman, Jimmy Saville, Arthur Brown, Jack Henry Moore, Robin Farquarson, Mick Lesser, Simon Tugwell, Wendy Sharkey, Spike Milligan, Hoppy & Suzy, Wild Child, Muzz Murray, Edward Heath.

Farquharson included amongst the 'Beautiful Freaks' in OZ

an important part of the underground press economy. *International Times*, for example, was nearly shut down by the Obscene Publications Unit for running gay personals. When the paper set up a bust fund to protect its directors from further raids, donations flowed from across London's closeted and out community. This was a temporary truce, however. The more confrontational wing of the GLF later staged a raid on the paper's offices for publishing what they saw as homophobic material.

Jim Anderson, one of *OZ*'s three founding editors, was one of the few openly gay members of what might be deemed the countercultural mainstream. In August 1969 Anderson's magazine produced a high-profile issue dedicated to the subject of homosexuality. The following issue focused on 'Beautiful Freaks', defined by the editorial as 'anti-hypocrites' who 'restore the Individual' and 'abolish the barriers between theory and action'. Amidst profiles of freaks famous and obscure, the issue included a semi-serious 'very abbreviated directory of international freaks'. Farquharson was featured alongside Abbie Hoffman, Ken Kesey, and Jimmy Savile, showing just how broad freakdom could be.

As for why Farquharson was chosen, art director David Wills remembered simply that the author of *Drop Out!* was seen as 'a professional oddball.'

OZ also put together a special issue dedicated to women's liberation (the so-called 'Pussy Power' issue), as did *Frendz* (renamed from *Friends* after the departure of founding editor Alan Marcuson) and even *Bitman*. But such one-off specials were felt by many to be tokenistic at best and objectifying at worst. How the various liberation movements interrelated and how best to depict them remained a problem for the underground press. The *Berkeley Barb*, one of the leading alternative papers in the US, was known for its close coverage of the Bay Area's growing gay militant scene; participants in the Stonewall uprising spoke of taking inspiration from the paper. But the same publication also deemed it acceptable to run a photo of two members of the MC5 having sex with an unknown woman, a feature which nearly saw them shut down by the Vice Squad. The arrival of *Suck*, 'The First European Sex Paper', further muddied the waters between underground culture and titillation, even if the new paper did make space for queer sexual identities.

At the same time, the first stirrings of gay pride showed another side to the moral panic of the Thorpe era. By early 1971, the GLF secured an office in the basement of the famous pacifist bookstore Housmans, opposite the flat of Farquharson's friend Anthony Howell. Farquharson was known to show up at the GLF tiny workspace and make long-distance calls to South Africa. Money was the last thing on anyone's mind and he was seldom stopped.

Farquharson was never going to be a straightforward supporter of the GLF's cause but he did find other ways of getting involved. The coming months saw the Rupert cartoon dominate the infamous *OZ* obscenity trial, propelling discussions over the relative merits of schooling to the front pages. Speaking to a documentary crew, the schoolboy cartoonist Vivian Berger explained that 'the whole point of the magazine was that we were really fed up with the school system today—we tried telling people this through other media, and it just doesn't work.'

Moving between Horton Hospital and his new home on Newport Street in Lambeth, Farquharson completely lost interest in the White Panthers' recording career. Copies of the single they had cut were left unstickered and unsleeved and were never properly distributed. Instead, alternative education became Farquharson's going concern. Depriving himself the chance of launching the British MC5, Farquharson returned to the idea of the anti-university with aplomb.

> ***International Times*, classified advert**
> ANTIUNIVERSITY OF LONDON, 23 Newport St., Lambeth Walk, SE11 (nearest tube, Westminster). Open since Oct 3 at new premises. Open to all. No fees. No fixed programme at present, but we do offer informal seminars most evenings. Call first & check. 24-hour telephone service REL 2662/3. possible small student loans. Gay counselling. Information & advice.

The anti-university scheme offered an appealing chance to put a number of varied, overlapping fights into active dialogue. With a secure institutional base, Farquharson's anti-racist organising could fuse with his interest in housing and the battle for gay rights. He could help to educate the masses and provide a platform for future struggles. These were the grand ambitions that underpinned the revival of Newport Street's long history of independent education. Within a few months a more formal programme for Farquharson's anti-university was devised, or at least announced.

> ***International Time*s, classified advert**
> Anti University of London programme for January-March 1971
> Saturdays: 12 noon—Lunch
> 3pm—Philosophy
> 5pm—Tea
> 7pm—Supper
> 8pm—Entertainment
> Sundays: 12 noon—Brunch
> 3pm—American Literature

5pm—Tea
7pm—Poetry

The Abbey Wood branch of the British White Panther Party reproduced this rather sketchy itinerary on the back page of the first issue of their new magazine. There were evidently no hard feelings about the Isle of Wight debacle. Alongside the programme was an ad for People, Not Psychiatry. The Panthers had lifted both ads from an issue of *International Times*. Alongside them was an ad explaining that 'Fleet Street producers require young good looking girls with very good figure', promising that all work would be 'according to existing British laws'. The underground press clearly remained somewhat conflicted on the subject of women's liberation.

Though his stance on gay rights was pretty clear, Farquharson's view of second-wave feminism was not. 'Homosexuality is nature's birth control' was as close to a public comment as he made on the matter. Gordon Winter claimed that his friend 'never liked women', quoting Farquharson as saying that they were 'plastic beings conned into titty Hollywood images by a sick capitalist society.' If accurate—there is obvious reason to doubt Winter's accuracy and motives—then this quote may have come as much from a dislike of women as it did from an intertwining distaste for traditional gender roles. A degree of flippant misogyny would not have been entirely uncommon in some of the militant gay circles in which Farquharson now moved. Historically marginalised groups were testing out and fine-tuning alliances and rivalries. The jury was out on who was on which side and why.

Fleet Street proper was starting to take an interest in Farquharson again. As things got 'anti-er and anti-er', in the words of the *Sunday Telegraph*, a reporter was sent to observe the activity surrounding the 'wandering scholar extraordinary' and his new university. 'Dr. Farquharson,' the reporter explained, 'has two PhDs and has been chucked out of most places you can think of.' In fact, Farquharson only had one doctoral qualification, and it was a DPhil, not a PhD. Whether this was a case of journalistic laziness or Farquharson muddying the waters is unknown. Coverage was nevertheless sympathetic, with the *Telegraph*'s reporter describing the anti-university's chief as 'witty, self-deprecating and dedicated' to his cause.

Gordon Winter

Robin popped into my office again. This time he invited me to attend his anti-university in Lambeth. It was, he said, a place of alternative learning. Having something of a short back and sides wartime formative years brainwashing attitude to learning, I must confess it seemed a shambles to me. But the thirty odd students, paying one quid a year, seemed to enjoy being educated by headmaster Robin, squatting barefoot, and reading them 'guerrilla poetry' with the fervour of Che.

Frater Choronzon

Among the assembled anarchist philosophers, Situationists, astrologers and crack-pots there was this eminently respectable gentleman, neatly turned out in a business suit. He presented a complete contrast to the tie-dyed majority of the delegates, and they were a little suspicious of him; police spy? CIA agent? His contributions were succinct and positive however, and I was struck by his ability to cut through the periphera of an issue and apply his thinking to the critical elements. He was a tall man, maybe 6ft 2ins, fortyish with greying, thinning hair and that wild-eyed look which comes across, for example, in some portraits of Beethoven.

Around this time, Farquharson's anti-university received an unannounced visitor in the form of Dom Sylvester Houédard. Known more commonly as dsh, his lowercase initials, the Dom was a Benedictine monk with an unlikely sideline in concrete poetry, exploring form and function with playful typography and linguistic trickery. He had recently held a retrospective exhibition at the Victoria & Albert Museum and was in demand across galleries, museums, and alternative spaces. Instead of moving into the commercial art world, dsh gradually retreated back towards theological study. For the time being, though, he found himself in his signature robes and dark sunglasses visiting the chaotic premises of the Newport Street anti-university.

What the Dom saw impressed him—not so much the freeform style of teaching on show but rather more literally what he saw as he entered number 23: namely the sign on the building's front door, which rendered the word 'anti-university' entirely in dashes, slashes, and brackets. The lettering was, the Dom noted, 'infinitely variable in size & weight', allowing users to reproduce text at whatever scale they wanted without needing to modify the font in any way. The Dom copied the sign down and used it to generate an entire alphabet, which he reproduced repeatedly on his trusty Olivetti Lettera 22 typewriter. Dropping the brackets, he referred to it as the 'farquharson-houédard slash-&dash alphabet'.

The Dom's monkish habit to one side, he was a visual poet interested in the symbolic weight of letters; here was a chance to collaborate with an eminent psephologist plugged into alternative London. The similarities didn't stop there. Prior to taking his holy vows, the Dom had studied at Oxford, narrowly missing being a contemporary of Farquharson's. He collaborated widely and was close to the poet Bob Cobbing, who worked at Better Books and helped to establish the London Film-Maker's Co-Operative as well as participating in Trocchi's project sigma. The Dom was also an active figure in the nascent gay liberation movement. The Dom and the dropout might have looked like an incongruous pairing but they were not an improbable one—not in the world of the anti-university.

Mozic
ND THE REVOLUTION

When Joshua fit the Battle of Jericho walls came tumbling down. That's elation. The holy Ghost talking. So it can done. The way to crack a mirror or ver a wineglass is to find the right quency and pound it. Like those strobe its that picked up the B-rhythms of some s dancing around in Ealing or somewhere, l threw them into epileptic fits. T.C. ows a cat in Australia who used to make ange music sitting between two huge umns and singing into them and feeding l feeding it back and back. Finally, he rst a blood vessel in his head and now he's zy. If you sit a man with a bucket on his ad and let a water-tap drip onto it, he'll be crazy within hours. The Japanese taught some Australians that. Music hath charms to tame the savage breast, as Shakespeare noticed. Music hath alarums to wild the civil breast, as well, as Tuli Kupferberg pointed out. It is partly a matter of the mode of the music, but then as well something to do with the ears the music exists in. He that has ears to hear, let him hear. The bell tolling in the desert makes no sound.

What then is the mode of revolutionary music in October 1969? And who's it for? Mick Farren is right to agonise over the superficiality of the rock revolution. The underground is falsely complacent, living on an exaggerated notion of its own importance and effectiveness, which Mick Farren tirelessly deflates and derides. He looks back with furious nostalgia at the time when ugly, desperate, grinding songs were million sellers. When shop-girls, mechanics, storemen, packers, gasfitters, wharf labourers and their girls, found dignity, lust and anger in the music of rock. It is painful to hear the skinheads saying as they look over the crowds, past the enclosure where the beautiful people bask in a cloud of Mick Jagger's spittle, "Well, the Stones are one of us, arnay?" Expensive drugs, more expensive butterflies, dead mates, Baby Jane Holzer's dildo, no, baby, the Stones are not one of you. By Marianne Faithfull's sacred Mars bar they are not one of you. They are being protected from you by the Underground's favourite scapegoats, the poor old phoney Hell's Angels. In the official souvenir of that concert there is a photograph of the groupies' enclosures backstage, which features, in filthy yellow plush trousers, Ibiza v dilly-bag, the undergro himself. The expression on the whole blind alley of rev "Why isn't it working" tl saying. "What the fuck hap

Why did Mick Jagg quarter of a million people city? Why did they behave up all their garbage? They their togetherness, boasted They showed the paren they were gentle an co-operative. Mick Farren was not how it was. The been contained. No one n the Rolling Stones any mo

CHAPTER 19
STARSHIPS IN GLENROTHES

In 1971, *Drop Out!* was issued in an affordable paperback edition by Penguin, introducing Farquharson to a far larger audience than Anthony Blond had ever managed. In internal communications, Farquharson's new publishers described his book as a kind of psychedelic *Down and Out in Paris and London*. Farquharson's book, Penguin believed, resembled the recent bestsellers of Carlos Castañeda and R. D. Laing. But persuading readers of the similarities would be a hard sell, which led Penguin to play up Farquharson's rebel scholar credentials. The author's potted biography once again claimed that Farquharson held not one but two doctorates, the second apparently awarded by Cambridge. There are no records of this degree ever having been awarded, nor a sense of when it could even have been possible.

Penguin's biography also described Farquharson as having been born 'in 1930 or 1940'. It is unclear whether this was an editorial conceit—an attempt at drumming up a bit of Castañeda-like mystery to help the new edition gain some legs—or genuine confusion on Farquharson's part. It's also very possible that they were simply unable to contact the author to confirm.

An air of mystery certainly did Farquharson no harm in terms of raising his outsider status. In the wake of being arrested for his act of shoelessness, Farquharson began to be referred to as an 'international freak' by the *Arts Labs Newsletter*, taking their lead from *OZ*. The informal tone of the *Newsletter* and other similar ephemeral publications offered a tantalising glimpse of Farquharson and his entourage. Word was spreading and things were clearly getting quite freaky.

Nicholas Albery

As reported in last month's newsletter, under the heading "INTERNATIONAL FREAK BEATEN-UP & COMMITTED" –Dr Robin Farquharson (ex-bit worker, author of *Drop Out*) was in Horton Mental Hospital, Epsom, as a patient–(thanks for the news Nick….) S.O.S. phone calls were immediately given by the Lab. people & the distress calls did not go unanswered………. it was quite a laugh in the end for when I visited Robin, a[nd] conducted tour of the hospital complete with informal chat with male nurse, social worker & psychiatrists………….

"Come on Robin, lets get out of here," said Batman Greg !!……… Now discharged, we had quite a time visiting odd Boots, (freaks, if you like Nick). Friday 13th will long be remembered, "freak now or forever hold your peace"………

Robin, you must send a copy of your book to the Lab. so as we can pass it round & get the new 'hang-ups' from the "Alternative Society"! As you (& Bob from Leeds, hitching to Italy right now) saw in Epsom town how reaction is to 'heads' etc. Conservative, Bourgeois–it's all around, can one escape, London maybe?! Switching people on even to the *Manchester Guardian* in Epsom is difficult! Let alone Lab. work, phew!…. It's almost hospital for me, in one way or another.

Epsom Arts Lab hasn't burnt any £5 notes on BBC TV or 'freaked' anyone lately, or got articles in the *Manchester*

> *Guardian*.......... BUT...................! If enough ROBINS got together in Epsom there would be quite a song & dance.

The bare facts of Farquharson's life were taking on an increasing fluidity. It was not clear how he ever returned to London after his spells in Horton. On this occasion, though, his return coincided with a skyrocketing of his ambitions. Having more or less settled in southern England, Farquharson now sought to live up to his friends' tongue-in-cheek moniker and embody the persona of the international freak.

By the summer of 1971 unemployment was extraordinarily high across the UK. Things were particularly bad in Scotland where economic downturn and mismanagement had left one of the country's major industries on the verge of collapse. Upper Clyde Shipbuilders consisted of five major firms operating in the Glasgow area, making them one of the largest employers in the region. In late July, employees were told that UCS was about to enter liquidation and that workers would lose their jobs. The company was refused an emergency government loan, directly risking the loss of some 10,000 positions. The people of Glasgow would not take this sitting down.

In an extraordinary display of solidarity, workers across the country joined the struggle. In late June, 100,000 union members went on strike to protest the government's inaction. Six weeks later close to 200,000 workers staged a half-day walkout in solidarity. The Angry Brigade then bombed the home of John Davies, Secretary of State for Business and Trade, and issued a communiqué encouraging workers in Clydeside to 'join the Angry side.'

The shipyards chose another tactic. Instead of striking, the unions opted to undertake a work-in. This meant that UCS continued to fulfil the jobs contracted to the company in the hope of proving that their labour was both necessary and viable. Things had gotten so urgent that John and Yoko felt compelled to send the workers a large amount of money for their solidarity fund in addition to a bunch of red roses. With the government committed to letting the shipyards go bust and workers committed to the escalating struggle, the situation at UCS was at breaking point.

In response to the mounting crisis, Farquharson initiated his grandest scheme to date. It all started by showing up unannounced at the offices of *Frendz*.

Rosie Boycott
Outside a tall, wild-looking hairy man was fighting with a cab driver. Breaking free of the driver's arm, he'd run up the office stairs. "I've just sold this building," he panted, "you can all retire. I know how to destroy the banking system of the country. Everyone must open six accounts and then transfer their overdrafts from one to the other, increasing them all the time. We'll bring the pigs down in a few months. It's easy…"

Jerome Burne
It's a pity we didn't pay more attention to Robin, but he was just another rather strange figure. We were at sort of a centre for some intriguing and interesting people who just happened to be on Portobello Road. We had one guy who came around and asked us if he could hoover the floor naked while the women from the advertising department shouted rude things at him.

I don't know whether it was actually robes but I remember Robin being kind of clad in white, like some sort of Old Testament prophet or something. And his plan was he was going to go up and buy the Clyde docks. There was a big strike going on and he was going to solve it, either solve it or just buy the whole thing outright and give a good deal to the workers. And he went off. I can't remember exactly what happened to him. But I do remember that, over a period of a couple of weeks when he was around, we would get visits from taxi drivers who would turn up and say, "There was this bloke who was in the cab and he couldn't pay for it but he gave us his watch and said to come and take it to you and then you'd pay." We probably gave an entire wage to pay for his cab bill.

Burne wasn't to know that other plans were afoot. More chapters of the British White Panthers had sprung up without Mick Farren's say-so,

The Glasgow White Panthers were more organised than many other branches of the Party, going so far as to produce their own letterhead

including a Glasgow outfit who formed a close alliance with Glasgow Advisory People (GAP), one of the city's leading alternative spaces.

John Hassan
GAP was situated in a tenement which was due for demolition because of the motorway which was running through Glasgow at the time. It was basically a very small baker's shop with a single counter running down the centre and a little back room with a small kitchen. The original people who ran GAP were no longer coming in—it was just the stragglers, you may say, who were hanging about. I was standing in front of the counter when the door flew open. It was a glass door. And in comes this guy dressed in gray flannel trousers, Bri-Nylon open-neck shirt, open-toed sandals, tall, balding. The first words that came out of this gentleman's mouth were, "Is this GAP?". I confirmed it was, to which he replied in a very demanding tone, "Come with me—it's important."

He opened the door and I followed him outside and there was a taxi. We got into the taxi and I said, "Before we go, can you tell me what this is about?" And he answered, "It's political." So I said,

"Well, you've got the wrong person!" So we went back into the shop and he basically explained that he wanted to try to save the jobs of the Upper Clyde shipbuilders. I had actually been unaware of the headlines because I wasn't watching television or listening to the radio. He asked if some of us would come with him, so two of the guys in the back did. One of them was called Alan—he was a very gruff sort of fellow, wore combat jackets, which were relatively in style at the time, and purported to be a member of the Angry Brigade, and of course he wasn't, just liked wearing the badge—and the other one was a schoolboy named Paul.

So we get into the cab and we drove to a Bank of Scotland and he got out of the taxi and went to the back but it was too early, so he got back into the taxi and we drove over to the Govan shipyard, which is on the south side of the river. And the gates were closed. Robin asked where the shop stewards would be, and they said, "They'll be over at John Brown's." So we drove back to the north side of the river, down to Clydebank, and at that point, we had to pay the taxi fare. That was perhaps the first point where our suspicions were slightly raised.

The gates were open and there was a little bothy on the right hand side with about 20, 25 ship workers inside. Robin asked who was in charge and told the fella that stepped forward that what he wanted to do was to buy the yard and save the jobs. "I have here a blank cheque," he explained, "which you can fill in for any amount up to £1." We three boys were standing behind Robin, so we could see the reaction of the ship workers. But Robin went on to explain the rest of his plan.

"Once I buy the shipyard, what I'll do is asset strip the place. Sell off the cranes and the materials and sell off the land. Your jobs will be quite safe. I'm going to use the income from the sale of the assets to buy a fleet of buses. Then we're going to open a factory in Glenrothes."

Now, Glenrothes is on the other side of the country. The workers were absolutely incredulous.

"But hey, there's no river over in Glenrothes—you cannae build ships in Glenrothes! What kinda ships are we gonna be making over there, then?"

And Robin replied, "Starships." At this point, we actually had to step forward and tap Robin on the shoulder and whisper, "Look, Robin, they're not listening to you, you're going to need to leave."

The four men were stared out of the shipbuilders' premises, not before Farquharson unsuccessfully attempted to block an oil tanker from entering the site. They returned to GAP, where Farquharson proceeded to make a number of calls from the shared telephone. After failing to be put through to the executive teams at Boeing and Pan-AM, Farquharson turned to his new friends with a different idea: 'Who wants to fly to Glenrothes?' He instructed Paul to grab one of the office's phones and stash it in a BOAC flight case. They then headed to the airport with a plan that recalled another of Farquharson's other recent schemes.

John Hassan

By this stage, Alan had had enough, but Paul and I both were up for it and there was another couple who volunteered to come with us as well. Robin came up with this idea that we would take on the part of a rock group. He asked us for a name, and we came up the name of a new, upcoming Glasgow group called Ciacona. Robin took on the guise of our manager.

We're in the taxi coming down to Glasgow airport and Robin loudly says to Paul, "Get on the phone with John and see if he can make it to the festival next week." So Paul goes into the bag, makes as if he's dialling this number, waits for a few moments, and says, "Yes, yes, I have Mr Farquharson to speak with you," hands the receiver to Robin, who says, "Oh, it's Yoko! Oh, hi Yoko. Yes, yes. Will John make it?" The taxi driver of course is totally mystified. We were having a little hilarity between ourselves: Robin was in character, playing a part, but it could only have been for the sake of the taxi driver, because he was the only other witness.

> We flew across Scotland and landed in a small field only to be met by two chauffeur-driven cars. We were gobsmacked. The cars took us to Glenrothes Development Corporation. We went upstairs, where Robin was asked to explain what he was doing. And out comes the telephone from the bag. On the end of the telephone wire he had attached this cocoa tin. He proceeded to explain his prototype for what he called an Iron-Drive-Emission Radio Telephone. That's the point where it clicked for me that Robin was a bit of a genius, whatever that is: a futurist, or something like that.

The idea of a wireless telephone held great appeal in this isolated part of the Highlands. Whether such a thing was possible was another matter, but Farquharson was a highly plausible and self-aware storyteller. As ever, he simply played along for real.

The men from the development board looked Farquharson up and down and eventually decided to have him to fill out a grant application. He and his friends were then returned to the airfield where the pilot raised the tricky question of payment. Farquharson offered to pay with a stamped piece of paper in lieu of cash, which the pilot rejected. They were promptly ferried to a nearby train station and left to fend for themselves.

As Farquharson busied himself with the business of procuring train tickets with no money, Hassan and his friends quietly discussed making their own way back to Glasgow and drawing a line under their involvement with Farquharson. The man himself suddenly burst back onto the platform, tickets in hand and promising the hungry teens a hot meal courtesy of some friends in Edinburgh. Hassan, Paul, and Alan sheepishly stepped onto the train and decided to play it cool. True to Farquharson's word, a well-meaning if mystified middle-aged couple welcomed them in for a meal, after which the group finally boarded a train back to Glasgow.

It was now evening. Walking back from the station to GAP, the tired men passed a club popular with Glasgow's small hippie set. Top of the bill of that night's entertainment were none other than Ciacona—the real band, this time.

John Hassan

After a couple of numbers they asked for a bit of silence because they were wanting to record a demo to send to London, so they started a bit more of their prog-style stuff. And in the middle of the song, Robin appears in front of the stage, outstretched arms, almost in a crucifix position, and began shouting, "Gay liberation has come to Glasgow! Gay lib has come to Glasgow!" So we kind of ushered Robin in a little room to the side and tried to calm him down and then went back to the gig.

After Ciacona had finished their set we went back into the side room to get Robin and saw that he was standing in the middle of the otherwise-empty room locked in an embrace with a man named Neil. It was probably the first time any of us had seen a public display of men in a full-blown kiss. At that point we all left, and that was the day finished.

In one day, Farquharson had managed to make his way up to Glasgow from London, undertake an all-expenses paid business tour of the country, get with a stranger, and avoided spending a single penny of his own money. Inevitably, though, his Scottish adventure would end the way all of his other recent plans did.

Andy Roberts

The story I remember being told is that Robin was confined (on this occasion) after successfully ordering a (military?) aeroplane—or aeroplanes.

The truth was more parochial. The day after the UCS-Glenrothes escapade, Farquharson tucked his head into GAP to say hello and goodbye and hailed a taxi to take him to the bank. After once more refusing to pay for his journey, he was finally arrested. Farquharson's attempt to save the shipbuilders' jobs was over.

A particularly weird and winding episode, the UCS debacle testified to Farquharson's ability to penetrate almost any environment through a combination of bluster, arrogance, and genuine lateral thinking. But as was so often the case, he contrived to squander an impossible opportunity, leaving spectators baffled as to quite what it was they had just witnessed.

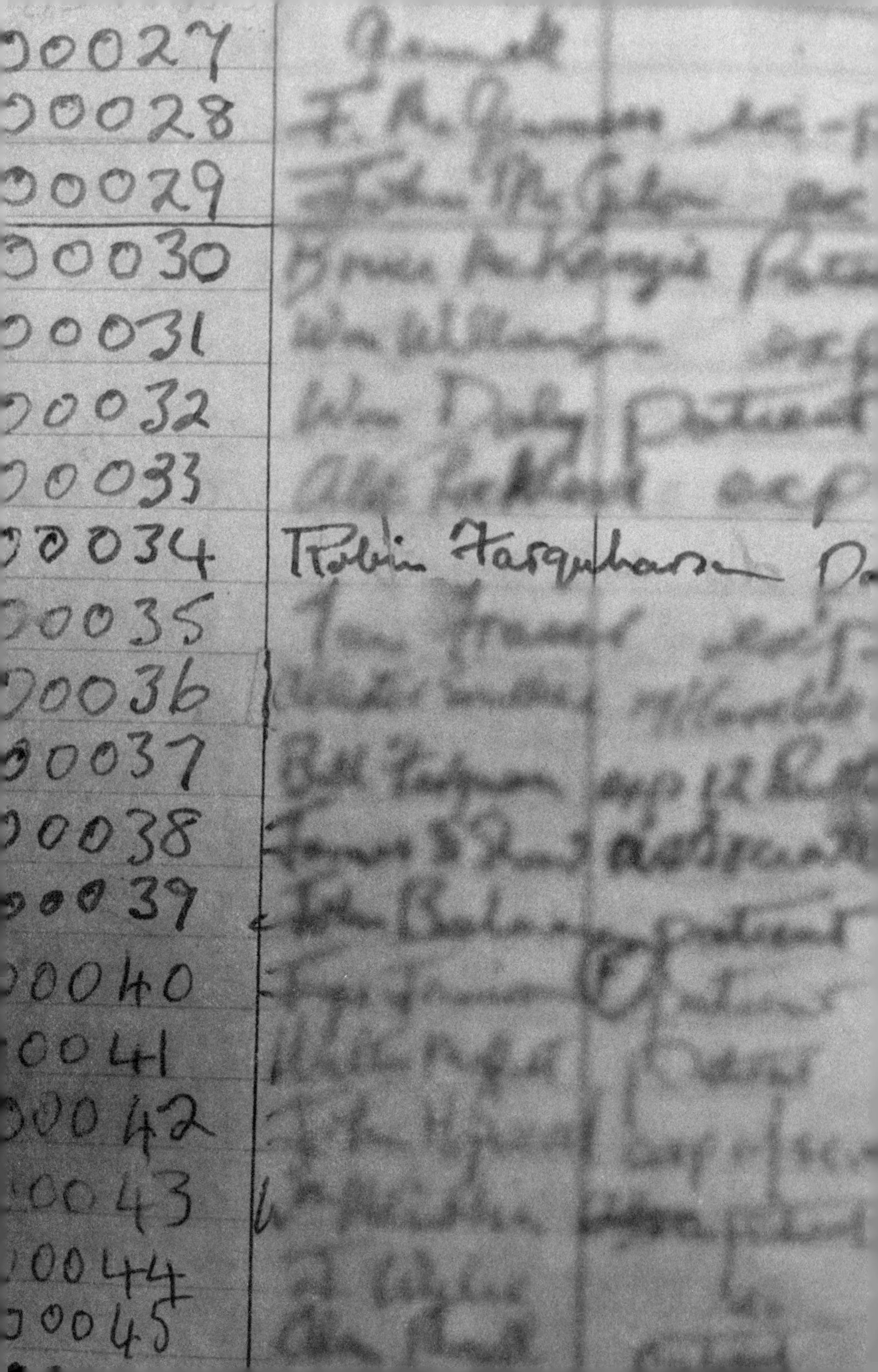
00027
00028
00029
00030
00031
00032
00033
00034 Robin Farquharson
00035
00036
00037
00038
00039
00040
00041
00042
00043
00044
00045

CHAPTER 20
THE YTISREVINU OF LONDON

After a brief period of incarceration, Farquharson was moved to Gartloch, a mental hospital located to the east of Glasgow. Though his second attempt at being a White Panther had ended as badly as the first, Farquharson's brief sojourn in Scotland led to an important breakthrough in his campaigning.

The nearby Hartwood Hospital housed a man named Thomas Ritchie, who had been a drifter, petty criminal, and occasional pollster for the Conservative Party when he became a patient in 1963. Some eight years on and still at Hartwood, Ritchie decided that enough was enough and began to agitate for the rights of his fellow psychiatric patients. When Farquharson was transferred from Gartloch back to the familiar surrounds of Horton, he and Ritchie kept in touch. For the time being, though, Farquharson was in a bad way.

Guy Legge

Robin appeared with a broken arm. He had been mistakenly sent to Long Grove [Hospital] across the road and was so

> heavily drugged that he fell down some stairs. He had a sort of lumberjack's jacket on, big red and black checkers. He used to wander around the ward swinging his arms about singing, "Jesus Christ, superstar/Just who the hell do you think you are?" He approached me one morning on the ward and asked if I would appear in his movie. I asked what it was called and he said *Ivan the Woodcutter*. I asked where the cameras and equipment were and he said we were only going to have a dress rehearsal. I asked about costumes and he said I could wear his clothes. I declined his invitation. He refused to leave me and I eventually swung a fist at him and I had the experience of this crazed South African with a handle-bar moustache squaring up to me. The staff cooled things down.

From hospital, Farquharson continued to try to organise and promote his anti-university, placing adverts in the underground papers back in London.

> ***International Times*, classified advert**
> The Ytisrevinu of London is more or less decentralised, indeed existent only in this ad. But its courses continue so if you are interested, phone up. (Dialecture! an antiuniversity lecture in the privacy of your own phone) or just come along.

This announcement promised far more detailed information than had previously been forthcoming: classes were going to be offered on logic, poetry, meditation, artificial intelligence, 'communication & anti-social work', economics, alternative law, 'and hopefully courses on I Ching and the Alternative Society when Robin returns in a few weeks time.' Farquharson also announced that he had enlisted the services of Keith Armstrong, a wheelchair-bound concrete poet and disabled rights campaigner.

Armstrong—the anti-university's 'professor of poetry'—produced a prospectus for his class on Farquharson-Houédard alphabet-headed paper. But whether any of these organised sessions ever ran or not was unclear. Tom Fawthrop, the journalist listed as running a class on alternative law, later insisted that his course never took place and that he had no memory of ever even meeting Farquharson.

The anti-university struggled on for several more months, appearing in different guises at different locations, but its commitment to decentralisation made gaining a stable foothold impossible. Nor did Farquharson's repeated hospitalisation help matters. For every detailed course listing there would be an ad that was pared down to the most basic possible information: 'Robin Farquharson is back', read one notice he placed in *International Times*. 'He can be written to in Ward 5, Horton Hospital, Epsom, Surrey or telephoned on Wednesdays… Alternative Society. Contact Robin.'

In the interim, Thomas Ritchie had liaised with members of GAP and his fellow patients and was now ready to launch something he called the Scottish Union of Mental Patients (SUMP). Despite Ritchie's lack of organising experience, SUMP represented probably the first organisation to use collective action to fight for the rights of psychiatric patients. It was a lateral move to the kind of anti-psychiatry practiced at Kingsley Hall—highly influenced by Laing and his peers, but driven by patients and social workers rather than doctors.

As SUMP saw it, this was not a problem specific to Scotland. Something similar had recently been attempted in West Germany. The Socialist Patients' Collective sought to link patients' rights with an explicitly anti-capitalist agenda, 'turning sickness into a weapon'. This was a genuinely revolutionary notion. Few were surprised when members of the SPC were duly accused of participating in Baader-Meinhof actions.

In a distinctly British mode, Ritchie chose to announce the formation of his group in the pages of *Ink*, a new underground paper launched by one of the founders of *OZ*. As several of his causes overlapped in one place and time, Farquharson promptly signed up as a member of SUMP, making him the group's 34th member and the first based outside of the confines of Hartwood Hospital.

Keith Armstrong around the time he made Farquharson's acquaintance

Ink wasn't the only new paper in the offing. Around this time, *Frendz* journalist Rosie Boycott was involved in discussions around launching an explicitly feminist publication. Boycott paired up with Marsha Rowe, who had been part of both *OZ* and *Ink*. The result was *Spare Rib*, a pioneering magazine that linked second-wave feminism with the values of alternative London. Foregrounding its connections to the underground, the magazine's very first issue carried an advert for People, Not Psychiatry. Michael Barnett's group were still based in the house Rhaune Laslett had found them from which Farquharson had been expelled.

Farquharson was meanwhile on the hunt for stable housing for himself and his fellow psychiatric patients. In March 1972, he and a number of former Horton patients took over a pair of abandoned houses on Elgin Avenue in Maida Vale, a ten minute walk from the offices of BIT. The police soon had them physically removed, despite the lack of a court order permitting them to do so. Farquharson was once more on the streets.

As his peers and associates developed what looked like stronger structures and more stable organisations, Farquharson was adrift. Sensing even greater instability, Anthony Blond contacted Rupert Murdoch to see if there was a way they could help their mutual friend. Murdoch declined, believing Farquharson to be beyond help.

Shelley Lee

I didn't know Robin as a friend. We spoke only restrained greetings. But I lived next to him in an empty boys school where thirteen of us were squatting last winter. The people shifted in the room next to mine and I cannot remember when Robin came to live or when he left. My knowledge of him is the sounds that passed through the paper thin walls and the spout of chaos I occasionally glimpsed when the door to his room was left open. Through the whole of the time he lived next to me the basic elements in the room never changed. A mattress with a grey dirt stained piece of cloth partially flung over it. An old brown leather suitcase always open in the middle of the floor. Out of it spouted books of every sort from detective stories to sociology to occult. And always newspapers strewn everywhere, page after page. A few articles of clothing lay on the floor. On the table the last occupier had left were the bits of food he would keep. The rest of the room was empty.

I usually was out during the greater part of the day so what he did at that time I have no idea. The experience through the walls came only in late night usually between 2 and 5am. It would begin with loud breathing and hurried uneven stepping of feet, as if he was running from one space in the room to another, but always in jerks and starts. Then things would be thrown or dropped, bottles crash, books fall. Still always the hurried feet. And then the groaning which would build to suppressed cries began—not cries as in sadness or sex, but as if he were suppressing vicious frantic internal screams. I don't know in fact what was happening, but the sounds would set my own body into such a state of tension and fright that I was incapable of doing anything but to lie there rigid and listening. Once the fierceness passed, the noise and uneven footsteps settled. The next hour or so would be low groaning sounds. Not a sound that could terrify, but an utterly despairing moan. Sometimes I would weep to listen. Now as I write I wish I had been strong enough then to go to him, but I was terrified and incapable. That is probably the story of his life.

During the day I sometimes saw him walking through Camden Town. Mostly I remember how his head was thrown back in a distorted position, with his mouth open and talking to himself. His eyes never focused on anything outside, but rolled, dealing with whatever horror was in his head.

I left the house in the beginning of summer and did not see Robin until the fall. Again he was walking the streets. I watched from the top of a bus how his stride had lost even the semblance of evenness. How he looked as if he were being thrown about the road instead of walking his own body. How his head with mouth open continued to jerk backward. I again lived the sick frightened feeling that I'd experienced night after night in the house.

In an unpublished note written around this time, Farquharson explained that 'because of what is going on in my head they want to take me away and shut me in a room for a year and they can. But I like what is going on in my head and I am troubling no-one. All I need is someone to talk to.' Despite the turmoil of the past few years, he still had hopes of maintaining a successful writing career. Even though he was now drifting between homelessness and temporary accommodation, Farquharson managed to attract some interest from Penguin in publishing two new books. One was simply called *Alternative Society* while the other was provisionally titled *Games and Society*.

> **Robin Farquharson**
> In the world of the transformed, paradoxically, a higher level of welfare is achieved at a lower level of consumption. The new objectives of satisfaction are human, not material. The major object of delight is in people, not things, and the total level of production for use is lower. This is the enriching paradox of the transformed society.

Penguin also explored the idea of having *Drop Out!* issued in the United States, but the publisher's New York wing rowed back their initial interest. Neither this nor any of Farquharson's other book plans come together. Instead, the would-be author circulated scraps from another work which he called *I am God*. It was based on a series of transcripts of wide-roaming conversations taped in various squats and communes. By this stage, even the sympathetic staff at Horton no longer offered themselves as a viable option.

> **Peter Johnston**
> In practice, they filled him up with sedatives. Came the depressive stage and Robin was set loose, with medication which, if taken, kept him a cabbage. He obviously resented this and eventually sooner or later—mostly sooner—threw the pills away and tripped again. Eventually, his relationship with Low-Beer

deteriorated to the extent that he no longer trusted or was trusted and his downward flight accelerated from there.

Richard Adams

I do remember him coming to the office one evening at a time when the issue was being put together. He arrived to a room full of people and there were a lot of distractions where he was another. He was known to some of the members of the *Gay News* editorial team and I think he set people's teeth on edge, someone with a reputation for being unpredictable and in a constant state of agitation. He conducted himself in a way that one would associate with somebody who's either experiencing a bad trip, had too much to drink, or experiencing the effects of psychosis. I didn't even know he was gay, though when I read his memoir I saw that he was outrageously gay. But he was not overt or anything else on that occasion: he was just off on a trip.

Woody Haut

I never really saw Robin in his totally manic state, but he was always very funny and very unpredictable and very nice with our kids. He didn't really intimidate them and they certainly weren't afraid of him—he was very playful and convivial with them.

Michael Dummett

The last time I saw him, sometime in the early 1970s, was an intensely distressing occasion. Answering a ring at the front door of my house, I found my children gathered just inside it; opening the door, I found Farquharson, obviously in a late stage of one of his manic phases, in the custody of some policemen: he had been showing my children some exceedingly pornographic drawings.

Gordon Winter

Although he favoured violence in the revolutionary situation of South Africa, Robin was, paradoxically, a man of great gentleness. Although a very naive amateur revolutionary he had a heart of gold. At all times, to all who met him, this crazy, lovable 42 year old intellectual beatnik was tremendously kind, superbly witty, generous to a fault, and without the slightest trace of vanity.

Anthony Howell
He then got an extremely important job in Regent Street with a firm doing computer analysis. It was a very, very technical job and might have given him stability for a while. But Robin's condition continually fucked him up because there he was, in a pretty excellent job, and then he flipped and invited all the tramps in London to come and have breakfast in the office. And of course, when all the employees walked in and found all the tramps all over the office, Robin got the sack.

Frater Choronzon
Robin Farquharson would not have thought of himself as a magician, nonetheless in the eyes of his beholders he certainly appeared to be able to exhibit what might pass for a magical power. People on the verge of mental instability frequently 'hear voices'; Robin's talent was in being able to recognise what it was he was hearing.

Michael Barnett
I heard he had joined the White Panthers and was using his power and magic in their cause. The last time we met he was very depressed. He had been brainwashed into believing that after all schizophrenia was organic and incurable, and so was manic-depression. He seemed to have resigned himself to a flawed life. I told him I thought he was copping out, letting go into hopelessness. He seemed to chirp up at this but also to resent it. If I was right he would have to start hoping and fighting again. Or so I fantasized. But this man, this giant, this mixture of David

Cooper, Aubrey Beardsley and General de Gaulle, is, I believe, indomitable. Survive he will, I am sure, endure and come again. I find in me that faith in him.

CHAPTER 21
THE DUST HEAPS OF SOMERS TOWN

Somers Town is a small, triangle-shaped neighbourhood in central London. Sandwiched between Camden, Euston, and King's Cross, the area is easy to miss. Despite its diminutive size, Somers Town has long been seen as symbolic of both the glories and failures of the British colonial project. In part this was because one of the major historical landowners was Cecil Rhodes, the infamous colonialist and founder of Rhodesia. The Rhodes family had strong ties to the neighbourhood; their family burial plot is located in the grounds of St. Pancras Old Church.

This affluent connection notwithstanding, Somers Town was once better known for its famous dust heaps. These enormous mounds of soot and ash were formed in the early eighteenth century as a result of decades of poor sanitation. With this deprivation came a keen sense of local pride, making Somers Town home to some of the earliest campaigns for social housing and a reputation for political radicalism. Community flourished, as did alcoholism and crime. These combined most noticeably in 1830 when a local cop named Joseph Grantham was killed by two drunk men, making him the first British policeman to be killed on active duty.

The construction of Euston Station in 1837 and King's Cross in 1852 wrought further chaos on the area, transforming impoverished Somers Town into one of the British Empire's largest hubs for transporting goods and people. In 1865, Charles Dickens based the plot of *Our Mutual Friend* on the Somers Town dust heaps and the hidden mysteries held deep within them. By this time the dust was itself a thing of the past, reportedly sold en masse to Russia for use in the enormous building works necessitated by the Napoleonic invasion of Moscow.

As modernity loomed Somers Town was in danger of becoming a well-connected slum. Residents old and new found themselves plugged into a long local history of collective resistance and resilience. At the tail end of the eighteenth century, the feminist pioneer Mary Wollstonecraft and the anarchist William Godwin called Somers Town home. So did Basil Jellicoe, the pioneering housing reformer. As the twentieth century dawned, this chain was bolstered by the presence of George Padmore, the Trinidad-born journalist and Pan-African activist who waged war on the British Empire from his flat on Cranleigh Street.

The spectre of destruction nevertheless continued to haunt Somers Town. Central London was heavily targeted in the Blitz. Though less damaged than the warehouse-heavy neighbourhoods in the east of the city, Somers Town was hit hard. It remained a wreck of bombed-out buildings well into the second half of the twentieth century. A concerted wave of slum clearance aimed to remedy things but progress was slow. Row after row of terraces crept closer to collapse and the former dust heaps gradually returned.

Towering above them was a new nine-storey art deco block, a living monument to the complicated status of social housing. The building was completed in 1950, offering safe and modern housing for local families. But to Padmore and his allies it represented a bitter reminder of the battle ahead, bearing as it did the name Cecil Rhodes House. Padmore himself died in 1959, leaving a large legacy in the local area and beyond, not least a keen eye for the abuse of power and the irreconcilable promises of empire.

Somers Town's ready access to important transport hubs continued to make the area important. In 1961, the famous arch of Euston Station began to be demolished, preceding the wholesale reconstruction of the station. Over the next few years the entire area was subsumed in redevelopment works until the new station was opened. Local residents meanwhile made do with an increasingly decrepit stock of Georgian houses. Homelessness and addiction began to haunt the neighbourhood as residents waited for the benefits of this upheaval to trickle down.

There seemed little obvious solution to these problems other than wholesale change. In 1969 the homelessness charity Centrepoint was launched, its name an ironic nod to the still-empty tower on New Oxford Street. As Centrepoint moved to set up its first night shelters, others decided to abandon the city completely. In 1970, Farquharson's former housemate Sid Rawle moved with a handful of followers to an Irish island loaned to him by John Lennon. Rumours circulated that Farquharson and Lennon were also in discussions, though it was unknown over what.

Others took smaller steps towards communal living. Many of those who came through London found a temporary refuge in Somers Town and at the Charrington Street squat, which was formed out of a series of semi-abandoned buildings between St. Pancras and Mornington Crescent.

Aidan Andrew Dun

I had been studying as a classical guitarist and was overzealous and ego driven. I over practiced and managed to destroy the tendons in both my arms. And then I went mad, essentially, and ended up in Charrington Street. I was extremely young—I hadn't even turned twenty—and was very raw and exposed by what had happened to me.

There were four or five hundred people in the Charrington Street squat at the time. There was Harmonica Keith, in a wheelchair. There were the clowns, but I didn't really hang out with them. There was an Irishman who traded in VW vans by the hundreds and had them parked all down the street. And then there was this guy called Paul Pawlowski, in whose house I was actually living. His apartment was incredibly basic and was just full of plumbing equipment, really, but high up near the ceiling there was this row of scholarly treatises on Greek religion. Paul was known as the Reverend Father Fuck. He had set up something called the Church of Aphrodite Pandemos. He was very altruistic with us and at some stage actually made me a priest in his church. Eventually it all got out of hand. He tried to sacrifice this goat he kept out back and we had to confiscate it from him and release it.

Centrepoint helped to make the lives of so-called street people newly visible. Itinerant living had nevertheless long been fetishised by artists and bohemians looking for a model of pre-modern existence. With this came the development of street poetry, which purported to tell the true stories of real people in unmediated fashion.

Though its origins were in the New York and San Francisco of the 1950s, it took until the late 1960s for the practice of street poetry and the lifestyle it represented to arrive in the UK. This came in part thanks to the efforts of a poet from Scunthorpe named Peter Baines, better known as Street Talk Pete.

Marilyn Weiss Baines

Unlike his two brothers and sister who found comfort and security in the old steel town, Peter Baines, a restless and untamed fifteen year old, finished school and having no definite direction in mind, hitch-hiked to London with just a few coins in his pocket. London lights and city people fascinated him and soon he learned the value of gaining an education by living life the hard way. Money was no object as having possessions was unimportant to him and he was prepared to live rough in order to 'be free'. He barely survived doing odd decorating jobs and labouring for his meal ticket.

Making his way to Greenwich Village, Street Talk Pete turned this interest into a creative practice.

> **Marilyn Weiss Baines**
> For the next four years, always carrying a pen and pad, Peter Baines carefully explored the times. He examined everyday mobility of the common people. He was intrigued by their speech patterns and political thinking. He stood on street corners and listened to gossip. He viewed the landscape. He studied street objects, their shapes and colours. He observed and listened. He walked the pavement and talked to people he met on the street. He jotted down notes which he would later on turn into a poem.

Returning to London, Street Talk Pete partnered up with a kindred spirit named Bongo Mike whom he encountered one day outside Better Books. Together the pair made a living from selling their work on the street. But the pair split when Mike learned that his collaborator was claiming the dole, which Mike considered an act of betrayal. Pete was left to find other avenues for his creativity.

While life on the road could be an inherently political or creative act, it was also a pragmatic one. Prominent hippie squats generated intense scrutiny from both the general public and the squatting community itself, but not all squatters were countercultural, nor was it always clear where an alternative squat ended and a more normative one began. Poor people relied on squats just as much as dropouts, making many squats an odd mix of politically radical professionals, itinerant workers, families with young children, out-of-work alcoholics, and stoned artists. George Price, the once-famous geneticist, was now squatting a house in Euston and giving away his belongings to neighbouring alcoholics. David Cooper was said to live in a squat on Buckingham Road in Dalston, though he was known to spend most of his time in the Duke of Wellington pub nearby.

When they worked, squats were symbiotic beings, balancing the needs of their residents with the capacity to adapt to anything and anyone. When they didn't work, they provided neither shelter nor respite. This was a hard way of life, a potentially treacherous half-space rooted around insecurity and improvisation.

Though some residents feared the presence of squats, fretting about the knock-on effects of having hippies in the area, others sympathised with and even joined their cause. In the summer of 1972, squatters erected barricades on Lesly Street to prevent Islington Council's demolition crews from gaining access to a series of houses just behind Pentonville Prison. Families of all kinds joined forces to ensure residents were granted stable accommodation elsewhere before letting the demolition proceed.

As actions like the Lesly Street squat became an increasingly common story, nearly every issue of the local *Camden News* was now dedicated to the subject of housing. Moving back and forth between his island and London, Sid Rawle lent his expertise in these battles.

> **Michael Child**
> I would describe what Sid and I did at that time as being unpaid pastoral workers to the hippie-squatting community centred around Chalk Farm, Somers Town, and Hampstead. Sid was very focused on the distribution of land and property: something along the lines of every citizen should have a share in the geography of their country.

Another regular topic of discussion was the activity of the Greater London Council. Since the mid-1960s, the GLC had been buying up streets across Somers Town, making use of compulsory purchase orders to complete the levelling of central London begun by the Luftwaffe. Many squatters now realised that they had technically been occupying government-owned property, whether they intended to or not.

Every so often, the cat-and-mouse nature of the squatting scene provided opportunities for marginalised groups to access space from which they would otherwise be excluded. By 1972, fires and inter-personal fractures had brought an end to Sid Rawle's Irish utopia. Returning to London, Rawle got involved in finding a home for a local outpost of the Gay Liberation Front.

Michael Child

Robin was connected with the GLF squat in Parkhill Road and got thrown out or left for some reason and was living in bad circumstances in a relatively small house somewhere in the middle of the devastation of the mostly demolished Chalk Farm. Both he and I were taking a lot of drugs; I got the feeling that he felt it would be impossible for him to live with other people because of his mental health.

Aidan Andrew Dun

One of the first nights that I spent at Charrington Street, I was woken up very early on a Sunday morning by this man in an enormous overcoat walking down the street barefoot. In one hand he was holding the largest alarm clock I have ever seen in my life and in the other hand was this huge sheaf of papers. He stopped on the pavement, put the alarm clock down, and started kind of dancing around it as he read from one of the manuscripts. I couldn't hear the words, but it sounded like poetry, and though I'd been overdosed on poetry at school this vision just gave me such a shock that I knew I had to track him down.

One way or another, the council machine ensured that symbolic figures like Rawle were soon moved on so that demolition could begin. When compulsory purchase orders didn't work, the GLC often turned to other less formal means. If properties were squatted, the council would often forcibly enter and remove key amenities, including those provided or repaired by squatters, so as to ensure that the building was unliveable.

Aidan Andrew Dun

At that time, Robin was living on the corner of Charrington Street. There was nothing there. There was no furniture, no water, no gas, no juice, nothing. There weren't even any doors or windows. It had been ruined by the wrecking gangs and was basically just a shell.

Fires were also often beneficial to the council, removing property they couldn't or wouldn't buy, evicting tenants they struggled to get rid of, and further justifying the need to redevelop land. Fires were also an occupational hazard in some squats, particularly those with improvised electrics. A significant blaze was sometimes just a matter of time.

In 1973, the GLC ensured that electrical engineers were refused access to fit the Charrington Street squat with a safe supply of power. By this stage, Street Talk Pete was amongst the residents there who had devised their own methods of resisting police harassment.

Aidan Andrew Dun

There was an old World War II siren mounted on the end of the street. In theory, somebody was up there who would sound the alarm if they saw any squad cars coming. There was an infamous raid after an IRA bombing—every single front door on Charrington Street was kicked down at dawn. They were looking for bomb factories. We were very lucky we didn't get searched because we were smoking opium in those days. We were very worried about being busted, so I wrote an article about it for the squat's little street paper and so did Robin.

'Screws of the World Orgy Correspondent'

Scandle at Palace—Naked Corgi seized…
Queen Arrested for Possession 4 a.m…

Late last night the Queen and Prince Philip were both arrested and taken to West End Central Police Station, where they were charged with possession of over 15 kilos of Cannabis Resin, said to be worth over $15,000,000 on the illegal market. A separate charge was brought over the arresting Constable's allegation that she had allowed her premises to be used for the illegal smoking of dangerous drugs.

Station Officer Ivor Plant declined to make a statement, but said that a full report is on its way to God and that an enquiry is to investigate firstly how long Royalty has been in the dope business and secondly to probe into the affair of the missing Crown Jewels. He went on to say that the Palace was busted after a phone call from the Kremlin gave info that 60 Heads of State were conducting a smoke-in at the Palace Banqueting Grounds last night a couple of hours after midnight Greenwich Mean Time.

A full report is to be issued by the Gnome Office.

Farquharson's intense intellectualism and surreal sense of humour made him a popular, mercurial presence at Charrington Street. By the end of 1972 he was one of the squat's longest permanent residents.

Michael Child
His sociopolitical talking at that time I think was focused on his period of rough sleeping and the impacts that rough sleeping has on people. He and everyone around him was very conscious of his schizophrenia which he talked about a lot. Secondly, he spoke a lot about being a published author and about his book which I don't think any of us had actually read. He also spoke a lot about his homosexuality although he didn't seem to have a partner.

Aidan Andrew Dun
Of course Robin was gay but I wasn't, however he was attracted to me. He became quite angry with me because I didn't and couldn't return his feelings, and he said to me very poignantly, "The point is, I always fall in love with people who aren't gay."

I remember very clearly this melancholy statement of his that he was too old to be a hippie. He was an outsider among outsiders. We all loved him and, frankly, we were proud to have such a luminous ruin of a man living amongst us. He clearly wasn't a hippie—he didn't carry a hash pipe around with him or sit around rolling joints—but he would smoke a joint with you, with the most catastrophic conversational results. But it was captivating to sense such a strong visionary will in the midst of this fluid chaos. He wasn't a hippie and yet he was fascinated by what we were doing. His presence somehow gave us hope.

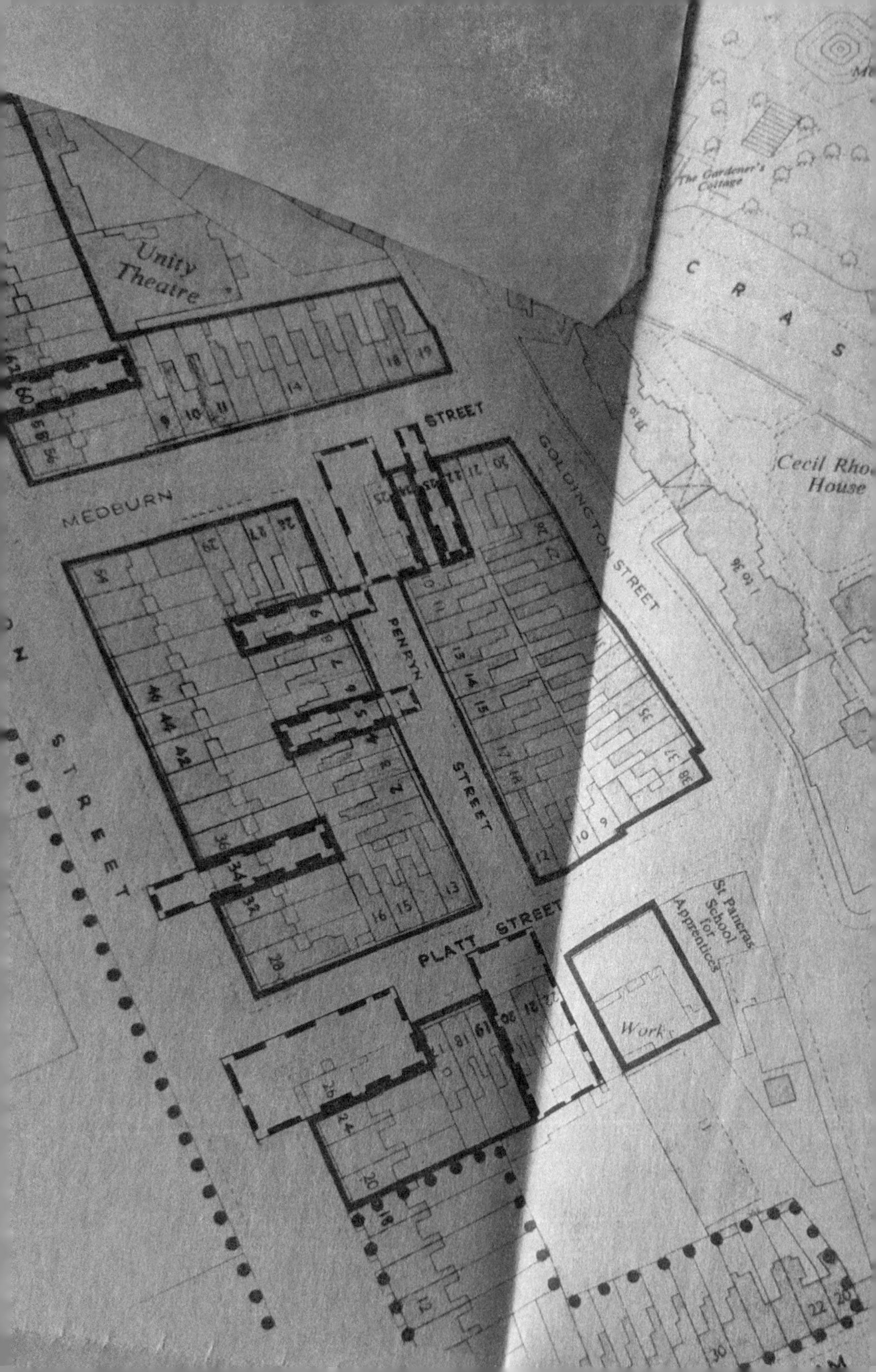

Unity Theatre
MEDBURN
STREET
GOLDINGTON STREET
PENRYN
STREET
PLATT STREET
St Pancras School for Apprentices
Works
The Gardener's Cottage

CHAPTER 22
A STRANGE THING HAPPENED TO ME LAST WEEK

Life at Charrington Street was a permanent battle—with the authorities, with the politics of communal living, and with the physical structures of the buildings themselves. Though Farquharson had long since given up on the prospect of employment, the daily demands of life at the squat made work impossible. The dole became his sole source of income.

More often than not, the council made a hard life harder. Evictions were commonplace and often without warning. Though the stated aim was to provide safer social housing, repossessed squats were commonly sold off to private developers. Despite its listed status, the building at 144 Piccadilly that had been squatted by the London Street Commune was demolished in 1972 and replaced with a luxury hotel.

Drifters and dreamers like Sid Rawle moved to remote parts of Ireland to try to bring about their vision of utopian living. In return, underpaid labourers from Ireland—commonly known as 'navvies'—were brought over to Britain to turn formerly communal squats into marketable assets. In the process, these workers inadvertently contributed to the reduction in affordable housing stock available to disenfranchised migrants like themselves.

The writer John Healy memorably dubbed this world 'the grass arena' in honour of its unique mix of combat and contingency. Healy knew of what he spoke, having spent fifteen years in and around post-war London's underclass of itinerant Irish labourers. Theirs was a world of precarity, petty crime, and police persecution. Squats were often navvies' best and only option.

More often than not, squats were demolished only for the land to be left undeveloped. The reasons were never entirely clear. The Charrington Street squat would soon be broken up, though not before Farquharson could up sticks.

Aidan Andrew Dun

At that time, I didn't think of myself as a poet: I was a ruined musician. When Robin found this out he said that he wanted me to sing this song that he'd written. He spent a lot of time on the Circle line, where it was warm and where he could write. He was translating the work of Catullus but sometimes wrote verse as well, and so he came to me with this song he wrote about the tube. It was basically a piece of doggerel, quite endearing but very stupid. Then he said that he wanted me to sing his song as a calypso. I grew up in the West Indies and so, like Robin, African culture had had a huge influence on me, but I tried to explain that I didn't really deal in calypsos and was more into Bob Marley. But he didn't really see the difference and just said, "I'm going to hire you a recording studio."

Well, maybe a week or so afterwards, I saw him in the street and he said that I never showed up at the studio. And I said, "Robin, I know you said some airy fairy stuff about hiring a recording studio, but, you know, I never heard any more about it." He just lunged at me and punched me really hard in the face, drawing blood. It was the worst blow I've ever had in my life. Some time later he said he was sorry about it and that he'd been in a manic state and couldn't control these manic moods, but we never really reconciled after that.

As part of their broader slum clearance project, the GLC had for some years been buying up parts of Platt Street. This was a typical row of terraced houses in the heart of Somers Town, just around the corner from Charrington Street. As with so many other buildings subject to compulsory purchase orders, the goal was to level a series of streets in order to construct a larger unified housing block. Around the end of January 1973, the last formal tenants moved out of 21 Platt Street and squatters soon moved in.

At the beginning of March, Farquharson joined the Platt Street squat, moving into the back room on the building's top floor. Having studied at Rhodes University and fought so desperately against racial injustice in his home country, Farquharson now once more lived in the shadow of the infamous colonialist, his eponymous tower block looming large over Platt Street.

Farquharson joined six other tenants who typified the varied mix of characters then squatting in the area. Sharing the top floor with Farquharson was a 45-year old man named Bill, about whom little was known. On the first floor was a 28-year old Scottish mechanic called William Watson who occupied the front room with his girlfriend. Watson had been working on the construction of the A12 motorway at Chelmsford when he met Michael O'Connor, a 26-year old from County Cork, Ireland. O'Connor had left school at 14 to work as a labourer. In 1971, he had been sentenced to 12 months hard labour for robbing a restaurant, after which he had moved to London to find work.

O'Connor had been living in Tufnell Park with another labourer named Charles McGinn while the pair worked on the construction of the A12. On that job they met Peter Hilditch, a largely illiterate 18-year old from County Antrim. Hilditch himself had recently moved over from Ireland, where he had been working as a gardener, groundsman, and labourer. Once the Platt Street building became available, the three men decided to move there together in order

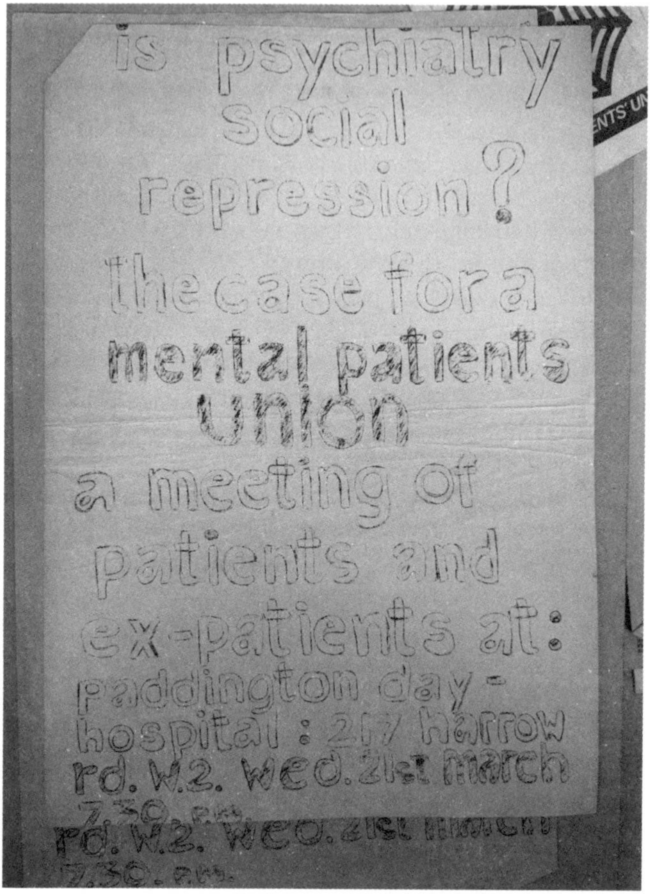

The inaugural meeting of the Mental Patients Union was incredibly well attended

to make the drive to work easier. Watson, his girlfriend, O'Connor, McGinn, and Hilditch shared the front room on the building's first floor.

On March 21st, this motley crew were joined by another housemate: none other than Street Talk Pete, who took a room on the ground floor after leaving a squat a few doors down. Pete brought with him three boxes filled with papers and a healthy supply of books. After dropping off his stuff, he headed out to try to procure a lock. On his return Pete found that his mattress had been moved back next door by parties unknown. Unsure what had occasioned this hostility, he decided to walk the streets of Somers Town until dawn and clear his head.

As Pete worked out his next move, Farquharson was back in West London in order to attend a meeting at Paddington Day Hospital. The hospital was located in an area Farquharson knew well, just a few minutes walk from his old squat on St. Stephen's Gardens, but Farquharson was not there to be institutionalised. In fact, it was an exciting time to be visiting Paddington Day. The pioneering therapeutic community had recently survived the threat of closure and after months of administrative frustrations, things were beginning to change. Patients started to take a more active organisational role in ensuring that Paddington Day was able to carry on functioning. Part of this was the organisation of a large discussion entitled 'Is Psychiatry Social Repression? The Case for a Mental Patients Union'.

The meeting had been heavily promoted in underground papers for the past few weeks. The turn-out was still remarkable: around 150 people showed up, the vast majority of whom were current or former patients, including Tommy Ritchie of SUMP, who had been discharged from hospital a few months earlier.

Liz Davies

We were absolutely stunned at the response we got. People had come down from Scotland or escaped from mental hospitals and psychiatric units and somehow managed to find their way to us. Robin was one of them. We hadn't met before — in fact, I don't think I'd even heard of him — but he was quite inspiring. Very tall, wearing a kind of suit and looking quite dignified. I think he'd been sleeping rough.

That night saw the official launch of the Mental Patients Union MPU), with Ritchie and Farquharson registered as founding members.

Farquharson then led a delegation back to Charrington Street, where he promised the use of a squatted room as an office. MPU members excitedly visited the space only to discover that the room in question lacked floorboards. Feelings were nevertheless very positive.

Brian Douieb

There was this really strong bond that we all felt at the time, a terrific sense of intimacy that meant you didn't need to meet someone more than once to feel on the same page. It was like that with Robin. His involvement with us was extremely short-lived because of what happened to him, but he immediately gained our affection because of his interest and his willingness to talk and his enthusiasm for what the MPU was planning to do. He was instantly likeable and unpretentious and didn't in any way try to insinuate himself into the organisation or into people's lives. He was just there wanting to be helpful.

Street Talk Pete returned to Platt Street as soon as it was light enough to write. Having retrieved his mattress, he began to set up his new room, installing a door and some shelves. He also hoped to improve the plumbing situation. This led to a brief argument with Hilditch, his new housemate, who thought it was pointless to call a plumber given that the house was condemned. The argument didn't get very far. Pete went back to his room, lit a small number of candles, and carried on with his writing.

Farquharson was out and about on the 22nd. He spent most of the day catching up with Peter Johnston, a friend who had designed a number of letterheads for various companies Farquharson had attempted to launch.

Peter Johnston

He seemed reasonably settled, had a commission from Jack Harwell (Data Processing) and seemed able to accept the usual couple of pounds with something like the old spirit (an addition to the state of Zembla's loan account). He smiled when I refused to 'lend' him £10 for a business venture. He left, I'm sure, with the intention of coming back.

After a little while Pete headed out for the evening, as did Farquharson, who went over to the Charrington Street commune for dinner with his friend Roni. He returned with two sleeping tablets. Watson, Hilditch, and O'Connor had headed off to the bar at Euston Station. McGinn, their other housemate, joined for a few drinks and left. The other three drank until closing time.

On the night in question, Watson claimed that he'd drunk ten pints of Guinness and the others six or seven each by the time the bar closed. The three men stumbled home, after which Watson remembered falling asleep immediately. The fog of alcohol smoothed good and bad together and made one indeterminate constant.

Watson later stated that he was awoken by O'Connor with the news that the house was on fire. As the men got dressed, O'Connor smashed the windows to let out some of the smoke. Hilditch arrived to hurry them up, and the three men rushed out of the front door. Just before midnight, a petrol attendant returning home from work saw that Platt Street was burning and called the fire brigade. Several witnesses saw O'Connor head back inside twice. Watson said that O'Connor was convinced that nobody else was home.

Apart from already being in a state of disrepair, 21 Platt Street had wooden floors, wooden windows, wooden doorframes, and a wooden staircase. The fire brigade later estimated that the blaze stripped 90% of the plaster off the ground floor, with the rest of the ground and first floors severely damaged as well. Farquharson's precious unpublished manuscripts were little more than kindling.

Roni, the friend with whom Farquharson had dined at Charrington Street, saw the flames out of her window. She rushed into the street and alerted the emergency services to her friend's presence. Entering the second floor of the house, the firemen found Farquharson lying unconscious beside his bed. His body was found on the floor, indicating that either the sleeping pills had taken effect suddenly or that Farquharson had been trying to leave the room before passing out. His body may also have been found on the floor because he had been trying to get to the window. Whether he was trying to jump or deliver one final lecture cannot be known.

An ambulance arrived and took Farquharson away just as the building's other tenants returned. Watson, O'Connor, and Hilditch headed to another squat nearby to discuss what had happened. Watson recalled O'Connor stating that the fire must have been started by the new tenant on the ground floor.

The police sergeant who attended the scene later said that he didn't believe Hilditch and O'Connor had in fact been drinking. Another policeman noticed that the back of O'Connor's right hand was slightly burned between his middle finger and thumb. It wasn't clear at what stage in the night this injury had been obtained. O'Connor declined medical assistance, though it later emerged that he did pay a visit to a hospital for the burn.

One or two details notwithstanding, the fire seemed like an open-shut accident. A police inspector who visited the scene didn't believe there to be any suspicious circumstances. He explained that the fire had probably started in the back ground floor room after an unattended flame caught ahold of some loose papers, likely the miscellaneous jottings of the newly-arrived poet. Friends in the underground press stated that a paraffin stove had been knocked over. Both scenarios were possible.

By 00:23, the fire was out. Farquharson was already being treated at the nearby University College Hospital, where he was semi-conscious and in the care of a visiting doctor.

Ping-Chung Leung

I was called for an emergency at 1am for the first time in my service. My impression of Mr. Farquharson was that of a destitute hippie. On admission his wet, burnt clothing was filthy and mud stained. I was surprised to find this hippie so desperate and miserable, so unlike the American counterparts who were stylish and powerful. I overheard that he was driven out of his illegal dwelling with suspected arson.

He tried to talk to me but never succeeded. Mr. Farquharson was in bad shape: unconscious and 40% burnt which affected his respiratory system. We all believed that he would not survive but he did after ICU treatment. He woke up the day after.

It took three days before it was deemed safe to take Farquharson off the respirator. He then began treatment for further burn management. Letters were sent to friends to reassure them of his progress. A note at the bottom of each page indicated that Farquharson was having to dictate his correspondence; he had yet to regain the use of his hands.

Robin Farquharson
A strange thing happened to me last week (on March 22). I was miraculously saved from a fire and am now in hospital and am assured of a complete recovery.

Apart from the issue with his hands, progress was good. Doctors made preparations for skin grafts.

Brian Douieb
We went to see him in the hospital and had to be gowned up because he was being kept inside this sterile plastic tent. He'd been so lively and enthusiastic so it was unbearable to see him lying in that bed like that. He couldn't talk a great deal. All he kept saying to us was, "It was very silly of me, wasn't it?" That really stuck in my head.

Liz Davies
We couldn't really see much of his face because of all the bandages and the isolation tent, but I remember Brian saying, "Well, I can still see your beard." We all laughed but there wasn't much else we could say to be honest.

Ping-Chung Leung
My morning visit found him conscious but a little confused,

> mumbling, "How could they do this to me?" I asked him to speak less because his crusting lips must be hurting him. On the next day, he recovered further but was troubled with early infection and fever. On the last day that I attended him, he said slowly, "You are not from this country. You are kind. How could they do this to me?" I refrained from further explorations which would not be good for him at this stage. He died in the evening before my morning visit.

It all happened relatively quickly. A nurse had seen that Farquharson had thrown up and was struggling to breathe. Oxygen and resuscitation efforts yielded no results and within the hour Farquharson was pronounced dead.

It was eight years to the day since the execution of his friend John Harris. Separated by what felt like a world and several lifetimes, the two friends were united by one final quirk of history, both of them having died on April Fool's Day.

Classified

Rates: 2p per word (20p minimum) Box Numbers, 5p extra. Discounts: 5% for 5 insertions, 10% for 10, and 15% for yearly contract.

Personal

THE LOVELY Robin Farquharson, manic visionary, notorious squatter and author of **Drop Out**, died from fire injuries on April 1. We are compiling an account of some of his most mind-blowing exploits. Please send your experiences of the man to Bitman magazine, c/o BIT, 146 Great Western Road, London W11.

HOW ARE THE MIGHTY FALLEN! Get well soon, oh mighty Wezzel. Get back where you belong, the Wesley back!

CALLING ALL NUDIST libertarians in Central London (later farther afield): let's strike a shattering blow for freedom and progress, and withal peace, by working joyfully together in the true libertarian spirit of mutual friendly co-operation towards the abolition of the shameful nudity taboo and the glorious advent of nudist liberation. All replies, if patently genuine, shall be gladly answered. Desmond Hunter, c/o Box 985.

NOMADIC BUSKER (male), folk, baroque, renaissance music seeks female partner. 01-855 1774.

SHOPPING FOR PEACE NEWS. Send your Co-op dividend stamps to the Accountant, Peace News, 5 Caledonian Road, London N1.

STILL CALLI
and footballe
staff have p
football tear
women so fa
Peace News.

"I RENOUN
support or
pledge signe
basis of the
for details
Sheppard H
London WC1.

TURN VEGA
environment
tion. Inform
partment L.
head, Surrey

Books '

THE COMMO
letter of the
conciliation,
Spiritual Co
Avyaktananc
charge. Plea
Vedanta Mc
Batheaston,

WANTED R
moderate pa
50p). Keep
women arou
copy: Call
Grove, Weyb

BOOKS/PAM
smith Books
SW13. 876 72

CHAPTER 23
A WREATH AND THREE TOMATOES

A few days later, members of the incipient Mental Patients Union gathered in Belsize Park to hold a wake for Farquharson. There was little time for mourning. The following day, the MPU held their first general meeting, marking the beginning of a highly successful movement. Farquharson's recent and tragic death only served to underline the urgency of their cause.

The group took a notably more aggressive approach than other previous patients' rights organisations. Where Gerald Low-Beer raised awareness of the use of psychiatry as a form of abuse abroad, the MPU made clear that the same methods were employed in the UK as a means of silencing all sorts of 'deviant' behaviour.

Brian Douieb

The view that the MPU took and to which Robin subscribed was that the whole process of labelling people as 'mentally ill' was a way of controlling so-called deviant behaviour in all its forms. So we had this sort of multi-Marxist approach which led us to try to link up with unions and other traditional left wing organisations. They didn't want to know. Like everyone else, they saw people who had been through the mental health system as incapable of having political views or making very much sense or having any kind of analysis of society of their own, but that's not how we saw things.

This Marxian understanding of mental illness led to a highly confrontational style.

MPU members soon heard that young women were being placed into asylums as a punishment for their having been forced into sex work. Working quietly but efficiently the MPU arranged to break a number of these women out. They also arranged to meet with other groups working at the intersection of reform and revolution, including one meeting in France which led to their van being searched at the border. Customs officers found a tranche of Red Army Faction leaflets the MPU had agreed to distribute in the UK. The nervous activists somehow escaped with only a warning. They returned to the UK more determined than ever to break with the psychiatric establishment.

Liz Davies
I remember very clearly this one meeting where a man, who I guess was a carer of some kind, led this other man into the room by what almost seemed to be a lead. We all turned to each other to wonder who he was and word quickly went around that it was David Cooper. It was very obvious that he was an alcoholic. All he kept on saying was "Psychiatry is dead, psychiatry is dead," over and over and over again.

In the meantime broadsheet coverage of Farquharson's death had been largely muted and brief. In part this was because the news was dominated by a surge in hostilities between Israel and the Palestinian Liberation Front. Britain hesitated to get involved. Though the *Times* dispatched a crime reporter to cover Farquharson's passing, the story of the 'Cambridge don [who] died a drop-out squatter' paled in comparison to the latest turn in the global struggles he had once tried to influence.

The *Sun* covered the fatal fire in more salacious detail. The article was entrusted to music journalist Mike Nevard, one of Murdoch's most loyal reporters, who proceeded to get just about every key fact wrong. Nevard breathlessly explained that 'a 50-year-old ex-Cambridge fellow has set Scotland Yard a mystery' by having 'dropped out so completely that detectives can find no trace of any relative who they can tell about his death.' Fittingly for a man so determined to make his name, the *Sun*'s brief article on the 'riddle' of 'Robert Farquharson' was included in the paper's showbiz section. Alongside it was a feature on Ringo Starr's burgeoning acting career.

In 1967, footage of Kensal Green Cemetery had been used in *The London Nobody Knows*. Shots of overgrown gravestones segued into the sequence of down-and-out drinkers, one of whom bore an uncanny resemblance to Farquharson. The scene was intended to make a heavy-handed point about the likely fate of those who called the street their home. Six years later the very same cemetery would now host Farquharson's cremation.

Kensal Green was in other ways a suitable final resting place for Farquharson the scholar. A large number of fellows of the Royal Society were buried there, including the pioneering mathematician Charles Babbage. Farquharson himself received no commemorative marker of any kind. His address in the crematorium's register was incorrectly listed as 'Pratt Street', his occupation simply given as 'author'.

Churchill College sent a wreath, next to which a friend placed three tomatoes; it was unclear whether they were meant to symbolise Farquharson's enduring hopes for a simpler world or a vaudevillian gesture of disdain for his former employers. Farquharson's brother Tony and his wife Janice happened to be in the UK and made up part of the small crowd of mourners. A few unknown men in trench-coats watched on as friends speculated as to their identities.

The three labourers carried on living together in a squat near the site of the fire. After a few weeks, Watson noticed O'Connor becoming oddly standoffish. On April 10th the inquest began at St

Pancras Coroner's Court. O'Connor stated that on the night of the fire, he, Hilditch, and Watson had gone out drinking—Watson was drunk, O'Connor recalled—and then returned to Platt Street and gone to sleep. O'Connor explained that he first noticed the smoke when he had gotten up to go to the bathroom. At that point he tried to force his way into the burning room on the ground floor. He couldn't gain access and so went to wake up Hilditch and Watson. In his statement to the court, Hilditch confirmed the majority of Watson's account, explaining that they had fled the burning building when they realised that they couldn't get close to the source of the fire.

Camden News reported on this routine court appearance, filing it away as part of a larger wave of local house fires.

> ***Camden News***
> South African author Dr Robin Farquharson who had written a book called "Drop Out" which was about squatters, died after fire swept through a derelict house in Platt Street, Camden, where he was squatting.
>
> At the first part of the inquest into the death of the 42-year-old doctor of mathematics, the court heard evidence from his friends which revealed that he was "a very excitable character". In his book, he described himself as a manic depressive.
>
> Nursery nurse, Miss Roni Shaw, who is squatting in Charrington Street, Camden said that Dr Farquharson did a "lot of good work in the community". He formed an organisation called BIT to help young people.
>
> Mr Michael O'Connor, one of his fellow squatters now living in Penryn Street, Camden, told the court how he ran back into the blazing house three times in an attempt to rescue the doctor.
>
> Pathologist Dr James Faccini said the cause of death was aspiration of gastric contents, bronchial pneumonia and severe burns. The inquest was adjourned until April 17.

Despite numerous errors—Farquharson was not the founder of BIT, for starters—the local coverage depicted O'Connor in a rather brave light.

After their court appearance, the former tenants of 21 Platt Street repaired to their new home. With O'Connor out and about, Hilditch suddenly turned to Watson and told him that the fire was not accidental and that it was O'Connor who had started it. Hilditch now said that after trying and failing to wake Watson up, O'Connor had lit the fire in a drunken attempt to get his friend's attention. He wanted to leave grotty Platt Street and he wanted to leave right away.

Very early in the morning after Hilditch's private confession, Watson was awoken by the sound of Hilditch and O'Connor fighting. At 2.45am, police at the nearby station in Holborn received a call from a man in distress. 'I've been to the coroner's inquest this morning on the drop out,' the man began. 'They're going to bring in an accidental verdict,' he continued, but 'the fire was started on purpose and I know who did it.' The man then broke off into mumbles.

A policeman headed over to the phone box to collect the unidentified man. On their way to the station, the man began to cry in the back of the car. When the policeman asked if he was the person who had started the fire, the man said yes.

Placed in detention, O'Connor told a different story to the half-confession Hilditch had made the night before. On the record, O'Connor explained that he and Hilditch had started the fire together in Pete's room to get back at the poet after the argument about the plumbing. The police and O'Connor returned to Somers Town and arrested Hilditch, who admitted to what he had done.

Through his tears Hilditch said that nothing but bad things had happened to him since O'Connor came into his life. The facts of the matter were that they had been drinking, Pete had been 'bossy', and one thing had led to another. In response to their new housemate's behaviour, O'Connor and Hilditch scattered his papers and his books and lit them on fire. The result was fatal.

The two men were arrested and charged with two counts of criminal damage and one count of manslaughter. The second and more minor charge of criminal damage was subsequently dropped. The suspects pled guilty to the other two charges and were sentenced at the Central Criminal Court, more commonly known as the Old Bailey. Sir Phillip Wien, the presiding judge, told O'Connor that 'any ordinary person would have regarded your conduct as quite crazy.' Wien was nevertheless relatively lenient. O'Connor was sentenced to three years imprisonment on each count to be served concurrently. With good behaviour he would serve between one and two years total. The eighteen-year old Hilditch pled guilty to the same charges. Due to his age, he was sent to borstal.

There remained several unresolved parts to what was now the official story of Farquharson's death. How could O'Connor and Hilditch not have not known that Farquharson was home? Did O'Connor refuse medical treatment in order to hide having tampered with the evidence? And why did he and Hilditch suddenly decided to come clean?

Michael Child, a fellow squatter, suspected that Farquharson was a target of violence 'most probably because he was a homosexual'. This might well have been the case. The police seemed disinterested in looking too deeply at the story and the two defendants ended up receiving what felt like particularly short sentences. The sad reality, however, is that bad verdicts can be reached without the need for any kind of conspiracy or cover-up.

Whatever stories may have swirled around Somers Town, the reasons for the trial going the way it did are likely straightforward. Given the status of the defendants—two drunk, white working class immigrants, one underage, the other with a criminal record—and the circumstances of the victim, an essentially homeless former mental patient living in one of the city's poorest neighbourhoods, there would have been little pressure to pursue lengthier and more complicated charges.

There was also the role of BOSS. If there was indeed a mark on Farquharson's name, as local rumours had it, then the Platt

Street fire served its purpose well: Farquharson was gone and so was most of the evidence. A small amount of press coverage was to be expected, but there was very little here to engender any kind of sustained scrutiny. Farquharson had been a persistent thorn in the side of the South African government and was now an easy target. But by the time of his death he was surely low down on any list of potential international threats to apartheid. In truth, by 1973 BOSS had no need to kill him. Nor was there any suggestion that the trial had been anything other than a run-of-the-mill affair—the exact sort of case the authorities were happy to conclude quietly and quickly.

The general contours of the official story remain plausible, even if some details have been lost to fire, booze, and time. More telling, though, is the fact that murder was not one of the charges faced by Hilditch and O'Connor, nor was it probably ever even considered to be a charge. In material terms, the wanton destruction of GLC property was simply the more important offence.

***Peace News*, classified advert**

The lovely Robin Farquharson, manic visionary, notorious squatter and author of *Drop Out*, died from fire injuries on April 1. We are compiling an account of some of his most mind-blowing exploits. Please send your experiences of the man to *Bitman* magazine, % BIT, 146 Great Western Road, London W11.

Matthew Hilton

I never saw him after Horton, and I only found out about his death when, for whatever reason, I was thinking, "I wonder what happened to that guy I once..." By then I was working in the fire brigade in Yorkshire, ironically. It didn't surprise me. There were people who might have wanted to wreak their revenge and there was the accident strewn nature of that lifestyle. I mean, it absolutely fitted.

Aidan Andrew Dun

Robin wasn't completely convinced by any means of the beneficence of acid. At the same time, he was very aware that quite a number of establishment figures were worried that he might become another Timothy Leary figure. So when it happened, the whole street was rocked by Robin's death, and like everybody else, I was convinced that he had been murdered, and not by the Irish labourers. I felt very certain that they had been set up. Life in those days was so turbulent and mercurial that I never even heard about a trial, but the whole thing left a bad taste in my mouth.

Michael Child

There is a niggling feeling that there was something that didn't fit about Robin, perhaps to do with him appearing more sane than he claimed to be—almost as though he had entered a plea of diminished responsibility against the process of having to be alive.

Shelley Lee

I don't know if Robin was a seer or a mystic. I cannot think of him as lovely. To my eye he was one of the saddest, most distorted of human beings. He had lost all sense of unity between body and mind until finally he was a mass of guts and flesh his body would toss about like it was shit. He was incapable of looking people directly in the eye. He had not one ounce of harmony or peace on any occasion I watched or was near him. Certainly his nights were not filled with beatific visions. Robin was a very sick and destroyed man. I cannot bear that people make him into a hero of a counter culture. I can only feel thankful that for him the trip is over.

Hoping to put an end to the speculation, Farquharson's mother made her first and only statement on the death of her son. Normally an intensely private woman, she decided to grant an interview to a reporter from South Africa's *Sunday Times*, the country's most widely read weekly newspaper.

Enid Farquharson

Robin was a tragically misunderstood personality whose character has been maligned in reports about his unconventional style of life. To emphasise this facet of what one might call his revolt against mediocrity and conformity to the dictates of hypocritical social conventions, without also acknowledging his intellectual brilliance and academic achievements, is so unfair that I feel I must put the record straight.

ROBIN

ScrEws of thE WorLd

latest lies.

Scandle at Palace–Naked Corgi seized...

BUCKINGHAM PALACE BUSTED!

QUEEN ARRESTED FOR POSSESSION 4 a.m...

by Robin Farquharson, Screws of the World Orgy Correspondent

Late last night the Queen and Prince Philip were both arrested and taken to West End Central Police Station, where they were charged with possession of over 15 Kilos of Cannabis Resin, said to be worth over $15.000.000 on the illegal market. A seperate charge was brought over the arresting Constable's allegation that she had allowed her premises to be used for the illegal smoking of dangerous drugs.

Station Officer Ivor Plant declined to make a statement, but said that a full report is on its way to God and that an enquiry is to investigate firstly how long Royalty has been in the dope business and seconly to probe into the affair of the missing Crown Jewels. He went on to say that the Palace was busted after a phone call from the Kremlin gave info that 69 Heads of State were conducting a Smoke in at the Palace Banqueting Grounds last night a couple of hours after midnight Greenwich Mean Time.

A full report is to be issued by the Gnome Office.

Robin (photo G.Winter)

RIP OFF PRICE 25 p HELP BIT SURVIVE

FREE 24-HOUR-A-DAY, 7-DAY-AWEEK

BIT INFORMATION & HELP SERVICE

HAS NOW MOVED TWICE IN THE LAST TWO MONTHS. OUR NEW ADDRESS: FOR THE NEXT THREE YEARS IS A COUPLE OF HOUSES DOWN AT:

146 GREAT WESTERN ROAD

LONDON W.11.

'EX-BITMAN ROBIN' 8/5/

this special issue of BITM
-besides all the regular ne
and info- recounts some o
the more inspired exploits
the life of Robin Farquhar
ex-BIT worker, notorious
squatter, manic visionary
author of 'Drop Out' and 'I

AFTERLIVES AND CONCLUSIONS

In July 1973, a philosopher named Allan Gibbard published a mathematical proof of Farquharson's conjecture regarding the dictatorial effects of voting. The economist Mark Satterthwaite later developed a further proof of Farquharson's theory. As Satterthwaite recalled, his encounter with 'Farquharson's beautiful little book catalyzed my thinking'. The resulting Gibbard–Satterthwaite theorem is now seen as a watershed moment in the development of social choice theory.

A few months after Farquharson's death the GLC's tactic of compulsory purchase orders hit another roadblock. A collective of squatters moved into a series of condemned Victorian buildings just off the Euston Road on Tolmers Square. The squatters counted George Price amongst their number. The resultant land rights battle became one of the most high-profile cases of the decade.

Squatters also occupied Centre Point tower in order to protest at the building's ongoing empty status. The block finally obtained its first official tenants in 1975, some nine years after construction had been completed. The local council approved a new scheme for Tolmers Square soon after, forcing developers to relinquish the site. George Price didn't live to see the end of the occupation, having died by suicide a few months earlier. The Situationists Housing Association also ceased to operate around this time. At its height the organisation oversaw 80 properties across London.

By 1975, the squat Farquharson began on Elgin Avenue had grown into an entire row of buildings. Together with the adjacent Walterton Road squat they housed around 250 people and formed a powerful front in the campaign for squatters' rights. The GLC insisted that the buildings were earmarked for redevelopment but refused residents the right to be rehoused. A large wave of publicity followed, fuelled by the music of the 101ers, a pub rock group named for the address of their Walterton Road squat. After two years of battles, the council finally caved.

Though its legacy would be disputed, the Elgin Avenue case was a landmark moment in the history of British squatting. Soon afterwards key BIT worker Nicholas Albery helped to launch the Free and Independent Republic of Frestonia, a set of squats and community buildings on nearby Freston Road which claimed to have seceded from the rest of the UK. In the interim, the frontman of the 101ers joined a group called the Clash, changed his name to Joe Strummer, and became an icon of rebellion. The spokesman for the Elgin Avenue squatters, an astrophysicist named Piers Corbyn, would later pursue the same status by other means.

Michael Barnett, the founder of People, Not Psychiatry, became a devoted follower of the Indian mystic Osho. Barnett later became known as a spiritual leader under the name Swami

Anand Somendra. Jenny James, Farquharson's rival in the PNP house, moved to County Donegal, where she established the Atlantis Commune as a continuation of PNP's mission. Atlantis eventually settled in a rural part of Columbia, where it continues to this day.

John Sinclair was freed from prison in late 1971 in part due to the publicity generated by a campaign song written by John Lennon. The MC5 disbanded the following year, having tried and failed to establish themselves on the UK scene. In the summer of 1972 Pun Plamondon's conviction was overturned. The Supreme Court held that the Fourth Amendment protected private citizens from warrantless wiretaps, even when their private communications were dedicated to overturning the government. Though local White Panther factions continued for some time, the original party eventually fizzled out.

In August 1972, Michael X's commune in Trinidad burned down. Police discovered two dead bodies buried in the grounds of the commune: a cousin of Michael's named Joe Skerritt and Gail Benson, the daughter of a Conservative MP. Evidence suggested that Skerritt's throat had been slit and that Benson had been attacked before being buried alive. Michael was sentenced to death. Despite a large campaign organised by friends in alternative London, Michael was hanged in 1975.

Inspired by the White Panthers' activities at the Isle of Wight, Sid Rawle and Nicholas Albery helped to spearhead the rise of the free festival movement. After the Windsor free festival was attacked by police in 1974, Rawle and his friends moved on to stage decentralised, admission-free events at Stonehenge. These ultimately led to the development of the long-running Glastonbury Festival. A corporate behemoth in New Age clothes, Glastonbury continues to serve as a stark reminder of Mick Farren's warnings surrounding the corporatisation of rock.

Between 1972 and 1973, *Frendz*, *OZ*, and *International Times* all shut down. BIT continued to operate until the end of the decade. *Spare Rib* carried on for another twenty years. Rosie Boycott, the magazine's co-founder, later became the first woman to edit a Fleet Street daily newspaper. She was eventually made Baroness Boycott on her nomination to the House of Lords.

The London Lesbian and Gay Switchboard opened in the Housmans building just under a year after Farquharson's death. Drawing on the tradition established by BIT, Switchboard (as it later became known) continues to provide confidential and free advice to this day.

Within a year of its founding the Mental Patients Union had over 1,000 members. It established a series of communal homes, the first of which opened in Hackney a few months after Farquharson's death. In memory of their fallen comrade the MPU referred to the building as Robin Farquharson House. It lasted for three years and played a major role in establishing what became known as the psychiatric survivors' movement.

In 1983, the government of Margaret Thatcher made good on Enoch Powell's recommendation to shut down the Victorian asylum system. The scheme was dubbed 'care in the community', leading to the closure of dozens of mental hospitals. Most were left more or less to rot, including Horton Hospital. Parts of Horton have since been redeveloped into housing, a sensible if slightly creepy fate for future residents of the once-great asylum. In Scotland both Hartwood Hospital and Gartloch Hospital were also abandoned. In 2022, parts of Gartloch served as a filming location for the poorly-received Robert Pattinson film *The Batman*. The abandoned hospital stood in for the orphanage said to have housed the young Bruce Wayne.

Having missed every Olympics since SAN-ROC's intervention in 1964, a non-segregated South Africa competed at the games for the first time in 1992. In 2007, Dennis Brutus was nominated for the South African Sports Hall of Fame. He refused the award.

After a long and fraught consultation, Cecil Rhodes House was renamed Park View House in 2021. In 2023, plans were announced for the construction of a nearby museum dedicated to the history of the British anti-apartheid movement, the first such public institution of its kind.

The area around Lambeth Walk has been transformed since the time of Farquharson's anti-university. The Lambeth Ragged School has been repurposed as Beaconsfield Gallery, a contemporary art space. A few buildings over, Mara's Scene Painting Shop was reopened in 2015 as Damien Hirst's Newport Street Gallery. The building on Newport Street which Farquharson ran as his anti-university has since been knocked down.

21 Platt Street and most of the neighbouring buildings were levelled in the wake of the fire in 1973. They have since been replaced with a low-rise housing estate.

The extent of surviving archival material relating to Farquharson is unknown. The vast majority of Churchill College's additional files on their former star academic are closed to the public on the grounds that they contain distressing material.

On the completion of his doctorate Farquharson presented a copy of his thesis to the Bodleian, the main library of the University of Oxford. This left Farquharson with the only other copy, which was normally retained by the author himself. For reasons unknown, Farquharson gave this final copy of his thesis to the poet Anthony Howell.

It wasn't an obvious prize asset. Both the thesis and the book it became were incomprehensible to Howell, who saw Farquharson's gift as something of a burden. Nevertheless, by the time I examined it, Howell had kept ahold of the volume for over half a century, torn between resentment and reverence. As Farquharson had once pressed this bequest into Howell's hands, so Howell now pressed it into mine.

I wasn't entirely sure whether I warranted such a gift or really wanted the responsibility of looking after it. If nothing else, the thesis was in terrible condition, having been stored in a shed on Howell's mother's farm for the best part of the 1970s. Dried mud covered the top third of the cloth cover, which was otherwise faded and fraying. The initial thrill of seeing Farquharson's signature on the inside flap was tempered by the presence of an ownership slip bearing the name of an Oxford college library. Farquharson had evidently either decided against donating this spare copy or had done so and simply stolen it back. I then found tucked inside the volume's cover a note addressed to Farquharson from a disgruntled creditor. It had first been mailed to Farquharson's Cambridge college and then forwarded to ward 5, Horton Hospital.

The content of the thesis itself was hardly more promising. The pages were flaking and the type had long since faded—all, that was, except for the illustrations. Farquharson had drawn up grid after grid of lines and circles in a variety of coloured pencils in order to represent his selection of electoral possibilities. Running my finger across the page I could feel the indent of the author's lead pushing through the paper. It wasn't hard to sense the urgency with which these marks had been made some fifty years earlier. Howell's disinterest meant the thesis had seldom if ever been consulted. A lack of exposure to light had kept the colours as vibrant as the day they were drawn.

Farquharson drifted from scene to scheme, finding solutions and creating problems. Along the way he developed a network that stretched from the most determined enemies of apartheid to the founding fathers of computer science. In hindsight, it seems obvious that this trip without a ticket would come to an abrupt end. His archives destroyed and dispersed, his friends departed or ambivalent, telling the story of Farquharson's life is no more possible now than it was in 1973. The unanswered letter, the scrawled signature, the coloured pencils, the mud, the theft, the gift, the fantasies, the revelations—each of these are little more than a fragile and minor clue of a world just as out of reach to us as it was to him.

MUSIC MAKERS
... THE DREAMERS OF DREAMS
OZ
LOVE
BROWN POWER
UNC
DON PAY TAX
ONE WORLD OR.... NONE
een the Bird of Paradise, she has spread herself
, and I shall never be the same again.
nothing to be afraid of. Nothing.
I am trying to grasp is the me that is trying to
we are all learning to become VIETCONG
A man must make his move before his move is made
CANNABIS
NT REVOLVE...EVOLVE
NG IS REVEALED
SMILE
GUER WARFA THE M
WE ARE GIVE US NOT D
eternity
why
HO!
DROP OUT.
IF I COULD TURN YOU ON..... IF I COULD DRIVE YOU OUT OF YOUR WRETCHED MIND IF I could TELL you
i would let
?

VOICES

Richard Adams Influential graphic artist and later designer of *Gay News*

Nicholas Albery BIT organiser, founder of Frestonia, and 'social inventor'

Michael Barnett Founder of People, Not Psychiatry, later known as Swami Anand Somendra

Jonathan Bennett One of Farquharson's peers at Oxford, later a celebrated philosopher

Rosie Boycott *Frendz* journalist and *Spare Rib* co-founder, later nominated for a life peerage

R. B. Braithwaite Philosopher who served as one of Farquharson's doctoral examiners

Dennis Brutus Poet, anti-apartheid activist, and founder of SAN-ROC

Jerome Burne *Frendz* journalist

David Butler Psephologist

Michael Child Squatter and bookseller

Frater Choronzon Chaos magician, also known as Charles Brewster

Frank Cioffi One of Farquharson's peers at Oxford, later recognised as an expert on Freud

Liz Davies Mental Patients Union co-founder

M. W. Dick Philosopher who served as one of Farquharson's doctoral examiners, later known for being the father of Cressida Dick, the first female and homosexual head of the Metropolitan Police

Brian Douieb Mental Patients Union co-founder

Michael Dummett Logician, tarot expert, and collaborator of Farquharson's

Aiden Andrew Dun Poet and Charrington Street squatter

Robin Elliott Friend of Nick South

Mick Farren Underground organiser and British White Panther Party leader

Enid Farquharson Mother of Robin Farquharson

George Firsoff Resident of 101 St. Stephen's Gardens

Ray Foulk Co-founder of the Isle of Wight Festival

Frank Hahn Economist and prominent critic of Margaret Thatcher's economic policies

John Haldane Philosopher and papal advisor

John Hassan Glasgow White Panther

Woody Haut Writer

Matthew Hilton Artist and director of *Leila the Hijacker*

Anthony Howell Poet

Jenny James People, Not Psychiatry housemate, later known as the founder of the Atlantis Commune

Peter Johnston Graphic designer

Adam Kisch Lyricist of 'Leila the Hijacker', later a well-known roller skater and fixture of Portobello Road

R. D. Laing Psychiatrist and writer

Richard Lancaster BIT worker

Shelley Lee Squatter

Stephen Lee *International Times* ad manager and BIT worker

Guy Legge Painter and patient at Horton Hospital

Ping-Chung Leung Honorary Senior Registrar, Plastic Surgery Department, University College Hospital

Colin Leys Voltaire Society member, later a political economist and co-founder of the Centre for Health and the Public Interest

Alan Marcuson Journalist and oriental carpet dealer

Iain McLean Historian of social choice theory

Ved Mehta Oxford student in the late 1950s, later known for his memoir, *Continents of Exile*

Barry Miles Co-founder of the Indica Gallery and *International Times*, later a well-known biographer

Paul Minns Member of Third Ear Band, an influential improv band in alternative London

James Mitchell One of Farquharson's peers at Oxford

Daniel Morgan Patient at Horton Hospital in the 1960s

John 'Nosher' Neal Dealer and UFOlogist

Anatol Rapoport Mathematical psychologist

Andrew Rigby Peace researcher and author of *Communes in Britain*

Andy Roberts Mental Patients Union co-founder

John Sinclair White Panther Party founder

Phillip Tobias Paleoanthropologist and NUSAS president (1948-1951)

Randolph Vigne Anti-apartheid activist and founder of the African Resistance Movement

Michael Weigall Voltaire Society co-founder, later a filmmaker

Ernie Wentzel Lawyer and NUSAS president (1955-1957)

Gordon Winter Journalist and BOSS informant

Marilyn Weiss Baines Collaborator and wife of Peter Baines

WHITE PANTHER PARTY UK

ACKNOWLEDGMENTS

A number of archives were essential in piecing together Farquharson's varied institutional lives. In London, my thanks go to the archivists at the Bishopsgate Institute, the British Artists' Film and Video Study Collection at Central Saint Martins, the British Library, the London Metropolitan Archives, and Special Collections at the LSE Library. In Oxford: Brasenose College, the Churchill Archives Centre, Merton College, Nuffield College, the Queen's College, and the Oxford University Archives at the Bodleian Libraries. I also drew on material kept at the National Archives, the Penguin Random House Archives at the Special Collections of the University of Bristol Library, and the R. D. Laing Collection at Archives & Special Collections of the University of Glasgow, the latter thanks to the research assistance of Catriona Perry.

A number of archives outside of the UK were also important. In the USA: the Beinecke Rare Book and Manuscript Library, the John Von Neumann and Klára Dán Von Neumann Papers, Manuscript Division, Library of Congress, the Ruth and Marvin Sackner Archive of Concrete and Visual Poetry at the University of Iowa, and the Lilly Library, Indiana University, Bloomington, Indiana. In Canada: the Bertrand Russell Archives at McMaster University. In South Africa: the Alan Paton Centre and Struggle Archives at the University of KwaZulu-Natal and, thanks to the research assistance of Laurence Stewart, the Historical Papers Research Archive at the Library of the University of the Witwatersrand. My thanks go to the archivists at each of these institutions for their help in accessing materials.

The following interviewees and correspondents kindly replied to my queries with generosity and openness: Susan Ardill, Robert Aumann, Gerard Bellaart, the late Jonathan Bennett, Joe Boyd, Jerome Burne, Michael Child, Phil Cohen, Caroline Coon, Liz Davies, Stanislav Demidjuk, Brian Douieb, Aidan Andrew Dun, Robin Elliott, Damien Enright, Tom Fawthrop, Stuart Feather, Ray Foulk, Jean Jaskold Gabszewicz, Allan Gibbard, Jonathon Green, Peter Hain, John Handelsman, John Hassan, Woody Haut, Jeremy Helm, Lesley Hilton, Matthew Hilton, Brian Hinton, Mike Holt, Anthony Howell, Russell Hunter, Jenny James, Ronnie Kasrils, Ken Keable, Adam Kisch, Jean-Jacques Lebel, Stephen Lee, Guy Legge, Ping-Chung Leung, Colin Leys, John Lifton, Pearce Marchbank, Alan Marcuson, Iain McLean, Barry Miles, Charles Shaar Murray, John 'Nosher' Neal, Glenys Parry, Nettie Pollard, Leon Redler, Andrew Rigby, Janine Rogalski, Marsha Rowe, Paul Rudolph, Craig Sams, Mark Satterthwaite, Effie Schultz, Amartya Sen, John Sinclair, Leni Sinclair, Nick South, Josefine Speyer, Peter Tatchell, John Tiberi, Lynne Tillman, Michelene Wandor, Nigel Waymouth, John Weymark, Esther Whitby, David Wills, Robert Wilson (Stanford), Robert Wilson (Wisconsin-Madison), Antony Wood, Emily Young, and Richard Zeckhauser. Thank you each for helping me to understand Farquharson's world and your place in it.

My thanks also go to Richard Adams, Rob Chapman, David Curtis, Gareth Evans, William Fowler, Mark Gallagher, Tom Gill, Mike Goldmark, Paul Gorman, Stewart Home, Juliet Mitchell, Brian Patten, Victor Rees, Luke Roberts, Iain Sinclair, Fabian Tompsett, Martin Village, and Ken Worpole each of whom offered valuable pointers, mediation, and advice during the process of assembling this text. Esther Leslie and the People's Museum Somers Town provided a small but powerful reminder of the strength of feeling held by residents of a remarkable corner of the city.

Phil Baker offered a full and fulsome edit of an early draft. His advice was clear, funny, and basically entirely correct. Any shortcomings of analysis are mine and mine alone. Clara Vlessing offered feedback on a full draft much later in the day, for which I am very thankful. Dimity Torbett kindly provided unpublished material relating to Farquharson's time in the Voltaire Society. Iain McLean offered illuminating feedback on passages relating to Farquharson's academic research. My father Murray helped me to translate some important legal documents into English. My thanks to him and my mother Lesley for their love, care, and *seykhl.*

The Strange Attractor HQ seldom bore any resemblance to the Pompeian brothel maintained by Anthony Blond, at least not when I visited. What it lacked in debauchery it made up for in extreme proximity to my flat. This good fortune probably suited me more than it did Mark and Jamie, who were nevertheless as tolerant and patient a pair of publishers as one could hope for. My thanks go to them for their support throughout this project.

A special acknowledgement is owed to the writer Adam Steiner, who worked for many years to produce his own biography of Farquharson. Adam managed to speak with several important figures in Farquharson's life before they passed away, including Dennis Brutus, David Butler, Michael Dummett, Mick Farren, and Frank Hahn. Though Adam's book didn't come to fruition, his decision to share his research with me came at a crucial stage in my project and provided several important early leads. I hope to have vindicated Adam's generosity and remain very thankful for his support.

My greatest thanks are to Aleph and to Bobby. This book is dedicated to them with love.

— M. Syd Rosen, May 2025

JOB WITH travel and good bread wanted for Tony (20) phone 656 2240 (Croydon) after six or at weekends

PERSONAL

PERSONALIZE your L.P.'s. Custom record labels from 50p a pair. SAE for details. Rod, 3 Grosvenor Street, Eland, Yorks.

YOUR Manchester day and night male escort low charges. BOX 125/4

WE ARE two heads with a baby girl, cats, motorcycle combination, a pottery and gardening gear looking for a country scene with others sharing the hustles and good things. Any ideas? Write or call (weekdays) Jackie, Houseboat Ellen Gordon, Hedgecocks Yard, North Street, Maldon, Essex.

I AM A likeable, attractive, well-heeled, 24 year old spare time poet, who has recently terminated a 2 year relationship with girl friend. I seek a sincere female friend, living on Merseyside, who would be interested in sharing some of my hectic life. Age immaterial. Possibility of also being able to make pots of money in spare time by assisting me in enterprising new venture in near future. My interests at present include, poetry, theatre, travelling, music, booze and orgies (really. I am invited to many) I am, however, extremely adaptable and can adjust to other people's interests. If interested, reply and I will meet you to discuss further. BOX 125/5

YOUNG Christian and gay. Find it a problem. For support contact Don BOX 125/6

YOUNG gay good looking student or similar wanted for genuine relationship Photo and details please. BOX 125/7

FEMALES—children—men. Wanted £2—£8 per hour for TV/photo/film advertising No previous experience necessary. Tel 764 7946

MASSAGE taught by qualified physical therapists. Six individual 1½ hour lessons only £24. £20—£30 per week can be earned part time once you have this new skill at your fingertips. Please write to "Masseur", The Dance Centre, 12 Floral Street, WC2 giving telephone number.

PEACEFUL man, 26, wants uncomplicated relationship with woman, 30's, own flat. BOX 125/8

VERY INEXPERIENCED gay (22) seeks friends. All letters definitely answered BOX 125/9

DYLAN, Beatles, Stones tapes. SAE BOX 125/10

HEADS needed to start up Jewish Arts Lab. Any Thursday, 23 Hand Court, Holborn, WC1 or contact Val 226 9804

STUDIO PRINTS adult classical nude photographs, SAE for lists. BOX 125/11

YOUNG MAN wishes to meet youth as penfriend. Share companionship, weekends, etc. Hampshire. Write with photograph please. Richard. BOX 125/12

SLIM YOUNG man offers free continental jet holiday to slim goodlooking boy. Also seeks males under 24 (over 18) for friendship, especially those interested sunbathing, naturism, camping. Write fully. Photo appreciated—returned. All replies answered BOX 125/13

NOTES

The majority of this book's standalone quotations come from either new interviews undertaken over the course of the research process or from archival documents. A handful of standalone quotations draw from previously published materials. On occasion, these have been corrected for spelling or synthesised with minimal edits to maintain clarity. Full references to these and other sources are listed below. This section also points towards relevant scholarly literature where possible for those who wish to delve further into Farquharson's life and world.

INTRODUCTION — A STITCH IN TIME DISTORTS ETERNITY

'It would eventually be established': Mike Nevard (06/04/1973), 'Riddle of the dropout doctor', the *Sun*, p. 9

'The victim's distinctive name': Robin Farquharson, diplomat (1925-2008); Robin Farquharson, photographer (1944-), and Robert Farquharson (b. Robin de la Condamine, 1877-1966)

'Wandering around King's Cross': Iain Sinclair (1997), *Lights Out for the Territory*, Penguin, pp. 157-158

'But Sinclair's 250 words': For example, at the time of his death, Farquharson lived with seven people, not just the two hard-drinking labourers reported by Sinclair

'Short bursts of manic Morse code': Kenneth Allsop (25/10/1968), 'High low', the *Spectator*, p. 22

'As he wrote in *Drop Out!*': Robin Farquharson (1968), *Drop Out!*, Anthony Blond, p. 58

'The anti-apartheid campaigner Dennis Brutus': Dennis Brutus (2006), 'I Speak Their Wordless Woe' in Judith Lütge Coullie, Stephan Meyer, Thengani Ngwenya, and Thomas Olver eds., *Selves in Question: Interviews on Southern African Auto/biography*, University of Hawai'i Press, p. 156

'Friends from London's alternative scenes': The South Africa-born psychologist Andrew Colman is amongst the only scholars of game theory to be more than passingly familiar with the contents of *Drop Out!*, see Andrew Colman (1982), *Game Theory and Experimental Games: The Study of Strategic Interaction*, Pergamon, p. 215, n. The economist Amartya Sen likewise recognised the role of Farquharson's years in alternative London and confirmed in an email to the author that he knew Farquharson personally, see Amartya Sen (December 1971), 'Review of *Theory of Voting*', the *Economic Journal*, vol. 81, no. 324, pp. 1024-1026

'As the students-turned-militants': John Kifner (25/05/1970), 'A Radical 'Declaration' Warns Of an Attack by Weathermen', the *New York Times*, p. 27

'The freak scene presented': For an entertaining analysis of the freak scene by a commentator happy to admit his own bewilderment at the term's development, see Leslie Fiedler (1978), *Freaks: Myths and Images of the Secret Self*, Penguin, pp. 300-319

Chapter i — Merging into the Landscape

'As Farquharson later recalled': Robin Farquharson (1968), *Drop Out!*, p. 57

'Reginald, his father': Association of Cricket Statisticians and Historians, 'Reginald Farquharson', stats.acscricket.com/Archive/Players/2/2959/2959.html [accessed 01/10/2024]

'Deputy prime minister Jan Hofmeyr': Robin Farquharson to Alan Paton (03/03/1965), PC1/1/7-Hofmeyr, Alan Paton Centre & Struggle Archives, University of KwaZulu-Natal Pietermaritzburg; Alan Paton (1964), *Hofmeyr*, Oxford University Press, p. 483, p. 517

'The family's elevated status': 'Private and confidential/CC/6/65', CCAC/110/21, Churchill Archives Centre, Churchill College, Cambridge; Peter Johnston quoted in *Ex-Bitman Robin* (May 1973), no. 6, p. 7

'From this rather proper': Farquharson R R student file, Brasenose College Archives, Oxford; *The British Esperantist* (May/June 1948), p. 164

'As recalled by the novelist Wilbur Smith': Wilbur Smith (c. 2018), 'Meet Wilbur', www.wilbursmithbooks.com/meet-wilbur [accessed 01/10/2024]

'What distinguished it': Ibid.

'Appropriately, Farquharson's classes': 'B.E.A. Examination Success', the *British Esperantist* (May to June 1948), p. 164

'He also obtained his pilot's license': Nuffield interviewer, FA10/1/15, Oxford University Archives

'Rhodes was a small but prestigious university': John Darwin (2001), 'The Rhodes Trust in the Age of Empire' in Anthony Kenny ed., *The History of the Rhodes Trust: 1902-1999*, Oxford University Press, p. 496

'My personal association with him': Phillip Tobias (31/03/1950), untitled letter, Farquharson R R student file, Brasenose College Archives

'He was more than a brilliantly clever man': Ernie Wentzel quoted in *Rand Daily Mail* (07/04/1973), 'Exiled SA academic dies in UK', p. 3

'Reginald actively pursued': Reginald A. Farquharson to Brasenose admissions tutor (24/04/1950), Farquharson R R student file, Brasenose College Archives

'Oxford afforded Farquharson a number of freedoms': Huw Lemmey and Ben Miller (2022), *Bad Gays: A Homosexual History*, Verso, p. 276

'As I explained initially': Robin Farquharson (21/10/1952), travel report prepared for college, Farquharson R R student file, Brasenose College Archives

'The Voltaire Society had all the trappings': Neil Chenoweth (2002), *Virtual Murdoch*, Vintage, pp. 17-19

'The members prided themselves': Ved Mehta (1993), *Up at Oxford*, WW Norton, p. 196

'Its motto was': John Haldane (June 2019), 'Anscombe: Life, Action and Ethics in Context', *Philosophical News*, no. 18, pp. 71-72

'Every Oxford society needed': Bertrand Russell Archives, McMaster University Library; *Cherwell* (27/01/1953), 'Voltaire goes to Mahomet', p. 1; *Cherwell* (17/02/1953), 'Epigrams from Russell', p. 1; *Cherwell* (05/05/1953), 'Profile: Robin Farquharson', p. 2; John Searle (2003) in Gustavo Faigenbaum ed., *Conversations with John Searle*, LibrosEnRed, pp. 28-29

'It's very hard to say': James Mitchell quoted in Neil Chenoweth (2001), *Virtual Murdoch*, p. 15

'Both of them were Commonwealth': Michael Weigall quoted in correspondence with Dimity Torbett, privately held

'Robin Farquharson's aim in life': *Cherwell* (05/05/1953), 'Profile: Robin Farquharson', p. 2

CHAPTER 2 — A PHONE CALL FROM GOD

'Most accounts locate the origins of modern electoral theory': Jeffrey Sworowski (1995), 'Condorcet's education: haunted by the ghost of Rousseau', *International Journal of Lifelong Education*, vol. 14, no. 4, pp. 320-330

'The solution proposed by Condorcet': Historians of social choice now recognise the thirteenth century polymath Ramon Llull as having solved Condorcet's Paradox several centuries earlier than Condorcet himself.

'Dodgson began to focus his attentions': Iain McLean (2019), 'Voting', *The Mathematical World of Charles L. Dodgson (Lewis Carroll)*, Robin Wilson and Amirouche Moktefi eds., Oxford University Press, pp. 124-125, p. 139; Iain McLean and Arnold B. Urken eds. (1995), *Classics of Social Choice*, University of Michigan Press, p. 280, n1. In 1984, an original copy of *A Discussion* was donated to Christ Church by Robert Vernon Harcourt, the second cousin of one of Dodgson's friends.

'Instead, more parochially': Duncan Black (1958), *The Theory of Committees and Elections*, Cambridge University Press, pp. 198-200. Black goes as far as to link Dodgson's electoral work with his other obsession: Alice Liddell, the daughter of the dean of Christ Church. See also Duncan Black (February 1953), 'Discovery of Lewis Carroll Documents', *Notes and Queries*, pp. 77-79

'As one mathematical historian notes': Iain McLean (2019), 'Voting', p. 139

'Wartime research into military strategy': Max A. Woodbury (1971), 'The Analyst's Bookshelf', *Operations Research*, vol. 19, no. 2, p. 551

'Then, having corresponded with Duncan Black': Michael Dummett (2005), 'The work and life of Robin Farquharson', *Social Choice and Welfare*, vol. 25, nos. 2/3, pp. 475-476; Iain McLean, Alistair McMillan, and Burt L. Monroe (1995), 'Duncan Black and Lewis Carroll', *Journal of Theoretical Politics*, vol. 7, no. 2, p. 112; Iain McLean and Arnold B. Urken eds. (1995), *Classics of Social Choice*, University of Michigan Press, p. 280, n1

'As a friend wrote to Russell': Robert Shackleton to Bertrand Russell (08/11/1955), Bertrand Russell Archives, McMaster

'V. able, should get 1': Nuffield interviewer #1, FA10/1/15, Oxford University Archives

'Blue suit. Tall': Nuffield interviewer #2, ibid.

'As Farquharson later stated': Robin Farquharson (September 1961), 'Review of *Elections in Developing Countries*', *The South African Journal of Economics*, vol. 29, no. 3, p. 227

'As the political scientist William Riker put it': William H. Riker (1992), 'The Entry of Game Theory into Political Science' in E. Roy Weintraub ed., *Toward a History of Game Theory*, Duke University Press, pp. 214-215

'In the words of Howard Marks': Howard Marks (1996), *Mr. Nice*, Secker & Warburg, p. 59

'It struck him that the outcome': Michael Dummett (2005), 'The work and life of Robin Farquharson', p. 475

'He is nervous in manner': anonymous Cambridge referee (25/05/1958), OM354, Queen's College Archives, Oxford

'He was light in texture': Jonathan Bennett, email to author

'Leary, Alpert, and other public scientists': Leary famously told *Playboy* that LSD was a 'specific cure for homosexuality', *Playboy* (September 1966), Vol. 13, No. 9, p. 95, pp. 97-98, p. 102, p. 104, p. 106, p. 108, p. 112, p. 114, pp. 250-251, pp. 254-256. Alpert, meanwhile, lived much of his life as a closeted gay man.

'The result was a mammoth': Michael Crick (2018), *Sultan of Swing: The Life of David Butler*, Biteback

'By this time nearly all': Robin Farquharson (1955), 'Théorie des jeux—sur une generalisation de la notion d'equilibrium', *Comptes rendus hebdomadaires des séances de l'Académie des sciences*, no. 240, pp. 46-48

'The other participants': Colin Cherry ed. (1956), *Information Theory*, Butterworths Scientific Publications, vii-ix. The published version of Spencer Brown's thesis thanked Farquharson in the acknowledgements, G. Spencer Brown (1957), *Probability and Scientific Inference*, Longman, Green and Co., vii

'Some of those involved': Benjamin Breen (2024), *Tripping on Utopia: Margaret Mead, the Cold War, and the Troubled Birth of Psychedelic Science*, Footnote

'At first glance, the examiners': FT68, Queen's College, Oxford Archives, pp. 1-7. It is unclear whether the assessors' comments were in response to a viva or if Farquharson passed his doctorate without an oral defence.

'Candidates for All Souls': Michael Dummett (2005), 'The work and life of Robin Farquharson', p. 479

'On the occasion in question': Ibid., p. 480

'The questions had been very fortunate': Robin Farquharson (1965), 'My Affliction and I', GB 247, R. D. Laing papers, University of Glasgow

'The Warden achieved maximum dramatic effect': Michael Dummett (2005), 'The work and life of Robin Farquharson', p. 480

'The next morning my friends': Robin Farquharson (1965), 'My Affliction and I'

'Farquharson was treated': Sparrow's biographer deals at length with the warden of All Souls' homosexuality and the college crisis he oversaw in the mid-1960s: John Lowe (1998), *The Warden: A Portrait of John Sparrow*, HarperCollins, pp. 166-192, 193-224

———

Chapter 3 — Syllables of Brass

'During the period in which he was hospitalised': Robin Farquharson (October 1956), 'Straightforwardness in Voting Procedures', *Oxford Economic Papers*, vol. 8, no. 1, pp. 80-89

'He rented a room': Robin Farquharson to Mr Macdonald (30/06/1957) and 'Report on work in Paris from March to June, 1957', FT68, Queen's College Archives

'One time when I was lunching': Jonathan Bennett, email to author

'After my wife and I were leaving': Colin Leys, interview with author

'But this period of productivity': Application for late submission of thesis (29/01/1958), FA10/1/15, Oxford University Archives

'Nuffield granted Farquharson': CCAC/110/21, Churchill Archives Centre

'It was the shortest thesis': David Butler, interview with Adam Steiner, privately held

'My maths was hopeless': Colin Leys, interview with author

'It was the talk of the town': ibid.

'Mr. Farquharson's thesis': Braithwaite and Dick reports to the board of the faculty of social studies, FA10/1/15, Oxford University Archives

'On one occasion, David Butler': David Butler, interview with Adam Steiner, privately held

'In his manic phase': Frank Cioffi quoted in correspondence with Dimity Torbett, privately held

'I adumbrated vast enterprises': Robin Farquharson (1968), *Drop Out!*, p. 49

'He once succeeded in speaking': Michael Dummett (2005), 'The work and life of Robin Farquharson', p. 480

'These episodes notwithstanding': Nuffield College Annual Report (1958-1959), p.2; Application for extension (30/04/1957), FA10/1/15, Oxford University Archives; anonymous referee to warden of Merton (25/05/1958), OM354, Queen's College Archives

'Oxford's CND branch': The *Daily Telegraph* (17/03/1958), 'Less Than 50 p.c. Reply to H-Bomb Ballot', p. 17

'After explaining the basic thinking': Robin Farquharson (1958), *An approach to a pure theory of voting procedure*, DPhil thesis, p. 3

'Though Nuffield first admitted': Nuffield College Annual Report (1957-1958), p. 4

'In response, Farquharson donated': Robin Farquharson to 'Miss Bertie' (16/02/1959), R.2.1, Nuffield College Archives, Oxford

'He was also shuttling': Robin Farquharson CV, CCAC/110/21, Churchill Archives Centre

'Robin Farquharson said we should': Michael Dummett quoted in Rudolf Fara and Maurice Salles (October 2006), 'An Interview with Michael Dummett', *Social Choice and Welfare*, vol. 27, no. 2, p. 6

'This award came at the insistence': Thomas Schelling to master of Churchill (10/12/1963), CCAC/110/21, Churchill Archives Centre

'In fact, another Robin Farquharson': *Evening Post* (07/02/1962), 'Mais Oui! The Wine Was Excellent', p. 4 and the *Times* (22/11/2005), Robin Farquharson obituary, www.thetimes.co.uk/article/robin-farquharson-95f6zbjb985 [accessed 01/10/2024]

Chapter 4 — Bent but Not Broken

'Elections in South Africa': Robin Farquharson (1959), 'South Africa 1958', *Elections Abroad*, David Butler ed., Macmillan, pp. 229-275. An earlier form of this article appeared as 'The Psephology of April 16' (20/04/1958) in the *Sunday Times* of South Africa, p. 2

'For all the shortcomings': Ibid.

'Butler recalled having to spend': David Butler, interview with Adam Steiner, privately held

'My younger brother Roger': Colin Leys, interview with author

'Returned to the Maudsley': Robin Farquharson (1965), 'My Affliction and I'

Chapter 5 — The Pleasures of the Night Are Gone

'I was, I guess, about 17': Alan Marcuson, interview with author

'The former NUSAS head': Mabel Raisibe Maimela (1999), *Black Consciousness and White Liberals In South Africa: Paradoxical Anti-Apartheid Politics*, PhD thesis, University of South Africa, pp. 47-48

'Through the Liberal Party': Randolph Vigne (1997), *Liberals against Apartheid:A History of the Liberal Party of South Africa, 1953-68*, Macmillan, p. 210

'Through Vigne he became close': Randolph Vigne (1991), *A Gesture of Belonging: Letters from Bessie Head, 1965-*

1979, SA Writers, p. 4, p. 6, p. 17, p. 23

'The Federation of Rhodesia and Nyasaland': Robin Farquharson (February 1961), 'Rhodesia's Peculiar Politics', *Fighting Talk*, p. 12, p. 15

'He started to write for *Contact*': Other articles produced by Farquharson in this period include 'Economics: The Siege Sets In', *Fighting Talk* (May 1961), pp. 7-8, 'Swaziland: In the Melting Pot', *Fighting Talk* (August 1961), pp. 7-9, and 'Dr. Verwoerd's Exaggerated Victory', *Financial Mail* (27/10/1961), p. 8

'It was for *Contact*'s May 1961 issue': Robin Farquharson (May 1961), 'Mandela Calls', *Contact*, p. 3

'I worked for him': Dennis Brutus, interview with Adam Steiner, privately held

'Finally, and this is perhaps': Robin Farquharson (09/08/1962), 'A rising population is a blessing', *Rand Daily Mail*, p. 8

'The pleasures of the night are gone': Robin Farquharson (September 1962), untitled poem, the *New African* (September 1962), p. 10

'They said in madhouse': Robin Farquharson (October 1962), 'They Said in Madhouse', *Fighting Talk*, p. 14

'Northwards from Johannesburg's Centre': Robin Farquharson (March 1962), '*The Drifters*: Excerpts from a Work in Progress', the *New African*, pp. 8-9

'In this regard the subject': Lori Waxman (2017), *Keep Walking Intently: The Ambulatory Art of the Surrealists, the Situationist International, and Fluxus*, Sternberg Press

'The drifters waver on many boundaries': Ibid. Mkele was a psychologist described by *TIME* as 'South Africa's leading expert on the Bantu market', *TIME* (21/06/1963), 'South Africa: What Makes Bantus Buy', time.com/archive/6812656/south-africa-what-makes-bantus-buy/ [accessed 01/10/2024]

'Farquharson continued with his research at Wits': Around this time Farquharson was asked by the Liberal Party to conduct research into the possible impact of international sanctions on the South African regime, 'The Liberal Party', PC16/3 Peter Brown Collection - Liberal Party of South Africa (1953-1968), Alan Paton Centre & Struggle Archives; *Rand Daily Mail* (29/06/1962), 'Mines will go, but Rand has bright future', p. 2; *Rand Daily Mail* (25/10/1962), 'SA's Development Rate is Behind U.N. Target', p. 10

'While researching his biography': Robin Farquharson to Alan Paton (03/03/1965) and Alan Paton to Molly (18/03/1963), PC1/1/7-Hofmeyr, Alan Paton Centre & Struggle Archives

'Coming in the fraught years': Around this time, Farquharson had a public spat with government officials at a conference at which he was presenting, see Robin Farquharson (1963), 'The Southern Transvaal Seen from the Viewpoint of Regional Planning', *Proceedings of the Conference on the Problems of Regional Development and Planning in the Southern Transvaal, Johannesburg, 16-17 May 1963*, Southern Transvaal Regional Development Association, pp. 22-45, plus 9 pages of unpaginated material

'Before the police finally retreated': Gordon Winter quoted in *Ex-Bitman Robin* (May 1973), no. 6, p. 1; Robin Farquharson (1968), *Drop Out!*, p. 71; *Sunday Express* (11/08/1963), 'Host refuses police entry to multi-racial party', p. 11

'Besides his newly-found revolutionary politics': Mark Gevisser and Edwin Cameron eds. (2013), *Defiant Desire: Gay and Lesbian Lives in South Africa*, Routledge

'In later years Farquharson would concede': Robin Farquharson (1968), *Drop Out!*, p. 27

———

CHAPTER 6 — THE AFRICAN RESISTANCE MOVEMENT

'A few days after word': Robin Farquharson (13/08/1963), 'In and out and back in again', *Rand Daily Mail*, p. 5

'Farquharson knew of what he spoke': Gordon Winter quoted in *Ex-Bitman Robin* (May 1973), no. 6, p. 1

'The next hilarious incident': Ibid.

'Farquharson and the teacher John Harris': Dennis Brutus, interview with Adam Steiner, privately held; Dennis Brutus and Bernth Lindfors ed. (2009) 'Dennis Brutus' Great Escape in his Own Words (Part Three)', *Journal of the African Literature Association*, vol. 4, no. 1, pp. 58-76

'With little time to prepare': *Rand Daily Mail* (09/10/1963), 'Farquharson at Apartheid Meeting', p. 3

'In Baden-Baden': *Rand Daily Mail* (21/10/1963), 'Olympic Ultimatum', pp. 1-2

'But South African newspapers reported': Robin Farquharson to Alan Paton (03/03/1965), PC1/1/7-Hofmeyr, Alan Paton Centre & Struggle Archives; *Rand Daily Mail* (21/07/1964), 'S. African who startled town is Farquharson', p. 3; *Sunday Times* of South Africa (06/10/1963), 'Mystery trip by Rand researcher', page unknown

'One former South African intelligence operative later alleged': Piet Swanepoel (2007), *Really Inside BOSS: A Tale of South Africa's Late Intelligence Service (and Something about the CIA)*, self-published

'Whether or not the ARM': C. J. Driver (2015), *The Man with the Suitcase: The Life, Execution and Rehabilitation of John Harris, Liberal Terrorist*, Cane River

'In the words of his biographer': Ibid., p. 12

'Moody he may have been': Ibid., p. 43

'Some have speculated': The biographer of Farquharson's friend Patrick van Rensburg, the anti-apartheid organiser, has stated that Farquharson was a member of the ARM but does not provide any sources for this assertion, Kevin Shillington (2020), *Patrick van Rensburg: Rebel, Visionary and Radical Educationist, a Biography*, Wits University Press, p. 153

'Speaking to the *New African*': Robin Farquharson quoted in the *New African* (May 1965), 'John Harris, 1937-1965: An Obituary Profile', p. 54

'Within a few years the ANC': Ronnie Kasrils (1993), *Armed and Dangerous: My Undercover Struggle Against Apartheid*, Heinemann, pp. 100-121; Ken Keable (2012), *London Recruits: The Secret War Against Apartheid*, Merlin Press

'Soon after his arrival': Gordon Winter quoted in *Ex-Bitman Robin* (May 1973), no. 6, pp. 1-2

'Robin was a very sick man': Randolph Vigne (1991), *A Gesture of Belonging*, p. 4

'The journalist would later feature prominently': Robin Farquharson (1968), *Drop Out!*, p. 71

'It later emerged that Winter': Simon Freeman with Barrie Penrose (1996), *Rinkagate: The Rise and Fall of Jeremy Thorpe*, Bloomsbury, pp. 180-181; Gordon Winter (1981), *Inside BOSS: South Africa's Secret Police*, Penguin; James Sanders (2006), *Apartheid's Friends: The Rise and Fall of South Africa's Secret Service*, John Murray, p. 71. Winter heavily disputed some of Penrose's reporting, as laid out in written evidence supplied to the Select Committee on Culture, Media and Sport, publications.parliament.uk/pa/cm200203/cmselect/cmcumeds/458/458w116.htm [accessed 01/10/2024]

'Via Winter, South African intelligence': Robert Parker (1981), *Rough Justice*, Fontana, pp. 161-6, p. 221, p. 245, p. 249

'Winter later claimed': Gordon Winter (1981), *Inside BOSS*, p. 571

'Winter also alleged': Mark Israel (1999), *South African Political Exile in the United Kingdom*, Macmillan, pp. 185-186, p. 192

'Dennis Brutus went so far': Dennis Brutus (June 1983), 'Shall I be deported from the USA?', *Index on Censorship*, vol. 3, no. 83, p. 16

'For example, on 19 July 1964': *Rand Daily Mail* (21/07/1964), 'S. African who startled town is Farquharson', p. 3

'Robin stood laughing': Gordon Winter quoted in *Ex-Bitman Robin* (May 1973), no. 6, p. 2

'A few weeks later Farquharson was again': the *Daily Telegraph* (03/08/1964), 'Man Ejected from Hilton Hotel', p. 7

———

CHAPTER 7 — THE SUPREME LORD OF CHURCHILL

'He also began to take serious steps': 'Private and confidential/CC/6/65', CCAC/110/21, Churchill Archives Centre

'In September, he was well enough': Robin Farquharson (1966), 'The Application of Game Theory to Committee Procedure', J. R. Lawrence ed., *Operational Research and the Social Sciences*, Tavistock Publications, pp. 579-584

'Friends and advisors included': D. G. Kendall to master of Churchill (19/12/1963), CCAC/110/21, Churchill Archives Centre; Neil Chenoweth (2002), *Virtual Murdoch*, pp. 16-17

'Arrow went as far': Kenneth Arrow to bursar of Churchill (11/12/1963), CCAC/110/21, Churchill Archives Centre

'By the middle of the decade': Churchill College Fellowship Electors (03/01/1964), ibid.

'The new University of Essex went one step further': Robin Farquharson to master of Churchill (12/12/1963), ibid.

Farquharson was also contacted by representatives from Plessey': A. M. Brown to Robin Farquharson (23/10/1964), ibid.

'The pioneering game theorist John von Neumann': John Von Neumann to Robin Farquharson (28/11/1955), *John Von Neumann Selected Letters*, Miklós Rédei ed. (2005), American Mathematical Society, p. 115; miscellaneous Farquharson correspondence, Box 3, John Von Neumann and Klára Dán Von Neumann papers, Library of Congress

'Farquharson was also very particular': Robin Farquharson (June 1961), 'Review of Methods of Regional Analysis', *The South African Journal of Economics*, vol. 29, no. 2, p. 152

'It was well known at the time' Iain McLean, email to author

'In the meantime': Thomas Schelling, 'Harvard Reading List and Final Exam for Games and Strategy', www.irwincollier.com/harvard-reading-list-and-final-exam-for-games-and-strategy-schelling-1963/ [accessed 01/10/2024]

'Following a successful interview': Frank Hahn, interview with Adam Steiner, privately held

'Farquharson helped to organise': *Sunday Times* of South Africa (17/01/1965), 'Cambridge to Boycott S. A. Foods, Wines', p. 15

'Liberal exiles have a new focus': Robin Farquharson to Alan Paton (03/03/1965), PC1/1/7-Hofmeyr, Alan Paton Centre & Struggle Archives

'He landed at the Hilton': Robin Farquharson (1968), *Drop Out!*, p. 30; Robin Farquharson (1965), 'My Affliction and I'; *SIAM Review* (January 1965), 'Conference on Game Theory', p. 176

'At Churchill, he decided': Peter Johnston quoted in *Ex-Bitman Robin* (May 1973), no. 6, p. 8

I spent one afternoon': Frank Hahn, interview with Adam Steiner, privately held

'He also fiddled': Gordon Winter quoted in *Ex-Bitman Robin* (May 1973), no. 6, p. 2

'I think the key to Robin': Guy Legge, interview with author

'However discreet he may or may not have been': Churchill College Council, 'Dr Farquharson's Illness', CCAC/110/21, Churchill Archives Centre; Peter Johnston quoted in *Ex-Bitman Robin* (May 1973), no. 6, p. 8

'An extreme breakdown in late 1964': In *Drop Out!*, Farquharson refers to having briefly studied law 'at Gray's Inn', one of London's four inns of court. It is unclear when Farquharson's legal studies could have taken place, though in a surviving letter written during the Churchill debacle Farquharson states that he has moved into a flat near Gray's Inn: Robin Farquharson to bursar of Churchill (23/07/1966), CCAC/110/21, Churchill Archives Centre

'Whether this dossier was ever compiled': Churchill's archives hold a folder of correspondence relating to Farquharson's periodic hospitalisations, perhaps indicating that some kind of surveillance dossier was indeed assembled. The college steadfastly refuse access to these files on the grounds that they likely contain distressing material. It is at the archivist's discretion to decide quite what this distress might be and whether or not it is in the public interest; Farquharson is certainly not a household name. It is also the archivist's responsibility to protect the college from any backlash resulting from inappropriate distribution of private materials.

'In a bid to make their care': Bernard Dionysius Geoghegan (2022), *Code: From Information Theory to French Theory*, Duke University Press, pp. 52-84

'The most disastrous of his outbreaks': Michael Dummett (2005), 'The work and life of Robin Farquharson', p. 480

'A scholarly review': Robin Farquharson (March 1966), 'Review of Jacot's *Stratégie et concurrence*', the *Economic Journal*, vol. 76, no. 301, pp. 107-108

'While the full circumstances': CCAC/110/21, Churchill Archives Centre. For Farquharson's account, see Robin Farquharson (1968), *Drop Out!*, pp. 10-11

'In turn, the college arranged': according to the Bank of England's inflation calculator, www.bankofengland.co.uk/monetary-policy/inflation/inflation-calculator [accessed 14/10/2024]. Farquharson gives his account of this episode in *Drop Out!*, see Robin Farquharson (1968), *Drop Out!*, pp. 10-13

'A representative from the Ministry of Justice': Official Solicitor to bursar of Churchill (25/10/1965), CCAC/110/21, Churchill Archives Centre

'More or less burned': *Rhodes Newsletter* (November 1968), 'Old Rhodian News', p. 11

CHAPTER 8 — BASICALLY HOSTILE TO CONVENTION

'As one influential account puts it': Sukhdev Sandhu (2003), *London Calling: How Black and Asian Writers Imagined a City*, Harper, p. 142

'In the words of Colin MacInnes': Colin MacInnes (1961), *England, Half-English*, Random House

'Though thinkers like MacInnes': For a recent analysis of MacInnes and his place in British race relations in the 1960s, see Rob Waters (2018), *Thinking Black: Britain, 1964-1985*, University of California Press

'As the pioneering Trinidad-born filmmaker': Horace Ové quoted in Jonathon Green (1998), *Days in the Life: Voices from the English Underground*, Pimlico, pp. 51-52

'In 1961, architect Cedric Price': Ana Bonet Miro (2016), 'Sigma portfolio and Bubble City: Ludic sites for a mobile fun palace programme', *Architecture and Culture*, vol. 4, no. 1, pp. 137-161; Andrew Wilson 'Project sigma: An Interpersonal Logbook', Jo Applin, Catherine Spencer, and Amy Tobin (eds.), *London Art Worlds: Mobile, Contingent, and Ephemeral Networks, 1960–1980*, Pennsylvania State University, pp. 151-168

'For a while it looked like': Jeff Nuttall (1968), *Bomb Culture*, Paladin

'A similar project had recently': Helen Spandler (2006), *Asylum to Action: Paddington Day Hospital, Therapeutic Communities and Beyond*, Jessica Kingsley

'Users could be guided into a state': R. D. Laing, speech at the Annual Conference of the National Association for Mental Health (February 1966) quoted in Adrian Laing (1994), *R. D. Laing: A Biography*, Thunder's Mouth Press, pp. 120-121

'Joe Berke was hanging around': R. D. Laing quoted in Bob Mullan (1995), *Mad To Be Normal: Conversations With R. D. Laing*, Free Association Books, p. 194

'Though he missed the International Poetry Incarnation': Farquharson and Fainlight had numerous friends in common, though it is hard to place them together at the same place and time. An undated letter from Farquharson survives in Fainlight's papers, Box 5, Folder 6, Harry Fainlight mss., Lilly Library, Indiana University, Bloomington, Indiana. Mark Hyatt, Fainlight's sometime boyfriend, also dated Anthony Blond and wrote a poem entitled 'To a Romantic (Robin).' that may be about Farquharson, see Mark Hyatt (2023), *So Much for Life: Selected Poems*, Sam Ladkin and Luke Roberts (eds.), Nightboat, p. 157, and Luke Roberts to author

'Farquharson was a frequent presence': Anthony Howell, interview with author; Robin Farquharson (1968), *Drop Out!*, p. 65

'Nick had been two or three years ahead of me': Anthony Howell, interview with author

'As Farquharson later recalled': Robin Farquharson (1968), *Drop Out!*, pp. 12-13

'Like Farquharson, David Cooper was': Adrian Chapman (2016), 'Re-Coopering anti-psychiatry: David Cooper, revolutionary critic of psychiatry', *Critical and Radical Social Work: An International Journal*, Vol. 4, No. 3, pp. 421-432

'It is possible that Cooper': with thanks to Paul Gorman for suggesting Adler as the possible link between Farquharson and Cooper. For more on Adler, see Paul Gorman (2020), *The Life & Times of Malcolm McLaren*, Little, Brown pp. 72-77

'Leon Redler, one of the Hall's founders': Leon Redler, interview with author

'Robin Farquharson had a bright idea': R. D. Laing quoted in Bob Mullan (1995), *Mad To Be Normal*, p. 207, p. 198

CHAPTER 9 — CONCENTRATING WITH MY EYES CLOSED

'Despite his recent ups and downs': Robin Farquharson (01/04/1966), 'Voters' Preference', the *Spectator*, p. 14

'Instead, by the end of the summer': Robin Farquharson (1968), *Drop Out!*, pp. 49-50

'Robin Farquharson answered an ad': Peter Johnston quoted in *Ex-Bitman Robin* (May 1973), no. 6, p. 7

'World currency stability': Robin Farquharson quoted ibid., p. 8

'As ever, Robin's starting point': Peter Johnston quoted ibid.

'I met Robin again in 67': Gordon Winter quoted ibid., p. 2

'Many of the new underground papers': Nigel Fountain (1988), *Underground: The London Alternative Press, 1966-74*, Routledge

'As Farquharson later explained': Robin Farquharson (1968), *Drop Out!*, p. 15, p. 76

'Lawson was thanked': Robin Farquharson (February 1956), 'Straightforwardness in Voting Procedures', *Oxford Economic Papers*, Vol. 8, No. 1, p. 89

'Nigel Samuel was the heir': John L. Williams (2008), *Michael X: A Life in Black and White*, Century, pp. 125-126

'Many of them were unaware': Miles quoted in Jonathon Green (1998), *Days in the Life*, p. 213

'Samuel's sister was Nicky Waymouth': Nigel Waymouth has denied being Farquharson's entrée to the underground, email to author.

'There he found a place': Jeremy Lewis (20/06/2004), 'Review: *A Jew Made in England* by Anthony Blond', www.thetimes.co.uk/article/review-memoir-a-jew-made-in-england-by-anthony-blond-xcbr25p99m9 [accessed 01/10/2024]

'Born into a wealthy': Anthony Blond (2004), *Jew Made in England*, Timewell, p. 20

'Raven's biographer later described': Michael Barber (1996), *The Captain: The Life and Times of Simon Raven*, Duckbacks, p. 194

'In the UK a former employee': Jack Harwell (1965), *A Plain Man's Guide to Software*, www.geonius.com/emett/guide.html [accessed 01/10/2024]

'British data theorist': Eden Medina (2011), *Cybernetic Revolutionaries: Technology and Politics in Allende's Chile*, MIT Press

'At the end of May 1967 he attended': Anti-Apartheid Movement newsletter (31/05/1967), 'Minutes of the National Committee meeting', p. 4

'One bunch of Brit hippies': Frater Choronzon quoted in Robert Kyle (2025), *Voices of Chaos: An Oral History of a Magical Revolution*, Strange Attractor Press (unpaginated pre-publication version)

'The Tribe of the Sacred Mushroom': Paul Minns, ghettoraga.blogspot.com/2010/02/time-music-in-third-ear-bands.html [accessed 01/10/2024]

'It was like a coffin': Nosher, interview with author

'When Farquharson took to the podium': Robin Farquharson (1969), 'Sophisticated Voting and an Example due to Kreweras', in *La Décision*, Georges-Théodule Guilbaud ed., Editions du Centre Nationale de la Recherche Scientifique, pp. 115-122

'Inspired by the words of Timothy Leary': Robin Farquharson (1968), *Drop Out!*, pp. 12-13, pp. 45-48

'As he later wrote': Robin Farquharson (1968), *Drop Out!*, p. 103

Chapter 10 — A Dirty Mind for Such a Holy Man

'The combination showcased': Robin Farquharson (1968), *Drop Out!*, p. 55

'As Farquharson wrote': Ibid., p. 109

'One encounter with the police': Ibid., p. 81

'Born a member': Ibid., p. 67

'Farquharson's favourite hospital': For more information on Horton, see Ruth Valentine (1996), *Asylum, Hospital,*

Haven: A History of Horton Hospital, Riverside Mental Health Trust

'When I arrived': Daniel Morgan (2008), 'Three months in Horton Hospital, Epsom, Surrey–1966', studymore.org.uk/mpur2.htm [accessed 01/10/2024]

'Though Low-Beer was no anti-psychiatrist': *New Scientist* (11/07/1974), p. 88

'God was speaking to Robin': Peter Johnston quoted in *Ex-Bitman Robin* (May 1973), no. 6, p. 8

'He was born in 1930': Benjamin Breen (2024), *Tripping on Utopia*, p. 3

'I ran into Robin': Barry Miles, email to author. Farquharson refers to Sue Miles's efforts to have him banned from the Arts Lab in *Drop Out!*, see Robin Farquharson (1968), *Drop Out!*, pp. 30-31

'As Farquharson bitterly recounted': ibid.

'One volume, whose title I don't remember': Robin Farquharson (1968), *Drop Out!*, pp. 68-69

'Despite the chaos surrounding its writing': Alan Aldridge (2008), *The Man with Kaleidoscope Eyes*, Thames & Hudson, p. 31

'Matters probably weren't helped': *Private Eye* (25/10/1968), p. 11

'Two years later Farquharson was still burdened': Farquharson placed an ad offering remaindered copies of *Drop Out!* in *International Times* (24 September to 8 October 1970), #88, p. 12

'Instead, the book became a novelty': *Sunday Times* of South Africa (22/09/1968), 'I took LSD, says brilliant S. A. scholar', p. 5

'Moving about London under control': Robin Farquharson (1968), *Drop Out!*, pp. 63-64

'Had he had the chance': Mason and Blond almost certainly knew each other. Blond's partner in his publishing firm was Isabel Colegate, whose novel *The Shooting Party* was later turned into a film starring Mason.

Chapter 11 — Barefoot in Camden Underground

'By the time *Drop Out!* came out': George Firsoff (1980), *1968: Spring of Youth*, self-published, pp. 38-39, p. 108, pp. 199-200

'To embrace this reality': Norman Mailer (1957), 'The White Negro', www.dissentmagazine.org/online_articles/the-white-negro-fall-1957/ [accessed 01/10/2024]

'Michael X's own': Michael Abdul Malik (1968), *From Michael de Freitas to Michael X*, André Deutsch, p. 127

'But as the sociologist Ned Polsky': Ned Polsky (1959), 'Reflections on Hip', Norman Mailer ed., *Advertisements for Myself*, Putnam, pp. 365–69

'The *International Times*, in many ways the successor': Tom Vague (19/10/2019), 'It Happened Here: Hoppy's Notting Hill Interzone', internationaltimes.it/it-happened-here-hoppys-notting-hill-interzone/ [accessed 15/12/2023]

'The unique combination': Richard Hornsey (2010), *The Spiv and the Architect: Unruly Life in Postwar London*, University of Minnesota Press

'The transgressive status of these venues': John L. Williams (2008), *Michael X*, p. 122, p. 178, p. 188; Ishmahil Blagrove, Jr. ed., (2000), *The Frontline: A Story of Struggle, Resistance and Black Identity in Notting Hill*, Rice n Peas, pp. 288-289

'MacInnes's preference': Ed Vulliamy (15/04/2007), 'Absolute MacInnes', www.theguardian.com/uk/2007/apr/15/britishidentity.fiction [accessed 15/12/2023]

'He had recently been one': For more on the history of the Antiuniversity of London, see Jakob Jakobson (2013), *The Antihistory Tabloid*, MayDay Rooms and the PETT Archive and Study Centre

'He may have 'personified the interface'': John L. Williams (2008), *Michael X*, p. 99

'Once, I found him barefoot': Peter Johnston quoted in *Ex-Bitman Robin* (May 1973), no. 6, p. 9

'Robin was a good friend of my wife': Woody Haut, interview with author

'I think the model for him': Anthony Howell, interview with author

'Robin Farquharson in full cry': George Firsoff (September 1973), 'Robin Farquharson', *Bitman*, no. 8, p. 7

Chapter 12 — The King of Zembla

'I left South Africa': Alan Marcuson, interview with author

'Inspired by the Situationists': T. J. Clark and Donald Nicholson-Smith (Winter 1997), 'Why Art Can't Kill the Situationist International', *October*, vol. 79 (Guy Debord and the Internationale Situationniste), p. 20; Erick Corrêa (2023), 'The Internationalist Anti-Colonialism of the Situationists', brooklynrail.org/2023/02/field-notes/The-internationalist-anti-colonialism-of-the-situationists [accessed 01/10/2024]

'Led by Abbie Hoffman': Larry "Ratso" Sloman, Michael Simmons and Jay Babcock (November 2004), 'Out, demons, out!', arthurmag.com/2011/04/13/out-demons-out-the-1967-exorcism-of-the-pentagon-and-the-birth-of-yippie-arthur-no-13nov-2004/ [accessed 01/10/2024]

'Much of it bore the mark': Jim McCann reportedly came to the attention of the *Friends* scene when he arrived at the paper's offices bearing a shotgun. He was interviewed for the paper's 8 March 1971 issue and later introduced to his future associate Howard Marks by Charles Radcliffe, a British Situationist and hash smuggler.

'By November Farquharson was back': Peter Johnston quoted in *Ex-Bitman Robin* (May 1973), no. 6, p. 9

'Farquharson was also beginning': John Eggeling, email to author

'There is a common trend': There is also the case of schizophrenia being used as a descriptive category for a certain kind of scientific work: for example, see Errett A. Bishop (1985), 'Schizophrenia in Contemporary Mathematics', *Contemporary Mathematics*, vol. 39, pp. 1-32

'It's very troublesome': Robin Farquharson (March 1974), 'Some more extracts from the selected works of the late Robin Farquharson', *Bit-Human*, no. 10, x; Iain McLean, Alistair McMillan, and Burt L. Monroe (1995), 'Duncan Black and Lewis Carroll', *Journal of Theoretical Politics*, vol. 7, no. 2, p. 113

'Spencer Brown's book': Spencer Brown was invited to Esalen by John Lilly and Alan Watts as part of the AUM conference in March 1973.

'Blackwell's in Oxford': Yale released the book in the US in late 1969. Due to an unknown delay, Blackwell's issued the book in the UK market in February 1970.

'Reviews were exceptional': See Gerald H. Kramer (September 1970), 'Review of *Theory of Voting*', *The American Political Science Review*, vol. 64, no. 3, p. 916; Amartya Sen (December 1971), 'Review of *Theory of Voting*', the *Economic Journal*, vol. 81, no. 324, pp. 1024-1026; Roberto D'Alimonte (April 1972), 'Review of *Theory of Voting*', *Italian Political Science Review*, vol. 2, no. 1; and *Times Literary Supplement* (11/09/1970), 'Psephologia', p. 990

'Farquharson even garnered a mention': Jim Anderson (February 1970), 'Head books', *OZ*, #26, p. 47

'The great merit of the book': Anatol Rapoport (July 1970), 'Sincere and Other Strategies: a Review of *Theory of Voting*', *Science*, vol. 169, p. 269

'A few years later, Richard Niemi': Richard G. Niemi (1983), 'An Exegesis of Farquharson's "Theory of Voting"', *Public Choice*, vol. 40, no. 3, p. 323

Chapter 13 — Mother Country Madmen

'By the time he met Farquharson': References to 'Nicholas A-Z' can be spotted throughout Albery's personal papers, privately held

'Albery had also just begun to help Hoppy': Hoppy himself missed the majority of this period, as he was behind bars on a drugs charge. He later commented on the relationship between BIT and the London Free School in an interview quoted in Rozemin Keshvani (2019), *Better Books/Better Bookz: Art, Anarchy, Apostasy, Counter-Culture & the New Avant-Garde*, Walther König, pp. 228-9

'Originally spun out': BIT also published a travel guide from 1970 onwards. It went through several editions and was revered by some travellers as the 'Bible of the East'. Geoff Crowther, the guide's principal author, was later a founding contributor to Lonely Planet, see Ashley Crowther (24/12/2020), 'Before Lonely Planet - BIT Guides Ruled', www.ashleycrowther.org/post/before-lonely-planet-bit-guides-ruled [accessed 01/10/2024]

'Richard Neville, the founder of *OZ*': Richard Neville (1970), *Play Power*, Paladin, p. 41

'A group calling themselves Zenden': *Project London Free* was inspired in tone and content by a New York pamphlet called *Fuck the System* issued under the pseudonym 'George Metesky'. *Fuck the System* was in fact authored by Abbie Hoffman and funded through a complicated chain by City Hall itself.

'As we walked and talked': 'Alan Beam' [Nicholas Albery] (1976), *Rehearsal For The Year 2000 (Drugs, Religions, Madness, Crime, Communes, Love, Visions, Festivals and Lunar Energy); The Rebirth Of Albion Free State (Known in the Dark Ages as England); Memoirs of a Male Midwife (1966-1975)*, Revelaction Press, p. 68

'Robin Farquharson was a BIT night shift worker': Nicholas Albery quoted in *Ex-Bitman Robin* (May 1973), no. 6, p. 1

'BIT was set up very, very specifically': Stephen Lee, interview with author

'In recent months': Peter Johnston quoted in *Ex-Bitman Robin* (May 1973), no. 6, p. 7

'But after just a short time': Ibid., p. 9

'Robin had written to me': Michael Barnett (1973), *People, Not Psychiatry*, George Allen & Unwin, p. 191. Barnett announced PNP in an article titled 'The Sick Scene' in *International Times* (4 to 17 July 1969), #59, p. 3. This was a special issue dubbed the 'Insanity Times' and featured an interview with R. D. Laing by Felix Scorpio, the husband of Farquharson's friend Jane de Mendelssohn.

'Perhaps his most inspired venture': Nicholas Albery quoted in *Ex-Bitman Robin* (May 1973), no. 6, p. 1

'Though the Woodstock Music and Art Fair': Stephen Dowling (15/08/2009), '50 facts about Woodstock at 50: Money', www.bbc.co.uk/culture/article/20190813-50-facts-about-woodstock-at-50-money [accessed 01/10/2024]

'From inauspicious beginnings': BIT was also behind Cope, a mental health support line staffed by patients.

'Various other groups explicitly riffed':

Yohuru Williams (2006), 'White Tigers, Brown Berets, Black Panthers, Oh My!', Jama Lazerow and Yohuru Williams (eds.), *In Search of the Black Panther Party: New Perspectives on a Revolutionary Movement*, Duke University Press, pp. 183-190

'Detroit was one of the most populous cities': Katherine E. Watkins (2012), '"Freakin' Out": Remaking Masculinity through Punk Rock in Detroit', *Women & Performance: A Journal of Feminist Theory*, vol. 22, nos. 2-3, pp. 239-260; Joel P. Rhodes and Judson L. Jeffries (2010), 'Motor City Panthers', Judson L. Jeffries ed., *On the Ground: The Black Panther Party in Communities across America*, University Press of Mississippi, pp. 125-185

'Originally called 'Motor City Five'': Wayne Kramer (1996) quoted in Legs McNeil and Gillian McCain (eds.), *Please Kill Me: The Uncensored Oral History of Punk*, Grove Press, p. 36

'Though Sinclair had a relatively comfortable': See Paul Gilroy (1993), *The Black Atlantic: Modernity and Double Consciousness*, Verso, pp. 72-110; Steve Waksman (2001), 'Kick Out the Jams!: The MC5 and the Politics of Noise', *Instruments of Desire: The Electric Guitar and the Shaping of Musical Experience*, Harvard University Press, pp. 207-236

'We are not playing': John Sinclair (January 1969), 'Rock and Roll Dope,' *Fifth Estate*, vol. 3, no. 19, p. 16

'The actions of the Black Panthers': John Sinclair (14/11/1968), 'White Panther Statement', *The Fifth Estate*, p. 8

'These were white radicals': Mark MacAulay (2010), *Black Sinatras, White Panthers: Race, Genre and Performance in Detroit Black Pop and Rock, 1960-1970*, PhD thesis, Dalhousie University, pp. 151-160; Patrick Burke (2021), 'Honkie Soul: The MC5 at the Democratic National Convention', *Tear Down the Walls: White Radicalism and Black Power in 1960s Rock*, University of Chicago Press, pp. 19-44

'Whatever the complicated racial politics': Daniel S. Chard (2016), *Nixon's War on Terrorism: The FBI, Leftist Guerrillas, and the Origins of Watergate*, PhD thesis, University of Massachusetts Amherst

'Michael even published': Michael de Freitas (March 1966), 'Two Poems', the *New African*, p. 38; John L. Williams, *Michael X*, p. 105

'The Deviants, his new band': Russell Hunter quoted in Jonathon Green (1998), *Days in the Life*, pp. 174-175. Hunter first met Farren via Mike Laslett, the son of London Free School founder Rhaune Laslett. Mother and son both make brief appearances in *Drop Out!*, see Robin Farquharson (1968), *Drop Out!*, pp. 84-86

'The British White Panther Party': Mick Farren (2002), *Give the Anarchist a Cigarette*, Pimlico, p. 285

'Within weeks': Mick Farren (1972), *Watch Out Kids*, Macmillan, p. 100

'As Greer wrote': Germaine Greer (October 1969), 'Mozic and the Revolution', *OZ*, #24, p. 28. On Farren and Greer's relationship, Mick Farren (2002), *Give the Anarchist a Cigarette*, pp. 218-221

Chapter 14 — A Computer Programmed to Public

'Horace Cutler, then chairman': Patrick Cosgrave (04/03/1997), 'Obituary: Sir Horace Cutler', www.independent.co.uk/news/obituaries/obituary-sir-horace-cutler-1270966.html [accessed 01/10/2024]

'Horace Cutler suggested': Robin Farquharson quoted in Gerald Gardner (28/02/1970), 'Puking the system', the *Guardian*, p. 9. Arthur Chisnall was also named as a member of the housing association's committee. Chisnall was the manager of the Eel Pie Island Hotel, which he transformed into one of the major early venues for rock and R&B

in Britain. Bluesman Alexis Korner was a regular performer on Eel Pie Island; as recounted in Chapter 17, Korner's sideman Nick South later formed a band with Farquharson, which is possibly how Farquharson came to know Chisnall.

'But records showed': The *London Gazette* (05/08/1975), 'Legal Notices', p. 9982

'Gardner described his subject's voice': Gerald Gardner (28/02/1970), 'Puking the system', the *Guardian*, p. 9

'As Farquharson put it': Ibid.

'As Gardner noted': Ibid.

'He stood out, dressed in a dark suit': Michael Barnett (1973), *People, Not Psychiatry*, p. 191

'Barnett's People for a New Psychiatry': On PNP's connections to Laing's circle, see Nick Crossley (2006), *Contesting Psychiatry: Social Movements in Mental Health*, Routledge, pp. 132-3

'Through Farquharson and the Situationists Housing Association's dealings': Michael Barnett (1973), *People, Not Psychiatry*, p. 193

'From the moment they moved in': Ibid., p. 194

'His energy was frighteningly high': Jenny James, email to author

'Robin never slept': Michael Barnett (1973), *People, Not Psychiatry*, pp. 194-195

'Robin had (at last) been picked up': Michael Barnett (1973), *People, Not Psychiatry*, p. 196

'Farquharson for his part': Robin Farquharson (1968), *Drop Out!*, pp. 79-80

'One evening he turned up': Frater Choronzon (1990), *Liber Cyber*, self-published. Other friends of Farquharson's have independently recounted similar stories in conversations with the author.

'In 1970 Robin was living' Richard Lancaster quoted in *Ex-Bitman Robin* (May 1973), no. 6, p. 4

'He rang me up one night': Michael Barnett (1973), *People, Not Psychiatry*, p. 197

'By now Robin was getting quite freaky': Richard Lancaster quoted in *Ex-Bitman Robin* (May 1973), no. 6, p. 4. It hasn't proved possible to locate this broadcast, which was likely wiped along with many other BBC shows from this period. Based on television listings in *Radio Times*, it is plausible that the show in question was the fifth episode of the *New Horizons* series 'A Matter of Degree?' on BBC One. The catch-all term 'alternative society' was made popular in the context of hippie organising by Nicholas Saunders, a close friend of Nicholas Albery who later played a key role in rejuvenating Neal's Yard.

'As Richard Lancaster put it': Ibid.

'Nicholas was a very organised person': Andrew Rigby, email to author

'Though Farquharson's replies': Robin Farquharson interviewed by Andrew Rigby (May 1973), *Ex-Bitman Robin*, no. 6, pp. 4-6

'As reported in *International Times*':, John Hopkins (13 to 26 March 1970), 'Time Travel & Mind Swap', *International Times*, #75 pp. 20-21; Hoppy (27 February to 13 March 1970), 'Real Time Television', *International Times*, #74, p. 10

'Funding for the event': Box 6, Folder 4, The Hoppy Hopkins Archive, Bishopsgate Institute. Another figure involved in the early days of TVX was the Australian filmmaker Albie Thoms, who had helped set up *Freek Press*.

'Unfortunately, like some of the rest of us': Nicholas Albery quoted in *Ex-Bitman Robin* (May 1973), no. 6, p. 1

'Shortly after the UFO+TV event': *Arts Labs Newsletter* (March 1970), 'International Freak Beaten Up & Committed', p. 1

'I was no longer working': Alan Marcuson, interview with author

'It reportedly took ten policemen': *Arts Labs Newsletter* (March 1970), 'International Freak Beaten Up & Committed', p. 1

CHAPTER 15 — THE MINISTER OF PROPAGANDA

'BIT now had its own newsletter': After its eighth issue as *Bitman*, the newsletter published six more times. Each remaining issue used a different variant of 'bit-' as a name: *BitWoman* (#9), *Bit-Human* (#10), *Bitbeing* (#11), *Bitmuch* (#12), *Bitbetter* (#13), and, finally, *BitTersweet* (#14). A large part of *Bitmuch* was dedicated to an extended history of the publication.

'The relentless and brutal treatment': For a contemporary discussion of whether gay liberationists should support *OZ* during the infamous obscenity trial, see Mick (August 1971), '*OZ OZ OZ OZ OZ*', *Come Together*, no. 8, p. 7

'In turn these companies relied': On freaks and the music industry, see Shawn David Young (2014), 'Apocalyptic Music: Reflections on Countercultural Christian Influence', Sheila Whiteley and Jedediah Sklower eds., *Countercultures and Popular Music*, Ashgate, pp. 109-122 and Kay Keister, 'The Long Freak Out: Unfinished Music and Countercultural Madness in Avant-Garde Rock of the 1960s and 1970s', ibid., pp. 141-156

'Suddenly any passing busker': For a roughly contemporary sociological analysis of freak culture, see D. Lawrence Wieder and Don H. Zimmerman (1976), 'Becoming a Freak: Pathways into the Counter-Culture', *Youth and Society*, vol. 7 no., 3, pp. 311-344

'*Groupie* was a curiosity': Jenny Fabian and Johnny Byrne (1969), *Groupie*, Omnibus, pp. 57-59

'April has been the month': Robin Farquharson (May 1970), 'Head Book Boom', *Bitman*, no. 1, pp. 33-34. 'Gameheadopoly' is a reference to 'Headopoly', a poster included in the hardback edition of Richard Neville's *Play Power*.

'When the baffled *Sunday Times*': Atticus (30/08/1970), 'Bear facts', *Sunday Times*, p. 9

'May that year': In 1992, the poet Anthony Howell oversaw the release of *Near Calvary: Selected Poems of Nicholas Lafitte*, The Many Press

'We could plainly see that Fiery Creations': Mick Farren (2002), *Give the Anarchist a Cigarette*, p. 284

'I spent the summer of 1970': Matthew Hilton, interview with author

'From the relative safety': Mick Farren later claimed that Fiery Creations had promised Alan Marcuson funds towards the cost of producing *Freek Press*. Instead, the festival's organisers reportedly threatened Marcuson and had him ejected from the site, see Mick Farren (10 to 24 September 1970), 'The Isle of Wight Festival: 5 Days of Peace, Music and Love', *International Times*, #87, p. 9

'While Farren and his associates': Ray Foulk, email to author

'In his account of the festival': Mick Farren (10 to 24 September 1970), 'The Isle of Wight Festival', p. 7

'Gentleman, in state of apparent agitation': Freshwater administrator quoted in Brian Hinton (1990), *Nights in Wight Satin*, IOW Cultural Services Department, p. 47

'According to an account in *Friends*': 'IOW 70' (02/10/1970), *Friends*, #15, p. 2

'Another witness held': *Freek Press* (1970), no. 2, Box 10, Richard Neville Papers, Beinecke Rare Book and Manuscript Library, Yale University Library

A subsequent broadside indicated': *Freek Press* (1970), no. 3, Box 10, Richard Neville Papers

---

CHAPTER 16 — LEILA THE HIJACKER

'A Situationist-inspired group': It is hard to work out to what extent Farquharson was personally familiar with the Angry Brigade. At the very least he maintained friendships with some of their associates in the underground press. Farquharson was friends with the writer Jane de Mendelssohn, who interviewed Jimi Hendrix for the 10 March 1969 issue of *International Times* and worked as a typist for Joe Berke. Jane's ex-husband was Felix de Mendelssohn (otherwise known as Felix Scorpio), who interviewed R. D. Laing for the 4 July 1969 issue of *International Times* and was involved in *Frendz* and *Suck* as well as presenting the classic documentary *Getting It Straight in Notting Hill Gate*. On 30 March 1971, Felix de Mendelssohn and Jill Marcuson, wife of *Friends* editor Alan, were arrested by the Royal Ulster Constabulary on suspicion of bombing Queen's University, Belfast. The perpetrator was believed to be Jim McCann, whom they had been sent to interview.

'London-based underground newspapers': for a good overview of this phenomenon and an example of it, see Peter Stansill and David Zane Mairowitz (1971), *BAMN (By Any Means Necessary): Outlaw Manifestos and Ephemera 1965-70*, Penguin, pp. 169-182. Both Stansill and Mairowitz were influential figures at *International Times*.

'The Weather Underground embodied': Bryan Burrough (2015), *Days of Rage*, Penguin

'Leary was smuggled out': Stewart Tendler and David May (1984), *The Brotherhood of Eternal Love: From Flower Power to Hippie Mafia - The Story of the LSD Counterculture*, Panther. Tendler covered Farquharson's death in his capacity as senior crime reporter for the *Times*.

'Republished in *International Times*': Timothy Leary (8 to 22 October 1970), 'Letter from Hiding', *International Times*, #89 p. 2, p. 15

'Reports circulated that the authorities': Sarah Irving (2012), *Leila Khaled: Icon of Palestinian Liberation*, Pluto Press, p. 57

'According to his friend Peter Johnston': Peter Johnston quoted in *Ex-Bitman Robin* (May 1973), no. 6, p. 10; *Sunday Times* of South Africa (08/04/1973), 'Brilliant Drop-Out Dies of Burns', p. 19D

'Speaking to the Associated Press': Robin Farquharson quoted in *Associated Press* (13/09/1970), 'Britain Will Free Hijacker', *Pensacola News Journal*, p. 12A

'It was an unexpected move': *Times Literary Supplement* (11/09/1970), 'Psephologia', p. 990

'After the Isle of Wight': Matthew Hilton, interview with author

'23 Newport Street fit the bill': Ibid.

'Robin was in a manic phase': Ibid.

'everytime you start': Matthew Hilton (October 1971), *Leila the Hijacker* artist statement, London Film-Makers' Co-Operative catalogue, addenda number 3

'While in South Africa': *The Frog Slave*: BFI identifier 196719, collections-search.bfi.org.uk/web/Details/ChoiceFilmWorks/150201126 [accessed 01/10/2024]

'He turned his attention': Matthew Hilton, interview with author

'The finished film': Ibid. For more on the London Film-Makers' Co-Operative, see Mark Webber ed. (2016), *Shoot Shoot Shoot: The First Decade of the London Film-Makers' Co-operative, 1966-76*, Lux

'It would appear that': David Curtis, email to author

CHAPTER 17 — HIGH ON DYNAMITE

'I had books of poetry': Adam Kisch, interview with author

'The backing band': Nick South, interview with author

'He rents Pye Studios': Adam Kisch, interview with author

'Leila the Hijacker': lyrics by Adam Kisch (1970), music by the White Panthers, Panther Records (unreleased)

'He's got these three session musicians': Adam Kisch, interview with author

'Let Us Return': lyrics by Robin Farquharson (1970), 'Let Us Return (Free Palestine)', music by the White Panthers, Panther Records (unreleased)

'Neither John nor Leni Sinclair': John Sinclair, email to author, and Leni Sinclair, email to author. On the White Panthers and Middle Eastern liberation movements: Pun Plamondon (2004), *Lost from the Ottawa: The Story of the Journey Back, a Memoir*, Trafford, pp. 191-205, Michael R. Fischbach (Spring 2020), 'The New Left and the Arab-Israeli Conflict in the United States', *Journal of Palestine Studies*, vol. 49, no. 3, www.palestine-studies.org/en/node/1650341 [accessed 01/10/2024]

'Farren wasn't entirely against this development': Mick Farren quoted in Rich Deakin (2008), 'Mozic and the Revolution Revisited', *Headpress*, no. 28, p. 48

'He may also have taken a dislike': Mick Farren (2002), *Give the Anarchist a Cigarette*, pp. 240-245

'Robin Farquharson—Britain's answer': 'Notice' (24 September to 8 October 1970), *International Times*, #88, p. 15
'The *Daily Mirror* dubbed': *Daily Mirror* (09/11/1970), 'The David Frost Freakout', p. 1

'National prude-in-chief': Mary Whitehouse quoted in 'Yippie King Puts David on the Spot', transdiffusion.org/2020/10/05/the-frost-freakout/ [accessed 01/10/2024]

'I was very young': Robin Elliott, email to author

'Robin wanted this': Matthew Hilton, interview with author

'At the height of the Front de libération': Jonathan Bennett, email to author

---

CHAPTER 18 — HEADMASTER ROBIN

'Two investigative journalists': Simon Freeman with Barrie Penrose (1996), *Rinkagate*, p. 181

'The eventual revelation': Ibid., p. 203

'Despite the legalisation of homosexuality': Probably the most well-known out gay man of the era was Tom Driberg, bon vivant and Labour MP. Driberg's scandalous behaviour and former Communist Party membership fuelled speculation that he was a Soviet spy. It's plausible that he and Farquharson knew each other. Driberg contributed on occasion to underground publications and supported Joan Littlewood's Fun Palace project. In a letter quoted in her autobiography, Littlewood states that 'If I let my feelings run away with me, I'd spend my time with sybarites like Robin Farquarson and Tom Driberg.' Though this seems like a concrete link, Littlewood is probably referring to the actor and dandy Robert Farquharson, whose birth name was Robin de la Condamine, see Joan Littlewood to 'Gerry' in Joan Littlewood (2016), *Joan's Book: The Autobiography of Joan Littlewood*, Bloomsbury, p. 268

'Soon enough there were two rival factions': The psychedelic wing of the GLF were known as the Radical Feminists, or RadFems. They should not be confused with supporters of the similarly named school of feminist thought. See Stuart Feather (2016), *Blowing the Lid: Gay Liberation, Sexual*

Revolution and Radical Queens, Zer0 Books

'In many ways this split': For example, see Nicholas von Hoffman (1968), *We Are the People Our Parents Warned Us Against*, Fawcett

'*International Times*, for example': *International Times* (5 to 17 December 1969), #69, p. 1; Peter Stansill (2006), 'The life and death of *IT*', *British Journalism Review*, vol. 17, no. 4, pp. 71–81; Mick Farren (2002), *Give the Anarchist a Cigarette*, p. 296

'The following issue focused': 'A Very Special Freak' (October 1969) *OZ*, #24, p. 10

'As for why Farquharson was chosen': David Wills, email to author

'But such one-off specials': for an example of the backlash to such publications, see the classic essay by Robin Morgan (9 to 23 February 1970), 'Goodbye to All That', the *Rat*, pp. 6-7

'The *Berkeley Barb*': Leo E. Laurence (04/07/1969), 'Gays Hit NYCOPS', *Berkeley Barb*, p. 5

'But the same publication': *Berkeley Barb* (21/03/1969), 'Kickin' Out the Jambs', p. 9

'By early 1971, the GLF': Rosa Schling (2023), *Peace! Books! Freedom! The Secret History of a Radical London Building*, Housmans, pp. 66-75

'Farquharson was known to show up': Nettie Pollard quoted in Lisa Power (1995), *No Bath But Plenty of Bubbles: Stories from the London Gay Liberation Front, 1970-73*, Continuum, p. 75; Nettie Pollard, email to author

'Speaking to a documentary crew': Vivian Berger quoted in 'Felix Dennis Obscenity Trial Documentary Clip', www.youtube.com/watch?v=n1YovxekV5c, 2m15s [accessed 01/10/2024]

'Copies of the single': Matthew Hilton, interview with author

'ANTIUNIVERSITY OF LONDON': 'Smalls', *International Times* (22 October to 5 November 1970), #90, p. 18

'Anti-University of London programme for January-March 1971': 'Anti University of London' (28 January to 10 February 1971), *International Times*, #96, p. 10

'The Abbey Wood branch': *Chapter?* (mid-1971), vol. 1, no. 1, p. 58

'Alongside the programme was an ad': 'Fleet Street producers' (28 January to 10 February 1971), *International Times*, #96, p. 10

'Homosexuality is nature's birth control': Robin Farquharson quoted in *BitWoman* (December 1973), p. 38

'Gordon Winter claimed': Gordon Winter quoted in *Ex-Bitman Robin* (May 1973), no. 6, p. 2

'Fleet Street proper was starting': Mandrake (10/10/1971), 'Anti-er and anti-er', the *Sunday Telegraph*, p. 11

'Robin popped into my office again': Gordon Winter quoted in *Ex-Bitman Robin* (May 1973), no. 6, p. 2

'Among the assembled anarchist philosophers': Frater Choronzon (1990), *Liber Cyber*

'The lettering was, the Dom noted': Dom Sylvester Houédard (1971), 'this is a lowercase abc i developed', CC-58890-10002094, Dom Sylvester Houédard papers, Ruth and Marvin Sackner Archive of Concrete and Visual Poetry, University of Iowa

'Dropping the brackets': Dom Sylvester Houédard and Robin Farquharson (1971), 'a farquharson-houedard slash-&-dash alphabet for broadsides', CC-48313-69338, Ruth and Marvin Sackner Archive of Concrete and Visual Poetry

---

Chapter 19 — Starships in Glenrothes

'In internal communications': 'Internal editor Q' (1970), Penguin cover brief, DM1952/596, Penguin Random House Archives, University of Bristol

'The author's potted biography': Robin Farquharson (1971), *Drop Out!*, Penguin, inside cover

'In the wake of being arrested': *Arts Labs Newsletter* (March 1970), 'International Freak Beaten Up & Committed', p. 1; 'A Very Special Freak' (October 1969) *OZ*, #24, p. 10

'As reported in last month's newsletter': Nicholas Albery, *Arts Labs Newsletter* (April 1970), p. 25

'Upper Clyde Shipbuilders consisted': John Foster and Charles Woolfson (1986), *The Politics of the UCS Work-in: Class Alliances and the Right to Work*, Lawrence and Wishart, pp. 9-12

'The Angry Brigade then bombed': The Angry Brigade (June 1970), 'Communiqué #10' in Gordon Carr (2005), *The Angry Brigade: Documents and Chronology, 1967–1984*, Elephant Editions, p. 29

'Things had gotten so urgent': John Foster and Charles Woolfson (1986), *The Politics of the UCS Work-in*, p. 204

'Outside a tall, wild-looking hairy man': Rosie Boycott (1984), *A Nice Girl Like Me: A Story of the Seventies*, Chatto & Windus, pp. 57-58

'It's a pity': Jerome Burne, interview with author

'GAP was situated': John Hassan, interview with author

'After failing to be put through': Ibid.

'By this stage': Ibid.

'After a couple of numbers': Ibid.

'The story I remember': Andy Roberts quoted in 'Survivors' histories' (c. 2010), studymore.org.uk/hissur.htm [accessed 01/10/2024]

'The day after the UCS-Glenrothes escapade': John Hassan, interview with author

---

Chapter 20 — The Ytisrevinu of London

'Robin appeared with a broken arm': Guy Legge, email to author

'The Ytisrevinu of London': *International Times* (16 to 30 December 1971), #119, p. 22

'Tom Fawthrop, the journalist': Tom Fawthrop, email to author

'For every detailed course': *International Times* (13 to 27 January 1972), #121, p. 11

'The Socialist Patients' Collective': Nick Crossley (December 1999), 'Fish, field, habitus and madness: the first wave mental health users movement in Great Britain', *British Journal of Sociology*, vol. 50, no. 4, pp. 647–670

'In a distinctly British mode': *Ink* (16/11/1971), 'Mental Prisons—Suicide and Despair', p. 4

'As several of his causes': Thomas Ritchie (1971), *Journal of SUMP Days*, SURVIVORS/3/1, Survivors History Archive, Bishopsgate Institute

'Foregrounding its connections': *Spare Rib* (July 1972), p. 37

'In March 1972, he and a number': Piers Corbyn (1980), 'We won, you should fight them too', Nick Wates and Christian Wolmar eds., *Squatting: The Real Story*, Bay Leaf Books, p. 131. Through Corbyn mentions the role of ex-Horton patients in establishing the Elgin Avenue squat, he doesn't identify any of them by name. We can, however, identify Farquharson as one of their number due to the address provided in an ad for his antiuniversity during the period in question, see *International Times* (24 March 1972), #126, p. 50

'Sensing even greater instability': Dimity Torbett, email to author

'I didn't known Robin': Shelley Lee quoted in *Ex-Bitman Robin* (May 1973), no. 6, p. 6

'In an unpublished note': Robin Farquharson (March 1974), 'Some more extracts from the selected works of the late Robin Farquharson', *Bit-Human*, no. 10, x

'In the world of the transformed': Robin Farquharson (c. 1971), excerpts from *The Alternative Society* quoted in *Bitman* (September 1973), no. 8, p. 8

'Penguin also explored the idea': DM1952/596, Penguin Random House Archives

'In practice, they filled': Peter Johnston quoted in *Ex-Bitman Robin* (May 1973), no. 6, p. 7

'I do remember him': Richard Adams, interview with author. *Gay News* eventually offered remaindered copies of *Drop Out* for sale by mail order, as seen in an advert in the March 1973 issue, p. 20

'I never really saw': Woody Haut, interview with author

'The last time I saw him': Michael Dummett (2005), 'The work and life of Robin Farquharson', p. 482

'Although he favoured violence': Gordon Winter quoted in *Ex-Bitman Robin* (May 1973), no. 6, p. 3

'He then got an extremely important job': Anthony Howell, interview with author

'Robin Farquharson would not': Frater Choronzon (1990), *Liber Cyber*

'I heard he had joined': Michael Barnett (1973), *People, Not Psychiatry*, p. 197

———

Chapter 21 — The Dust Heaps of Somers Town

'In 1865, Charles Dickens': Esther Leslie (2022), 'Dust Heaps', lostfound.aspaceforus.club/sample-page/origins/dust-heaps/

'In 1970... Sid Rawle': John May (15/09/2010), 'Sid Rawle obituary', www.theguardian.com/uk/2010/sep/15/sid-rawle-obituary [accessed 01/10/2024]

'Others took smaller steps': For an overview of London squatting in this period, see Alexander Vasudevan (2023), *The Autonomous City: A History of Urban Squatting*, Verso, pp. 40-66

'Rumours circulated': Stephen Lee, interview with author

'I had been studying': Aidan Andrew Dun, interview with author. A similar episode is related in a contemporary account provided to an anarchist newspaper, albeit concerning a sheep rather than a goat, see JR (08/09/1973), 'Lamb in Sheep's Clothing,' *Freedom*, vol.34, no.36, p. 7. For more on Father Fuck, see John Kruse (29/11/2022), 'Cultural Revolution II: the Church of Aphrodite', johnkruseblog.wordpress.com/2022/11/29/cultural-revolution-ii-the-church-of-aphrodite/ [accessed 13/11/2023]

'Unlike his two brothers': Marilyn Weiss Baines (1979), introduction to Peter Baines, *Concrete Poems*, Street Talk Press, pp. 1-2

'For the next four years': Ibid., p. 2

'Returning to London': Buskaction (c. 2008), 'Street Poetry', bak.spc.org/buskaction/streetpoetry.html [accessed 29/08/2023]. Bongo Mike became a high-profile defender of the rights of buskers to perform without a license. Alongside a later collaborator named Extremely Frank Jeremy, Bongo Mike ultimately took his case all the way to the European Court of Human Rights.

'But the pair split': Jeremy Helm, email to author

'George Price, the once-famous geneticist': Oren Harman (2010), *The Price of Altruism: George Price and the Search for the Origins of Kindness*, Bodley Head, pp. 295-301

'David Cooper was said': with thanks to Ken Worpole for the information on Cooper's Dalston life

'In the summer of 1972': Steve Platt (1980), 'Here there and everywhere', Nick Wates and Christian Wolmar eds., *Squatting*, p. 31

'I would describe': Michael Child, email to author

'Robin was connected': Ibid.

'One of the first nights': Aidan Andrew Dun, interview with author

'At that time, Robin was living': Ibid.

'In 1973, the GLC ensured': Steve Platt (1980), 'Mounting opposition', Nick Wates and Christian Wolmar eds., *Squatting*, p. 56

'There was an old World War II siren': Aidan Andrew Dun, interview with author

'Scandle at the Palace': Robin Farquharson (c. 1973), 'Buckingham Palace Busted!', *Joint Happiness Cooperation Community News* [?] quoted in *Ex-Bitman Robin* (May 1973), front cover

'His sociopolitical talking': Michael Child, email to author

'Of course Robin was gay': Aidan Andrew Dun, interview with author

---

CHAPTER 22 — A STRANGE THING HAPPENED TO ME LAST WEEK

'The writer John Healy': John Healy (1988), *The Grass Arena: An Autobiography*, Faber and Faber

'At that time, I didn't think': Aidan Andrew Dun, interview with author

'Around the end of January 1973': Unless otherwise stated, details relating to Farquharson's tenancy of 21 Platt Street come from surviving documents in the criminal case against Michael Christopher O'Connor and Peter James Hilditch, Clerkenwell Magistrates' Court (May 1973) and Central Criminal Court (September 1973). These are held at J267/236/ 362763, the National Archives (hereafter: TNA)

'We were absolutely stunned': Liz Davies, interview with author

'That night saw the official launch': List of original members, Mental Patients' Union minutes, SURVIVORS/1/15, Survivors History Archive

'There was this really strong bond': Brian Douieb, interview with author

'Street Talk Pete returned': 'Statement of witness: Peter Graham Baines', pp. 13-17, TNA

'He seemed reasonably settled': Peter Johnston quoted in *Ex-Bitman Robin* (May 1973), no. 6, p. 10

'He returned with two sleeping tablets': 'Statement of witness: Roni M. Shaw', pp. 38-40, TNA

'On the night in question': 'Statement of witness: William Watson', ibid., pp. 5-12

'The fire brigade later estimated': 'Statement of witness: Paul Dempsey', ibid., pp. 18-20

'Farquharson's precious unpublished manuscripts': George Firsoff (1980), *1968: Spring of Youth*, p. 199

'A police sergeant who attended': 'Statement of witness: Patrick Egan', ibid., pp. 46-51

'Another policeman noticed': 'Statement of witness: James Robson', ibid., pp. 42-43

'Friends in the underground press': This information was repeated widely, including in *Ex-Bitman Robin* (May 1973), no. 6, p. 1

'I was called for an emergency': Ping-Chung Leung, email to author

'A strange thing happened': Robin Farquharson (late March 1973), quoted in Hertzog Biermann (15/04/1973), 'SA Author of 'Dropout' A Tragic Genius', *Sunday Times* of South Africa, p. 20B

'We went to see him': Brian Douieb, interview with author

'We couldn't really see much': Liz Davies, interview with author

'My morning visit found him': Ping-Chung Leung, email to author

---

Chapter 23 — A Wreath and Three Tomatoes

'The view that the MPU took': Brian Douieb, interview with author

'Customs officers found': Liz Davies, interview with author

'I remember very clearly': Ibid. The MPU was involved in breaking girls out of Leavesden Asylum. They had been subject to hospitalisation under the Mental Health Act 1959. For more on the MPU's militancy, see Mental Patients Union (February 1974), 'Repression', *MPUnews*, no. 3, p. 6

'Though the *Times* dispatched': Stewart Tendler (11/04/1973), 'Cambridge don died a drop-out squatter', the *Times*, p. 4

'The *Sun* covered the fatal fire': Mike Nevard (06/04/1973), 'Riddle of the dropout doctor', the *Sun*, p. 9

'His address in the crematorium's register': 1973 cremation register, Kensal Green Cemetery, West London Crematorium, no. 31321

'Churchill College sent a wreath': Peter Johnston quoted in *Ex-Bitman Robin* (May 1973), no. 6, p. 10

'After a few weeks': 'Statement of witness: William Watson', pp. 5-12, TNA

'O'Connor stated that': 'Statement of witness: Patrick Egan', ibid., pp. 46-51

'In his statement to the court': 'Statement of witness: James Robson', ibid., pp. 42-43

'South African author': *Camden News* (13/04/1973), 'Author dies after fire', p. 44

'With O'Connor out and about': 'Statement of witness: William Watson', pp. 5-12, TNA

'I've been to the coroner's inquest': 'Statement of witness: Ian Finlay McIntosh', ibid., pp. 52-53. The coroner in question authored several articles on the process of conducting an inquest, see D. R. Chambers (1985), 'Medical Evidence in the Coroner's Court', *Medicine, Science and the Law*, vol. 25, no. 2, pp. 103-107 and D. R. Chambers (1989), 'The Coroner, the Inquest and the Verdict of Suicide', *Medicine, Science and the Law*, vol. 29, no. 3, p. 181

'Placed in detention': 'Statement of witness: Anthony Whitchurch', pp. 64-68, TNA

'Through his tears Hilditch said': 'Statement of witness: Ian David Russell', ibid., pp. 56-59

'In response to their new housemate's behaviour': 'Statement of witness: Ronald Dickinson', ibid., pp. 60-63

'Sir Phillip Wien, the presiding judge': the *Daily Telegraph* (11/09/1973), 'Two sentenced for drop-out don's death', p. 19

'Michael Child, a fellow squatter': Michael Child (29/05/2012), 'Margate Meltdown Mouse', thanetonline.blogspot.com/2012/05/margate-meltdown-mouse-and-ramsgate.html [accessed 13/11/2023]

'Whatever stories may have swirled': The two men were charged for three breaches of Section 1 of the Criminal Damage Act 1971: 1) damaging a property belonging to another, 2) damaging a property in a way likely to endanger life, and 3) damaging a property by fire. The third charge made against Hilditch and O'Connor related to the first breach above, a general accusation that is implicitly contained within the other two breaches. Though further evidence may one day arise, there is no reason to be suspicious about the fact that this charge was dropped. It's plausible that the court chose not to proceed with it once it became aware that the suspects would plead guilty. The same is also true with regard to the two men having initially provided misleading statements to the inquest. Though this was under oath, it probably didn't reach the threshold for a perjury charge, as it related to the principal offence itself—the fire—and didn't have any meaningful or damaging ramifications to the case.

'The lovely Robin Farquharson': *Peace News* (13/04/1973), 'Classified', p. 10

'I never saw him after Horton': Matthew Hilton, interview with author

'Robin wasn't completely convinced': Aidan Andrew Dun, interview with author

'There is a niggling feeling': Michael Child, email to author

'I don't know if Robin': Shelley Lee quoted in *Ex-Bitman Robin* (May 1973), no. 6, p. 7
'Robin was a tragically misunderstood': Enid Farquharson quoted in Hertzog Biermann (15/04/1973), 'SA Author of 'Dropout' a Tragic Genius', *Sunday Times* of South Africa, p. 20B

Afterlives and conclusions

'As Satterthwaite recalled': Mark Satterthwaite, email to author

'At its height the organisation': Peter Evans, 'Borstal 'does not help boys to cope with life'', the *Times* (04/05/1973), p. 6

'Pun Plamondon's conviction': 'United States v. United States District Court', better known simply as the '*Keith* case', after the judge who initially ruled against the government.

'Inspired by the White Panthers' activities': In later life Rawle began to work on his memoirs with the help of none other than Jeremy Sandford, the writer of *Cathy Come Home*. Traces of this unpublished text can be found on Sandford's website: www.jeremysandford.org.uk/jsarchive/sid-intro.html [accessed 13/11/2023]

'Between 1972 and 1973': John Spiers (1974), *The Underground and Alternative Press in Britain: A Bibliographical Guide with Historical Notes*, Harvester Press

'In 2007, Dennis Brutus': Cameron Duodu (23/02/2010), 'Dennis Brutus obituary', www.theguardian.com/world/2010/feb/23/dennis-brutus-obituary [accessed 13/11/2023]

''After a long and fraught consultation': Amelia Gentleman (21/06/2021), ''We didn't want it named after another person': how residents of Cecil Rhodes House feel about its new name', www.theguardian.com/uk-news/2021/jun/21/we-didnt-want-it-named-after-a-person-how-residents-of-cecil-rhodes-house-feel-about-its-new-name [accessed 01/10/2024]

IMAGES

For this book, the author has compiled rare archival images that don't necessarily meet contemporary expectations of quality. All reasonable efforts have been made to identify the sources of the images contained in this volume. The publishers would be glad to be made aware should any omissions be noted.

p. 8: Keith Wesley, 'Author badly burned', *Camden News* (30/03/1973), p. 48.

p. 12: collage based on following clippings: 'I took LSD, says brilliant S. A. scholar', *Sunday Times of South Africa* (22/09/1968), p. 5; 'Author dies after fire', *Camden News* (13/04/1973), p. 44; 'Squatters charged with killing', *Camden News* (19/04/1973), p. 40; 'Platt Street case', *Camden News* (04/05/1973), p. 40; 'Mystery Fire Death of Author', Camden News (11/05/1973), p. 5; *Arts Labs Newsletter* (March 1970), 'International Freak Beaten Up & Committed', p. 1; 'Particulars of applicant', Farquharson R R student file, Brasenose College Archives, Oxford; Advert for *Drop Out!*, the Observer (15/09/1968), p. 25; 'Brilliant Drop-Out Dies of Burns', *Sunday Times of South Africa* (08/04/1973), p. 19; Mike Nevard (06/04/1973), 'Riddle of the dropout doctor', the *Sun*, p. 9; Robin Farquharson (May 1961), 'Mandela Calls', *Contact*, p. 3.

p. 20: 'Maths-Politics Wins Him Prize', *Rand Daily Mail* (12/12/1961), page unknown.

p. 21: Ex-Bitman Robin (May 1973), no. 6.

p. 24: 'Left Pretoria', *Rand Daily Mail* (22/03/1957), p. 9.

p. 28: Rhodes University, Farquharson's alma mater.

p. 32: Farquharson's map of his European journey (1951), Farquharson R R student file, Brasenose College Archives, Oxford.

p. 34: The crest of the Voltaire Society, Bertrand Russell Archives, McMaster University Library, 81832.057302 5.51 RA1 710.

p. 36: Farquharson and 'Red Rupert', *Cherwell* (11/06/1952), p. 24.

p. 39: 'Profile: Robin Farquharson', *Cherwell* (05/05/1953), p. 2.

p. 40: Lewis Carroll/Charles Lutwidge Dodgson (1863), photograph by Oscar Gustav Rejlander.

p. 52: Butler (L) introduces Farquharson (in glasses) during the BBC's 1955 election coverage.

p. 60: Queen's College (1957), Farquharson is standing with arms crossed on the third row from the bottom fourth from the left.

p. 68: *Sunday Times* of South Africa (08/04/1973) p.19.

p. 76: *Contact*, May 1961.

p. 81: Dennis Brutus (c. 1965).

p. 87: 'Host refuses police entry to multi-racial party', *Sunday Express* of South Africa (11/08/1963), p. 11.

p. 90: 'Save These Lives' poster, World Campaign for the Release of South African Political Prisoners (1963).

p. 99: Gordon Winter (1970s).

p. 102: Robin Farquharson (1958), 'An approach to a pure theory of voting procedure', Doctoral thesis, Oxford, p. 34, author's collection.

p. 108: Letter to Farquharson (12/07/1968), author's collection.

p. 112: Kingsley Hall (c. 1965), author's collection.

p. 117: *Archigram* (1963), no. 3; Centre Point (c. 1970); the Roundhouse (c. 1964).

p. 123: Allen Ginsberg and Anthony Howell, *Sunday Times* (29/06/1973), p. 3.

p. 128: Farquharson (c. 1964).

p. 135: Anthony Blond (1968).

p. 140: Robin Farquharson (1971), *Drop Out!*, Penguin.

p. 145: Gerald Low-Beer, *New Scientist* (11/07/1974), p. 88.

p. 152: *International Times* (3 to 16 May 1968), #30.

p. 160: *Friends* (12/12/1969), #1.

p. 163: Michael X, Lennon, and Ono (04/02/1970).
p. 168: Nicholas Albery (c. 1975).

p. 171: The headquarters of BIT (c. 1969).

p. 182: UFO+TV flyer (1970), author's collection.

p. 185: 144 Piccadilly (1969).

p. 186: Gerald Gardner (28/02/1970), 'Puking the system', the *Guardian*, p. 9.

p. 198: Desolation Row (1970).

p. 204: *Freek Press* (1970), #4.

p. 207: White Panther Party, 'Bulletin on Isle of Wight Festival' (1970), private collection.

p. 212: *Evening Standard* (07/09/1970).

p. 219: Farquharson (c. 1970), *Sunday Express* of South Africa (13/04/1973), page unknown.

p. 222: Engineers at Pye Studios (c. 1970).

p. 232: Antiuniversity catalog, private collection.

p. 235: 'A Very Special Freak', *OZ* (October 1969), #24, p. 10.

p. 242: Germaine Greer (October 1969), 'Mozic and the Revolution', *OZ*, #24, p. 28.

p. 247: White Panther Party UK Glasgow Chapter letterhead, author's collection.

p. 254: SUMP membership list, Thomas Ritchie (1971), *Journal of SUMP Days*, SURVIVORS/3/1, Survivors History Archive, Bishopsgate Institute.

p. 258: Keith Armstrong (c. 1973), folder 35, Keith Armstrong papers, Bishopsgate Institute.

p. 266: Aiden Andrew Dun (1970s), private collection.

p. 278: Plans for Platt Street (13/06/1967), London Archives, GLC/DG/HG/12/050.

p. 282: MPU poster, MPU scrapbook, SURVIVORS/3/1, Survivors History Archive, Bishopsgate Institute.

p. 290: Classified ad in *Peace News* (13/04/1973), p. 10.

p. 300: *Ex-Bitman Robin* (May 1973), no. 6.

p. 308: *OZ* (April 1968), #11, back cover.

p. 314: British White Panthers solicit funds (c. 1970).

p. 318: *International Times* (9 to 23 March 1972), #125, p. 47.

INDEX